Europe:
Where the Fun Is

Other Books by the Authors:

The Rites of Winter: A Skier's
Budget Guide to Making It On the Slopes

The Rites of Spring: A Student's
Guide to Spring Break in Florida

You Too Can Be a Democratic
Candidate for President

EUROPE:

WHERE THE FUN IS

Rollin Riggs and Bruce Jacobsen

Mustang Publishing Company
New Haven, Connecticut

Distributed to the trade by Kampmann and Company, New York.

Library of Congress Cataloging in Publication Data

Riggs, Rollin.
   Europe: where the fun is.

   1. Europe—Description and travel—1971-   —Guidebooks. 2. Amusements—
Europe—Guidebooks.   I. Jacobsen, Bruce. II. Title.

D909.J23 1985   914'.04558   85-90178
ISBN: 0-914457-07-1 (pbk.)

10 9 8 7 6 5 4 3 2 1

Cover design by Deborah Daly.

Acknowledgements

A guidebook this big reflects the efforts of scores of people. We wish we could list the name of every bartender, waitress, cab driver, tourist officer, and friend who gave freely of advice, tips, or encouragement. Alas, they will have to remain anonymous.

However, there are many who have helped out whom we can name. Special thanks to the following: Court Chilton, Bruce Shaw, the Foleys (Michael, Beth, and Abby), Debbi Cohen, Bobby Jacobsen, Caitlin Doyle, Mary Ann MacDonald, Julie Williams, Amity Schlaes, Willie MacMullen and the good folks at Air MacMullen, Mike Natan, Michel Shavelson, Kathy Edrington, Leigh Boston, Leigh Green and his wooden shoes, and of course, our parents, Arthur and Elizabeth Jacobsen and Webster and Sandy Riggs.

Further, Stephen Hughes would like to thank the good folks at the Pensao Restauradores in Lisbon, Paolo Oliveira, and two Swedish blonds in Albufeira.

Also, this book would not exist without our distributor, Eric Kampmann, and our agent, Joy Harris — both outstanding professionals.

And we have one more favor to ask of all our friends: please go out and buy five copies of this book.

Bruce Jacobsen
Rollin Riggs

Table of Contents

Introduction

Writing this book was murder — dancing at another elegant Parisian nightclub, checking out yet another nude beach, exploring the best bars in Amsterdam. Believe us, we earned our money. We didn't limit ourselves to the easy stuff, like finding the American Express offices or the big museums abroad. No, we chose to travel the tough road and get the low-down on the high life. We think our mission was successful.

We felt we had to do it. For some reason, other travel writers seem to stop work about 7:00 p.m. — that's when we're just getting started. We think most guides to Europe are, frankly, boring: "This museum offers another fine collection of 18th-century Belgian paintings, and the snack bar prices are quite reasonable." Necessary, true, but boring nonetheless. When not discussing the 300 hotels in town *ad nauseum*, most travel guides describe the places you might go if you were on a sixth-grade field trip.

Now, we don't mean to denigrate Europe's lovely hotels, marvelous museums, or historic sights. It's just that we think there's a lot more to Europe than what you'll get in the standard travel guide today. By all means, hit the "sights;" that's probably why you're abroad, after all. But also go native for a while. Parisians don't go to the Eiffel Tower or Notre Dame any more than New Yorkers hang out at the Empire State Building or the Statue of Liberty. So if you want to meet Parisians, you'll have to go elsewhere, like to the cafes, nightclubs, and restaurants in town. And that's where we come in.

So please, buy a couple of other guidebooks before you go abroad. Most of them are extremely helpful and well-researched, and especially the first-time traveler will find them useful. But refer to them during the day, and use us at night.

The basic problem with Europe is that it's, well, so *foreign*. Language can be a problem, money an annoyance. But fortunately, the topic of this book — fun — adheres to fairly universal standards. Beer is beer, dancing is dancing, and a wink at the attractive blond at the next table transcends all cultural barriers.

Of course, we don't guarantee that you'll have a blast at any of the places we discuss; that's entirely up to you. We chose to write about a place because we thought it was fun ourselves and because others there seemed to be having a good time and recommended it to us. For the most part, you will have fun when you make an effort to participate, not just observe. Join in the slam-dancing at a punk club in London; go topless on a Greek beach; kiss all your neighbors at Chez les Fondus in Paris. When you make an effort to join the party, you will find that neither language nor political barriers make any difference.

To research this book, we organized a network of students, journalists, and experienced European travelers, most of whom are natives of the cities they covered. We then visited Europe ourselves, checking out the hot-spots to see how they compared to the reports we had received. We talked with hundreds of people everywhere we went: cabbies, bartenders, tourist officers, kids — anyone who might give us a good tip on where to have fun. We wanted to write a book that would tell people where to go as though a good friend from that city were advising them. If you were to describe the fun stuff in your city to a friend, what would you suggest? Well, those are the places we tried to find for Lisbon, Berlin, Vienna, etc.

All guidebooks suffer one common problem: by the time the book is out, a lot of names, prices, phone numbers, etc. may have changed. We apologize for any inconvenience this may cause you, but it's just the nature of the territory. And bear in mind that phone service in Europe, especially southern Europe, is not universal. Many small bars and cafes in Spain, for instance, have no need for a phone — or even for an official address, sometimes. But any place we mention that does not have an exact address or phone number should be simple to find if you just ask a native.

We hope that you will have a great time in Europe, and we hope that this book helped you make some memories that you otherwise would not have made. After exploring a city's past, make sure you save enough energy to discover its present — in the bars, cafes, and hang-outs where Europeans go to relax, find romance, and have a blast.

Send us a postcard!

The Typical Guidebook Disclaimer

Though we've tried mighty hard not to copy all the other European guides, there's one thing they all have that we've gotta have too — The Disclaimer. And it goes something like this: (*hit it, boys*)

We've double-checked all our facts — prices, hours, phone numbers, etc. — but please remember that due to inflation, taxation, the fluctuating dollar, floods, gypsies, and the Plague, a lot of the facts herein are probably wrong. So please don't curse us when you get to Paris and discover that dinner at **L'Entrecote** costs 52 francs instead of the reported 48. Blame it on the Socialists, or something.

And the same goes for typographical errors, too. We tried to catch all of them, but a few always manage to slip past. Those damn Socialists again.

Basically, all of this means that we refuse to assume responsibility for any damage you may incur due to a little boo-boo in this book. We won't even refund your $7.95.

Life's hell, huh?

The Typical Guidebook Appeal

Seriously, though, we want very much to hear from you — praise, criticism, new ideas, a good joke, anything. Tell us what you thought of this book, and how it can be made better for future editions. A guidebook's readers should be its best researchers, so please join our happy research family and drop us a line. If your suggestion is used in a future edition, we'll send you a free, autographed copy of the book. Whatta deal!

Write to us in care of Mustang Publishing, 4651 Yale Station, New Haven, Conn., 06520.

Of course, if your suggestion is not used, you'll just get on another obnoxious mailing list and get tons of junk mail.

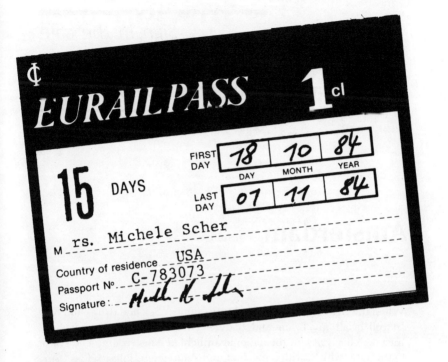

GET FIRST CLASS EUROPEAN TRAIN TRAVEL FOR ABOUT $18.00 A DAY. GET EURAILPASS.

Eurailpass gives you inexpensive and flexible First Class train travel through sixteen European countries for fifteen days. The total cost? $260. That's less than eighteen dollars a day.

Ask your travel agent about Eurailpass or send for our free, colorful and informative brochure today!

NAME

ADDRESS

CITY   STATE   ZIP CODE

Key #

EURAILPASS

*Sign in the cafe
of the Paradiso: 'Please
smoke your joints someplace else.'*

Amsterdam

When the British musician Ian Drury sang, "Sex and drugs and rock 'n roll/Is all my brain and body need," many people may have mistaken his lyrics for the national anthem of Amsterdam. The visitor to this city, which, with a touch of understatement, bills itself as "surprising" — will find prostitutes in the windows of 17th-century homes, bars which sell as much hash as Heineken, and night spots that offer encounter sessions and yoga classes along with rock 'n roll.

The tourism officials are right — Amsterdam, the fourth largest business and touristic center of Europe, will surprise the hell out of you. Here, tourism is regarded as serious business, and business is regarded as great fun. Amsterdam has long been noted as an especially tolerant city, where your work and your pleasure are nobody's business but your own. Back in 1631, Descartes wrote, "Everybody here except me is in business and so absorbed by profit-making that I could spend my entire life here without being noticed by a soul." These days, much of the profits come from beer-brewing, drug-dealing, and prostitution, so the city is as absorbed as ever.

Youthful European travelers all recognize something known as "Amsterdam amnesia." Its symptoms include bloodshot eyes, a hangover, a missing wallet, and tales of "some cute Swede" or snowstorms of cocaine. People who spend more than two days in the city usually acquire these traits, and recovery can take weeks. In Amsterdam, a one-night stand is an enduring relationship, and an alcoholic stupor is the expected mental state. Amidst the neatly organized grid of canals there are an awful lot of devious little angles.

Nightlife

Amsterdam's nightlife is, for the most part, split into three distinct sections: the Leidseplein, the Zeedjik, and the Rembrandtsplein.

For youths, the **Leidseplein** *is* Amsterdam. Take Fort Lauderdale during Spring Break, multiply it about ten times, and you've got the Leidseplein on a weekend evening. Packs of teenage girls giggle at spike-haired punks; drunken soldiers scope traveling American women lugging backpacks; Italians, Canadians, and Germans discuss the latest nuclear and Hollywood bombs.

The cheapest and most popular activity, of course, is simply hanging out, checking out the action and seeing who's picked up whom. The best loitering spots are the tables at the outdoor cafe on the Leidseplein itself, where you can sit and sip a cup of espresso or nurse a beer under the twinkling white lights strung through the trees.

The variety of bars and discos in this small area will astonish all but the most wordly. The current "in" place will in all likelihood be *passe* next week, and might even have changed its name. The **Bamboo Bar**, a reliable veteran, supplies live jazz in a tropical surrounding, and the wall-to-wall patrons provide the heat and the humidity. **La Bouteille** and **Club Atalaya**, two of the top discos in town, charge small membership fees and are renowned as especially fertile pick-up spots. While La Bouteille draws a more local crowd, Club Atalaya caters to young jet-setters, where dark-haired Italians go nuts for the Swedes. **'t Cafe** and **Jacob's Cafe**, both with fabulous locations, are fairly simple, somewhat grungy, easy-going bars. 't Cafe draws people with its huge Rolling Stones' style mouth-and-tongue logo and no-nonsense wood interior, and Jacob's offers easy entrance — since it lacks a front wall. Usually, the absence of the wall is hard to notice, since by 9:00 p.m. the gap has been substituted by a wall of hard-drinking Jacob's fans that stand side-by-side to view the passing pedestrian parade. **Pianobar Snobs**, much more friendly than its great name suggests, draws a slightly more mature, sedate crowd, where just an occasional line of coke can be seen. The **Revolution Bar** may make your head do many revolutions, and it attracts a mostly black crowd. The list could go on and on, but suffice it to say that there are two bars on the Leidseplein for every taste. There's even a spot for those who prefer absolute silence when they try to capture their kings or queens: **Het Hok**, a chess club/cafe right in the thick of the action, where you can buy a beer and watch the strategists, or sit down and play a game.

But the "big three" — Melkweg, de Balie, and Paradiso — all just off the main Leidseplein area, overshadow the smaller joints.

The **Melkweg**, a lively combination of dance hall, coffeeshop, and radical university, will probably make you say, "Only in Amsterdam." A maze of small rooms and cafes and a large theater area housed in a huge old milk factory, Milkweg (Milky Way) in a typical hour will offer a workshop on yoga, a leftist film about Chile, and a folk rock band, simultaneously. Although its somewhat somber, 1960's style "be-in" atmosphere has lost some appeal lately (a prominent bit of graffiti on a stairway wall says bluntly, "The Milky Way is a joke"), Milkweg remains the center of Amsterdam's young intelligentsia and counter-culture and is a magnet for traveling youth from all over the world. Though many Americans will regard Milkweg as simply a curious anachronism, this odd warehouse will both challenge and bemuse.

Just slightly less political than Milkweg, but quite a bit rowdier, de Balie and Paradiso offer top bands at cheap prices. **de Balie** seems more experimental and sometimes more punk, and its smaller size can be refreshing with the right band. The **Paradiso**, a cavernous former theater with all the seats removed, reigns as the city's top concert arena. Anything can happen, and something usually does. Top bands frequently appear, but the cover is rarely more than 15 guilders. Its expansive interior definitely puts the emphasis on dancing, though a small bar in the back and a cafe upstairs provide room for conversation. People smoke and sell hash openly and share their joints generously, except in the cafe, where a small sign requests, "Please smoke your joints somewhere else." Though a slim majority of Paradiso patrons seem to be in the slightly punk 20-25 age group, the mix depends on the band, and all kinds of combinations appear on the dance floor, including gay groupings, and some combinations you're just not sure of. The politics at the Paradiso are definitely left, but you won't want to leave, no matter what your views on El Salvador.

On **Reguliersdwarsstraat**, two blocks from the main Rembrandt-splein (a region we'll discuss in more depth later), a row of chic new watering holes has evolved, with gays on one side of the street, and the young "beautiful people" of Amsterdam on the other. Homosexuals can bar-hop all night and never walk more than 100 yards, as the bars **Vert**, **Downtown**, **Viking**, **April**, and **Traffic** stand virtually side-by-side. Traffic is the most accessible bar to non-gays, with the occasional live band or theme night, but it still caters primarily to men. Right across the street, **Rose's Cantina** and **Oblomow** attract a stunning collection of young professionals, preppies, and debutantes. Both serve food (Rose's is Mexican and Oblomow Italian), have large bar areas, taped, popular music, and become packed by 10:00. Less crowded and a good choice for a late dinner is **Los Gauchos**, a rustic Argentine restaurant with a strolling guitarist.

The Zeedjik consists of lovely, tree-lined streets whose old, narrow homes face canals that gently lap at the quaint bridges. Scantily-clad women, often knitting, sit in the windows under red lights and try to sell the world's oldest commodity. With a little encouragement, they'll wink, strut, and haggle in an effort to make you a client. This quarter, whose main streets are O.Z. Voorburgwal and O.Z. Achterburgwal, also houses a few dozen porno stores and movie houses, some live sex theaters, and street-side vending machines that sell condoms, but the women remain the prime attraction.

In the daytime, the Zeedjik hides its contradictions behind elegant, historic facades. At night, however, it becomes eerie and wild, with a blatant seaminess that titillates, irritates, and astonishes. Small groups of horny, slightly nervous young men linger on the bridges and corners, approached every so often by women in mini-skirts. Tourist couples, some with their children, stroll along the streets, trying to peek inside the windows and ignore them at the same time.

Most of the prostitutes wear negligees or bikinis and sit in rocking chairs, biding their time until someone likes what he sees and knocks on their door. Most of the women are either chubby or aging, but about one out of ten is remarkably beautiful. Laissez-faire economics gets full play here: price directly reflects the woman's desirability and the extent of her services required. Some prostitutes walk the street, too, but these women are considered much less safe than those in the windows.

Anyone who has been to New York's Times Square, Boston's Combat Zone, or any adult bookstore, for that matter, will be somewhat disappointed by the second main feature of the Zeedjik, the porn shops. Surprise, surprise — people make love for the cameras in Europe just as they do in America, and, in fact, many of the actors are American porn stars.

However, if you've always wanted "just to see what it's like," the famous **Casa Rosso** offers the most graphic, most complete live sex show around. First, you're treated to a brief adult movie, then a long strip-tease show featuring about six women. The squeamish should not sit in the front row, because one of the women invites audience participation. The show climaxes as four or five couples in succession make brief and passionless love a few feet from your face. The full show at the Casa Rosso costs 50 guilders (about three times more expensive than comparable fare in Times Square) and lasts about an hour.

For more discreet erotic entertainment, Amsterdam boasts a number of exclusive men's clubs, like **Chatterly** and **Yab-Yum**, that offer sex shows and massage services. Finally, escort services are numerous, and the reputable **Escort Guide Service** is probably your best bet for commercial companionship.

Next door to the Casa Rosso dwells the famous pink elephant of **Club 26**, a lavish yet informal casino. Look for the small gold plaque that says "Club Cabala," and walk down the red hall to the entrance. (You'll need a passport or driver's license to get in if you're not a member.) Those planning to become regulars will need to buy a membersh p, but entrance for the one-time visitor is free, as are the drin's and the cabaret-style show. Inside, you can bet on craps, roul tte, or blackjack, and the bingo game at the end of the night is extremely popular. The casino's interior is large and beautiful, and the gamblers are an interesting mix of middle-class, Zeedjik-area resid nts and wealthier locals and tourists. Technically illegal, Club 26 has been raided a few times, but it always re-opens without much problem. You can just come just to watch, too, as no one pressures you to bet.

There's a story about an Amsterdam bar in the Zeedjik that was raided once: it seems the bartender was cutting up a pound of hash on top of the bar in full view, when the cops rushed in. They searched everyone for drugs, found none, glanced at the hash, and left. They were looking for what Amsterdam residents consider "real" drugs — heroin, pills, and such — and they couldn't be bothered with just another pound of hash. On the other hand, despite the atmosphere, hash and coke *are* illegal, so you're at the mercy of the police. In the lower areas of the Zeedjik, there are a number of small, scary bars with standard sailors-bar names like "Skip O Hoy Bar" and "Casa Blanca." Obviously, unless you're really tough, you shouldn't venture into them alone. And there's really only one reason to go inside anyway, and that's to buy drugs. Hang out for a while with a beer, get the feel for the place by talking a little with the bartender, and soon you'll know whether it's safe to ask for some hash, coke, or sometimes even harder stuff. Remember, though, that in these joints you'll be drinking and smoking with some of the dregs of Amsterdam society, and neither their merchandise nor their friendship is to be trusted. Like everywhere else in the world, it's wisest to let a native whom you can really trust buy your drugs for you.

When you think of the classic nightclub scene, you may recall the 1950's style glitzy cabaret, with an M.C., a juggler, a singer or two, and a stripper. The **Rembrandtsplein** evokes this image, with its neon-filled arena of nightclubs, restaurants, and bars that cater mainly to an older crowd which still thinks a naked woman hiding behind some large feathers is pretty darn risque. While the Zeedjik offers drinking and a lot of sex and the Leidseplein offers drinking and a lot of music, the Rembrandtsplein strikes a happy medium, with drinking, a little sex, and a little music.

This square consists of a number of good, rather expensive restaurants (most with sidewalk tables), a multi-screen movie theater (most shows in English), and an assortment of regular-to-sleazy bars and nightclubs (most with a dress code). In the **Carrousel**, for example, there's no cover, but you must buy at least one beer (for five guilders), which will be served by a topless waitress. The half-dozen half-naked women who work there follow a curious French tradition: they will talk with you if you buy them champagne. Why men would want just to sit and talk with a woman without her shirt on is a question for Masters and Johnson, but it's a popular concept, and three or four bars in the area provide similar fare. (There's a back room, of course, where you are allowed to do more than talk, for the right amount.) Somewhat more beautiful women, with all their clothes on, work in the **Windsor Cabaret** and **Jenny's Bar**, and they enjoy champagne just as much as their exposed counterparts.

The **Piccadilly**, with its blazing neon sign, is the most popular cabaret in town. There's no cover, but the expensive drinks (beer 12.50 guilders, drinks 15 and up) make up for that, and the waitresses get rather surly if you don't re-order. The show usually has a juggler, a crooner, and a stripper of the old school, where strip-tease had more tease than strip. Definitely for the over-30 crowd, the Piccadilly will entertain those who can resist the angry looks of the waitress.

Finally, outside these three main entertainment districts, four spots deserve a pilgrimmage. First and foremost is **Hoppe**, the most popular, most famous, and one of the oldest (1670) traditional brown cafes — which resemble London's pubs. Not that it's really any different from the other brown cafes — lots of dark wood, beautiful bottles, sand on the floor, etc. — but, for some reason, *everyone* goes here for a drink, from the after-work businessman to the before-dinner tourist, and you should, too. At Hoppe you'll have the chance to mingle with regular Amsterdammers in an atmosphere of complete relaxation. (If you can't squeeze in through the front door, there's a back door a few yards down Spui.) Brown cafes in general are always good for a light meal and a good drink. The atmosphere can be either warm and intimate or warm and raucous, but it's always warm. Another excellent and convenient brown cafe is **Haarlemsch Koffiehuis**, right across the street from the Central Station. They serve omelettes and soup there, as well as Guinness, Heineken, etc.

You also should visit at least one of these two "tasting houses," the **Wynand Fockink Tavern** or the **De Drie Fleschjes** ("The Three Bottles," also known as "Bootz Tavern"). Antique liquor bottles and casks line the dark walls, colored light seeps through the stained glass windows, and the idea is to order "tastes" of a variety of liqueur. You'll find a wide assortment of the famous Dutch gin, *genever*, here. After that, a jolt of curacao or sherry might be perfect. By the way, there's a style to drinking from the delicate, brim-full tulip glasses. For the first taste, put your hands behind your back, bend over, and sip right from the glass, which remains on the bar. Sometimes it can be tough to return to an upright position.

Finally, the **Kosmos**, a more spiritually-minded cousin to the Milkweg, offers an extensive range of metaphysical workshops and such, and bills itself as a "meditation center." Unlike the Milkweg, Kosmos is not known as a "night-spot" as such, because it doesn't have music and dancing, but it does conduct seminars in the evening.

The basement bookstore alone, crammed with titles on witchcraft, reincarnation, and things holistic, is worth an hour's browse.

Daytime

Before you start your day, you'll need two basic things: a good map with large type, and a cheap umbrella. The chances are good that it will rain, but odds are even better that it will be rainy *and* windy, thus destroying most umbrellas, whether they cost $3.00 or $30.00. Probably the best solution to the showers is a quick dash into one of the scads of small bars (there seems to be one every block) for a quick Heineken or genever.

Most likely, your focal point will be the **Central Station**, the terminus for almost all the city's public transportation. Notorious for pickpockets and hash salesmen with an inferior product, the Central Station also plays host to itinerant musicians and jugglers demonstrating their talents or lack thereof, and it's always crowded.

The true heart of the city, though, is a few blocks up Damrak at **Dam Square**, a historic and noisy plaza where all of Amsterdam eventually comes to hang out. People feed the nasty pigeons, people take snapshots of people feeding the nasty pigeons, and a punk band "on tour" or an official ceremony of some sort tries to compete with the pigeons.

Up the Damrak (now it's called Rokin) is the lovely floating flower market at **Muntplein**. The market is over 200 years old, and on the barges that line the canal you'll be able to buy all varieties of freshly cut flowers and boxed tulip bulbs that have been cleared for customs.

Keep walking up Vijzelstraat a few more blocks, and then follow your nose. That pungent, tempting odor is, of course, the **Heineken Brewery**, which offers free tours at 9:00 and 11:00 in the morning (only at 10:00 from mid-September to June 1). Amsterdam is justly proud of this world-famous company (even though locals drink more Amstel than Heineken), and you'll find both Dutch and tourists in line to tour the facilities. The tour, which sells out quickly in the summer, costs only one guilder (which goes to charity) and lasts about an hour. After seeing the brewing process, you'll be seated in a huge dining hall and served a few glasses of the product, plus cheese and crackers. And if it's your birthday, you'll get a free mug. The Heineken tour is a lot of fun, and the smell of hops will linger in your nose for the rest of the day.

About three blocks from Heineken, you can treat yourself to a quick tour through the diamond cutters workshop of **A. Van Moppes and Zoon**. The cutters and polishers work in full view, and a large display room tempts brightly. Unlike Heineken, though, these guys don't give free samples.

Walk a few blocks east on **Albert Cuypstraat**, and you will encounter Amsterdam at its most unpretentious and, perhaps, its most charming. The open-air market which extends from Ferdinand Bolstraat to Van Woustraat attracts housewives, businessmen, secretaries, tourists, and kids — everyone and anyone looking for a bargain. The scores of stands offer a good selection of clothes and curios, but you'll be happiest if you're looking for food. Peaches to kiwi, and hamburger to live eels — you'll find it along Albert Cuypstraat.

If you couldn't find it at the Albert Cuypstraat, head for the Waterlooplein, and if you can't find it there, it doesn't exist. The flea market at the Waterlooplein is, simply, a bizarre bazaar. A favorite of local youths, the stalls offer old records, jackets, books, you name it, at unbeatable prices. A used bicycle here goes for $50, tops. And yes, for those of you wondering, you can get those hard-to-find multicolored jockstraps at the Waterlooplein. While supplies last. The stalls begin closing around 4:00 p.m., and bargaining is encouraged.

If you've made it this far on foot, you've had quite a day, so pop into the **Waterloo 77** right across from the flea market for some refreshment. A cozy local spot, the bar is typical of the hundreds of bars that exist throughout town. A glass of Heineken (draft) will cost about two and a half guilders.

A great alternative to this "see-the-city-by-foot" tour is a "see-the-country-by-bike" tour, sponsored by **Ena's Bike Tours** in the Amstel Station (*not* the Central Station), easily reached by subway or tram. The seven-hour, 25-mile ride, led by a guide, offers a contrast to the bustling city. Riding through the flat, green countryside, you'll visit a farm where they make cheese by hand, a working windmill, and a picnic spot accessible only by rowboat. (If the weather turns bad and the picnic gets cancelled, the guide buys everyone a drink in a pub in Ouderkerk.) The tours leave at 10:00 every day from June 1-October 1, weather permitting. For 27.50 guilders (which includes the bike but not the lunch), it can't be beat.

But no matter what sights you see or things you buy, the best daytime activity in Amsterdam is simply strolling — through the beautifully seedy red-light district; down Kalverstraat, the glitzy, pedestrians-only "shopping street;" along the wealthy, tree-lined, canal-side streets like Herengracht and Keizersgracht, with their fine bank buildings and embassies; or through the Jordaan (especially Angeliers Dwarsstraat), a Greenwich Village type area where many boutiques and small cafes cater to the young, upwardly-mobile set in town. On a stroll, you'll see people cooking in their houseboats along the canals, and workmen hoisting furniture to a third floor window. (Incidentally, it's not your hangover — the houses are slanted slightly so that furniture won't scrape against the walls when it is pulled up.)

Restaurants

Because of the vast colonization efforts of the Dutch in the past, Amsterdam boasts a remarkably varied selection of restaurants. Dutch food itself is not particularly exciting, but the variety of more exotic cuisine, especially Indian, should leave you sated.

Both breakfast and lunch can be rather boring affairs. Breakfast usually consists of bread, cheeses, and jam, while the lunchtime staple is the *broodje*, a soft roll filled with most anything. Amsterdammers especially like their pungent raw herring, eaten plain or with chopped onions in a broodje, or dropped into the mouth from above.

The most famous dinner entree in Amsterdam actually includes more than a dozen entrees. *Rijstafel* ("rice table"), a notoriously filling Indian dish, consists of a large bowl of rice and at least twelve side dishes, such as meatballs, fried bananas, pork, and various vegetables. Scoop some rice onto your plate, and then dump a dish or two on your rice. Eat, and dump another dish. And another. And another. **Bali**, right off the Leidseplein, is Amsterdam's most famous rijstafel restaurant, but the half-dozen establishments on Binnen Bantammerstraat (a block from the Zeedjik), like **Ling Nam**, **Lotus**, and **Kong Ling**, serve a rice table just as good and much cheaper.

What makes a meal enjoyable at a traditional Dutch establishment is the lovely decor of mahogany, stained glass, pewter, and Delft china that surrounds you as you eat. **The Five Flies**, probably Holland's most famous restaurant, sets the standard for everything "Dutch" in an eating establishment. Dark, cramped, and intimate, the five houses joined together to form the restaurant offer steep stairs and an unforgettable meal, although a bit expensive. Equally authentic in both atmosphere and food is the **Holland's Glorie**; it also costs half as much as The Five Flies.

Another typical Dutch dish, much cheaper and more fun than those above, is pancakes served with a variety of fillings. A great place for this is **The Pancake Bakery** on Prinsengracht, where you can order a pancake filled with everything from kiwi to caramel, with a large scoop of whipped cream on top.

And if you're desperate for some good ol' American barbecue, **Curly's**, a few blocks from the train station, will make you pine for a Willie Nelson tune with their large portions of chicken and ribs and big draft beers. Yee-hah.

Finally, fast-food in Amsterdam is not a last resort. Throughout the city you'll find *automatieks* (small, self-serve cafes, like automats, only better), which serve good chicken, egg rolls, burgers, etc. for a guilder or two. They can be a life-saver for the late-night munch, but stay away from the small pizzas.

LISTINGS

Nightspots

The Leidseplein:
Bamboo Bar, Lance Leidsedwarsstraat 66, phone 24-39-93.
Club Atalaya, Kleine Gartmanplantsoen 7, phone 26-35-73.
de Balie, Klein Gartmanplantsoen 10, phone 23-29-04.
Het Hok, Lance Leidsedwarsstraat 134, phone 24-13-33.
Jacob's Cafe, Leidsestraat 98, phone 23-60-36.
La Bouteille, Lance Leidsedwarsstraat 68-70, phone 22-78-23.
Melkweg, Lijnbaansgracht 234a, phone 24-17-77.
Paradiso, Weteringschans 6-8, phone 23-73-48.
Revolution Bar, Lance Leidsedwarsstraat 35, phone 25-42-26.
't Cafe, Leidseplein 18, no phone available.

The Rembrandtsplein:
The Carrousel, Thorbeckeplein 20, phone 23-45-38.
Jenny's Bar, Reguliersdwarsstraat 97, phone 26-63-81.
The Piccadilly, Thorbeckeplein 6-10, phone 26-84-94.
Windsor Cabaret, Thorbeckeplein 18, phone 24-30-94.

The Zeedjik:
Casa Rosso, O.Z. Voorburgwal 98, phone 26-22-21.
Club 26, O.Z. Achterburgwal 84-90, phone 26-02-02.

Reguliersdwaarstraat:
Rose's Cantina, Reguliersdwaarstraat 38, phone 25-97-97.
Oblomow, Reguliersdwaarstraat 40, phone 24-10-74.

Daytime Drinking

De Drie Fleschjes, Gravenstraat 18, phone 24-84-43.
Haarlemsch Koffiehuis, Prins Hendrikkade 36, phone 24-80-98.
Hoppe, Spui 18-20, phone 24-07-56.
Waterloo 77, Rapenburgerstraat 169, phone 37-99-18.
Wynand Fockink Tavern, Pijlsteeg 31, phone 24-39-89.

Jazz

Bimhuis, Oude Schans 73-77, phone 23-33-73.
De Kroeg, Lijnbaansgracht 163, phone 25-01-77.
Joseph Lam, Hoagte Kadijk 35, phone 22-80-86.

Gay Bars

April, Reguliersdwaarstraat 37, phone 25-95-72.
Downtown, Reguliersdwaarstraat 31, phone 22-99-58.
Homolulu, Kerkstraat 23, phone 24-63-87.
Traffic, Reguliersdwaarstraat 11, phone 23-32-98.
Vert, Reguliersdwaarstraat 43, phone 24-63-03.
Viking, Reguliersdwaarstraat 15, phone 24-06-60.

Restaurants

Bali, Leidsestraat 95, phone 22-78-78.
Curly's, Spuistraat 3d, phone 24-60-92.
The Five Flies, Spuistraat 294-302, phone 24-83-69.
Holland's Glorie, Kerkstraat 220, phone 24-47-64.
Kong Ling, Binnen Bantammerstraat 11, phone 24-26-14.
Ling Nam, Binnen Bantammerstraat 3, phone 26-65-79.
Los Gauchos, Geelvincksteeg 6, phone 26-59-77.
Lotus, Binnen Bantammerstraat 5, phone 24-26-14.
The Pancake Bakery, Prinsengracht 191, phone 25-13-33.

Sex Clubs

Chatterly, Zieseniskade 18, phone 23-01-33.
Satyricon, Roempotstraat 1, phone 76-24-20.
Yab Yum, Singel 295, phone 24-95-03.

Escort Services

Escort Guide Service, phone 24-77-31.
Euro Escort, phone 27-10-01.
She, phone 22-29-40.
Superb, phone 27-37-47.

Daytime

Amsterdam Diamond Center, Rokin 1-5, phone 24-57-87.
Bonebakker Diamonds, Rokin 86-90, phone 23-22-94.
A. Van Moppes and Zoon Diamonds, Albert Cuypstraat 2-6,
    phone 76-12-42.
Reuter Diamonds, Singel 526, phone 24-97-15.
Artis Zoo, Plantage Kerklaan 40, phone 23-18-36.
Ena's Bike Tours, basement of Amstel Station, phone (015)
    14-37-97.
Heineken Brewery,Stadhouderskade 78, phone 70-91-11.
Kosmos, Prins Hendrikkade 142, phone 26-74-77.

*Barcelona flourishes
almost as a city-state,
worldly and self-sufficient*

Barcelona

Call Barcelona "Spanish" at your own risk. The city, perched on the seacoast near France, has always looked outward to the Mediterranean and the world. Perhaps the statue of Christopher Columbus at the harbor symbolizes it best: he's facing the ocean and the colonies, turning his back on Spain. Residents of Barcelona consider themselves Catalan, not Spanish; some refuse even to converse in Spanish, calling it *"Castellano"* and considering it just another dialect. Spain's second-largest metropolis flourishes almost as a city-state, wordly and self-sufficient.

Many Spaniards consider the Catalans cold, aloof, and opportunistic. But if this is true, then it becomes a mystery why the city possesses so much vitality and charm, producing such artists as Casals and Picasso. Centuries ago, Cervantes described Barcelona as "the flower of the beautiful cities of the world, honor of Spain, gift and delight of its inhabitants and refuge of foreigners." Today, the visitor can view the city's zest for living in the daily spectacle at the **Ramblas**, Barcelona's center for strolling and scoping. Technically five or six smaller "ramblas," or streets, the Ramblas follows a straight line from the city center at the Plaza de Cataluna to the Puerta de las Pas at the port.

The Ramblas puts on an ever-changing show: in the morning, staid retirees quietly read their newspapers. Chic students mingle with mothers and their strollers in the afternoon, and the whole city comes out to strut under the moon and the stars at night. Of course, seats are sold for this performance: just 14 pesetas (pts.) for a chaise chair on the sidewalk. But better yet, the **Cafeteria of the Opera** — across from the Liceo (Opera) — offers *granizados de limon* (akin to lemon

23

slurpees) and a view of the show.

The character of the Ramblas changes as it stretches toward the port. On the upper Ramblas, vendors hawk flowers, birds, hamsters, and other animals. A little further down, kiosks sell international newspapers, books, and porno magazines. Sex shows, prostitutes, and drug dealers lurk near the port.

A nineteenth century architect named Gaudi designed some of Barcelona's most fantastic architecture. His masterpiece, the cathedral, has yet to be finished, but still rises magnificently over the city. Some of his other famous buildings include the **Parque Guell**, built into a cliff wall, with tiled caves and other exotic details. Four apartment houses, the **Casa de les Punxes**, **La Pedrera**, **Casa Ametlles** and **Casa Batllo** are other well-known examples of his work.

Nightlife

Barcelona contains three very different drinking and dancing sections. The most affluent zone lies outside the walls of the older city and is known as **Eixample**. Its clubs cater to the rich, cocaine-snorting crowd, who live in the nearby Art Nouveau apartments. The clubs are far enough apart to require a cab or car. The "in" clubs change from year to year, but **Boliche** and **Up and Down** were the hottest last year. A third, **Boccaccio**, has lost much of its past popularity. Be warned that the clubs are in-bred and affluent — fitting in will require perseverance and pesetas.

The antithesis of this crowd frequents the low-life neighborhoods located on both sides of the Ramblas. On the left side of the Ramblas (facing the port) is the **Barrio Chino**, which translated literally means China Town, but has nothing to do with China. This red-light district must set the record for number of sex-shops per square foot. The lower Ramblas also has its share of the same. On the left side of the Ramblas the bars sell cheap booze in dirty glasses. Working-class males over thirty-five hang out here. If curiosity takes you into these areas, don't go alone.

The third and most exciting area surrounds the church of Sta. Maria del Mar and the street Passeig del Born. This section of the town combines the best of two worlds: the atmosphere of a traditional city with the accoutrements of the twentieth century. It was renovated a few years ago, and its streets are both clean and safe. A young crowd (18-35) loves to spend the evening here, but surprisingly few tourists know about it. That means that when an American walks into one of these bars, a native will be more prone to say, "American? How interesting! What are you doing here?" not *"Otro yanqui, mierda."* The clubs and bars along these streets are less gaudily decorated, more reasonably priced, and a lot more welcoming than any of the clubs in the Eixample. And while in Eixample, some discos still play "disco" music, here they play the newest in rock and new wave.

Zeleste stands out as the one club to visit in Barcelona. In the eyes of young, progressive Barcelonites, it has been "the place to go" for the past couple years. Bands belt out jazz and rock almost every night and attract a friendly university and working crowd. The place orginally became popular for its presentation of experimental music by local bands, instead of the usual "imperialistic" U.S. tunes. Today the politics are less overt, but the music remains current. The 500 pts. cover on band nights includes a cocktail. Next to Zeleste is **Cal Rodriquez**, a tiny place where the local crowd stops for late night and early morning snacks or sandwiches as they leave the club. Another late-night/early morning tradition is to stop by the bakeries on calle San Ramon (near the Rambla) for an *ensaimada*, a sweet breakfast roll, just out of the oven.

The Passeig del Born houses quite a few night spots, but the best two keep most of their charm hidden from outsiders. Two doors apart from one another, **Miramelindo** and **Berimbau** have their names written on large, imposing, and rather uninviting doors. Once inside, you enter either a soda-shop (Miramelindo) or the heat of tropical Brazil (Berimbau). The latter will sweep you away with the samba and strong Brazilian cocktails. The atmosphere is intimate and mainly for couples. The soda-shop styled Miramelindo (the name means "look at me, pretty boy") has two floors, with table and bar seats, and snacks and sandwiches at fairly reasonable prices. Their pina coladas are great, but if you want rum in them, say so.

Barcelona boasts a fine set of popular and entertaining bars. **The London Bar**, near the Ramblas, attracts a native crowd. It was opened in 1909 according to pure Modernist (Spanish Art Deco) precepts and the mood and architecture have been kept intact. The clientele displays some appropriately nostalgic bohemianism. **Bodas**, also near the Ramblas and known as the king of cocktails, is duly famous for its elaborate drinks and zany bartenders. There are new drink specials every night, and a trendy, heterogeneous crowd. The bartenders are quite entertaining if nothing else is doing.

The Dry Martini must be Spain's only "martineria." The owner and bartender, Pedro Carbonell, has 80 types of gin and offers a new "Martini del dia" every day. It also has the other ingredients that make up a good bar — good booze and good boozers. For a more classical drinking experience, **Els Quatre Gats** furnishes a good example of a bar-tertulia style setting. Tertulias were informal intellectual gatherings held at the turn of the century. This bar draws its name from an early 20th century avant-garde movement that had its headquarters across the street. Glasses of champagne cost only 70 pts.

To play games, head for **El Casino**, located in one of the most "chic" quarters of the city. Although it looks like a traditional casino, El Casino features only skill games like dominos, parchesi, chess, and cards. One "regular" there told us that the prerequisites for entering are to be young, rich, good-looking, and lots of fun.

To be entertained for the evening, visit **La Bodega Bohemia**. Singers of anything from opera to flamenco used to get their start here. Now you'll see imitations of those nostalgic scenes along with some new and future stars looking for ready ears and applause. If you're a would-be singer, get up and show your stuff, and see what the Barcelona crowd thinks of you.

As far as daytime drinking, Barcelona is not as big as Madrid on tapas. If you got into the habit of bar-hopping for tapas in Madrid (it's a hard habit to break), try **Casa Tejada** for the best assortment in town. Or the very heart of the older quarter (Barrio Gotico) around the Plaza de San Jaume makes for good prowling grounds.

Restaurants

Since it stands near the sea, Barcelona is *the* place to eat seafood. And the place in Barcelona sits next to the water. Take the Metro to Ciutadella and walk down to the streets packed with moderately priced restaurants, their large windows overlooking the ocean. Not surprisingly, these places draw large crowds. The best choice on the menu in any of these restaurants is the *paella de mariscos* (seafood rice dish), which can be ordered for two or more people. Other specialties include fresh-caught *lenguado* (sole) and *merluza* (hake). Although Spanish meals usually consist of two dishes, it is quite acceptable to make a complete meal out of a paella and a bottle or two of red wine. If you decide to dine on just one dish, get a large salad, put it in the middle of the table, and share it Spanish-style. The **Barcelonata**, a metro stop and Barcelona's other maritime quarter, also is packed with seafood restaurants, but one, **Can Costa**, is really special. Brave the occasional line and enjoy a superior supper.

A place with tradition in another section of town is **El Born**. This bar and restaurant was once a cod-fish store, and the odd depressions in the bar were sinks, used to soak the dried cod. El Born was converted to a restaurant in 1976, when the entire quarter was cleaned up. The cuisine is strictly Catalan — in fact, the neighbors do most of the cooking. The cocktails are excellent and the people friendly. There is an all-you-can eat open buffet nightly that costs 850 pts. per person.

El Agut (not to be confused with El Agut d'Avignon which is also quite good but twice as expensive), remains the spacious working man's bar/restaurant it has been since its founding in 1924, with dinner running 500 to 600 pts. They don't serve such upper-class frills as aperitifs, champagne or coffee, but a great *sopa de pescadores* (fisherman's soup) costs just 110 pts. The cooking is Catalan.

Two small but special Catalan restaurants are **Quatre Barras** and **Raim**. Next to the old train station (by the port), Raim serves its food in a family-like setting. With slightly higher prices, but first-class food, Quatre Barras draws a crowd bigger than its quarters. Arrive early (8:30-9:30) to get into this restaurant near the Ramblas.

Theater can be combined with dinner at the **Teatre Iliure** *(teatro libre* in Catalan) and the **Restaurant del Teatre**. The restaurant, housed in the former bar and waiting room of the theater, is a hotbed of Barcelonan feminism. Irene, Reyes, and Gloria, the three young women who started the place, cook excellent family-style food, and will gladly discuss feminist politics in your country or theirs. Just ask for whichever one is cooking that week. The Menu del Dia, consisting of two dishes, wine and coffee served family-style, is but 425 pts. Before dinner, see a play (in Spanish) at the innovative Teatre lliure.

Cal Culleretes, established in 1786 as a pastry shop, is considered the granddaddy of good old Catalan cooking. The Menu del Dia is 700 pts, and a bottle of white Alella is only 300 pts. For a more expensive alternative (1,500 pts), **Jaume de Provenza** serves an imposing array of seafood and dishes of their own creation (a la Jaume). Their cuisine is international with a modernist flair. **Restaurante Tallers** is a working-man's restaurant, serving good dinners for 500 pts or less. The nearby **Restaurante El Siglo** shares the same diners, but charges even lower prices. The owner insists on speaking Catalan, though.

When you're on a low budget and hungry, the sandwiches advertised in bar windows for 70 to 100 pts. can look tempting. Resist the temptation, avoid the indigestion, and try **L'Espigo**. It's cheap, cozy, and has a three-dish meal (lunch only) with wine, bread and dessert for 320 pts. **Flash-Tortilleria** has been popular with local youths for a decade, who say it's the best restaurante-snack in the city. They stock over a hundred types of tortillas, from 145 to 415 pts., as well as regular dinners. It's one of the few restaurants open Sunday. For those who really miss sandwiches, **La Compania General de Sandwiches**, also popular with young folks, makes more than 80 kinds of sandwiches on great bread.

Escaping Barcelona

The two small mountains that rise on two sides of the city, **Monjuich** and **Tibidabo**, provide a welcome relief from the crowded streets. Montjuich (210 meters) can be reached by buses 1 and 101. But the funicular that begins at the port (walk down Ramblas toward the sea, make a right from Port to Jaime 1-Miramar) is more entertaining. Just remember the last funicular to return to Port leaves Miramar at 8:15 P.M. Of course, if you miss the last funicular ride down, there is still plenty to do on Monjuich, depending only on your company and your mood. The very young at heart can play at the **Parque de Atracciones** (Amusement Park) every day but Monday. For those not quite so young at heart, Montjuich offers gardens and winding paths to stroll in relative privacy. Naturally, the best place to go is to the top of the mountain, which can be reached by taking the road winding to the right once you leave the funicular. If you are lost, just ask for the **Museo Militar** (Military Museum), located at the summit. By the way, once you're up there, the museum warrants a visit. At a lower level of Montjuich, and more easily reachable by the Metro stop Plaza de Espana, are the **Juan Miro Foundation**, the **Museum of Catalonian Art**, the **Pueblo Espanol** (an anthology of typical Spanish architecture constructed in 1929 and definitely worth visiting), and the **Teatro Griego** (Greek Theater) where open-air concerts and plays are held over the summer.

The other small mountain rising above the city is Tibidabo (summit 530 meters), best reached by the purple line (F.C. Generalitat) to the stop Avda. Tibidabo. The very ambitious may walk the rest of the way up; others will take the tram that stops across the street from the Metro exit to the funicular, and then the funicular to the top. Awaiting you is another but larger Parque de Atracciones and a cathedral that gives the best view of Barcelona and the ocean beyond. The all-boy choir there also is spectacular. The woods behind the cathedral lend themselves to good wandering, but remember that if you miss the last funicular down (it leaves at 9:30 p.m.) in the summer, it's a long, long walk down. On the other hand, the woods also make for some fine illicit camping.

Shopping

Shops are usually open in the morning from 9:30 to 1:00, and in the afternoon from 4:30 to 8:00. **Corte Ingles** and **Galerias Preciados** are large department stores open from 10:00 to 8:00, where you can find just about anything at reasonable prices. The best clothes boutiques are in and around the Plaza de la Cucurulla — **Kary's** and **Zas** have nice fashions. **Fargas**, in the Barrio Gotico, makes the finest candies (bombones) and chocolates in Barcelona. For a local specialty and necessity, visit **La Cubana**, also in the Barrio Gotico. They sell hundreds of types fans (albaniques), with prices ranging from 150 to 750 pts.

Populart, next to the Plazuela de Montcada. specializes in "arte popular rustico" or Catalan folk-art. Don't think it's for tourists, because it's taken very seriously by the locals. **La Boqueria** market, a huge hangar-like enclosure, sells food and other items, with little cafes sprinkled about to take the edge off.

LISTINGS

Restaurants

Mentioned in the text:
Jaume de Provenza, calle de Provenza, 88, phone 230-00-29.
El Born, Passeig del Born, 26.
El Agut, Calle Gignas 16, phone 315-17-09.
Teatre lliure and **Restaurant del Teatre**, calle Montseny 47, phone 218-67-38.
Quatre Barras, calle Quintana 16.
Raim, Calle Pescaderia 6, phone 319-20-98.
Can Costa, calle Juicio, phone 319-5043.
L'Espigo, calle de Copons 2, phone 225-23-88.
Flash-Flash Tortilleria, La Granada, 25, phone 228-55-67.
La Compania General de Sandwiches, Santalo 13.
Cal Calleretes, Quintana 5, phone 317-64-85.

Not Mentioned:
Salon de the "Pot Petit", Rosellon, 277, phone 228-54-11. Two young women opened a small, chic, and original salon de the in 1980, and then expanded it into a restaurant. *Plato del Dia* between 325 and 500 pts.
La Troballa, Riera Sant Miquel 69, phone 217-34-52. La Troballa was a typical Art Nouveau home like the kind you'll find along Paseo de Gracia, and a group of young people took it over and converted it into a restaurant, leaving its interior as intact as possible. The *Menu del Mediodia* (lunch) is 375 pts.
La Carassa, Brosoli 1, phone 247-29-90. For history buffs: this is said to be the site of Barcelona's first house of prostitution. Don Pedro Gibert Vila will come around at the end of your meal to offer you a *kirsch*, so you can ask him yourself. Try a *fondue de carne* (meat fondue) for 650 pts.
Vegetariano, Canuda 41-43, phone 302-10-52. Barcelona's best vegetarian food. Menu del Dia: 250 pts.

Clubs and Bars

Mentioned in text:
Casa Tejada, calle Tenor Vinas 3, phone 200-73-41.
Zeleste, Calle Plateria 65, phone 319-86-41.
Cal Rodriquez, calle Plateria 67.
The Dry Martini, Aribau, 16.

El Casino, Diagonal, 612.
Miramelindo, Paseo del born, 17.
Berimbau, Paseo del born, 19.
The London Bar, Nou de la Rambla, 34, phone 302-31-02
Boadas, Calle Tallers 1, phone 318-95-92.
Els Quatre Gats, Montsio 5.
La Cava del Drac, Tuset, 30, phone 217-56-42.
La Bodega Bohemia, Lancaster, 2.

Not mentioned:
El Paraigua, Pas de l'Ensenyanca 2, phone 302-11-31. Not a bad place to take a date, though it might be hard to find one there. The setting is Modernist. You can relax in the basement to the beat of classical music.
La Ratrac, Descartes 5. Skiing is the central theme of this bar, whether in its decoration and atmosphere or in the general topic of conversation. It's a must-stop for skiers and would-be skiers. You can see films and slides and compare the slopes.

Shopping

Corte Ingles, Plaza Cataluyna.
Galeria preciados, calle Portal del Angel.
Kary's, Plaza de la Cuchurulla.
La Cubana, Calle de la Boqueria, 26.
Populart, Calle Montcada at Plazuela de Montcada

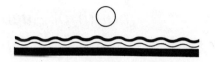

Europe's Hottest Beaches

Pyla-sur-mer
Etretat
The Algarve
Costa del Sol
Costa Brava
San Sebastian
Cinque Terre
Yugoslavia
The Greek Islands

*For the entire
month of August, all of
France goes to the beach*

Pyla-sur-mer and Etretat France

Every August, all of France goes to the beach. Not for a mere weekend, mind you, but for the entire month.

Luckily, France has long coasts on the Mediterranean Sea, the Atlantic Ocean, and the English Channel — all of them offering spectacular beaches. The Riveria is justly famous for its style and and its stunning mountains plunging down to the emerald blue sea. And in the north, there's Deauville's legendary chi-chiness and its large, white beach.

But during the summer season, and especially the madhouse August rush, these "in" spots are overcrowded and overpriced. So here are two suggestions for the "best" unknown beaches in France: Pyla-sur-mer on the Atlantic Coast and Etretat on the Normandy Coast.

Pyla-sur-mer has the best pure beach in France. Unlike many famous Riveira spots which have only stone beaches, Pyla has spar kling white sand. It is also a huge beach, stretching for miles down the coast from the bay of Arcachon near Bordeaux. Technically speaking, Pyla is one huge dune — the biggest in Europe.

The spot is popular with day-trippers from Bordeaux, but aside from some Germans, few foreigners have discovered it. English voices remain rare. Even in the summer, then, the dune is not too crowded. So it's easy to enjoy the wide open spaces, ringed by a gorgeous pine forest.

Camping is a real treat here. Locals often drive up, set up a hibachi, skinny dip, and spread out a sleeping bag to spend the night. Protection from the wind and the blowing sand is easy to find: just find a comfortable angle behind one of the large concrete bunkers built by the Germans during World War II.

For the less adventurous, Pyla offers a few inexpensive hotels. In town, there is the **Maminotte** and the **Ahurentzat**. Nearer to the beach is the **Oyana**. All are in the 80 to 100 franc range for a room. There are other, less expensive hotels in Arcachon, a few miles back on the road to Bordeaux. Contact the Tourist Bureau at the Place de la Gare for more details.

As for eating, the region is famous for its oysters, which are harvested in Arcachon's bay. Visitors get the freshest and best of the crop. Restaurants in the area, though, are not known for their culinary excellence. They are also, in general, quite expensive. But there are numerous cheaper tourist spots, pizzerias, creperies, and the like.

Near the Pyla beach, there is one nice restaurant for a special occasion, the **Corniche**. Meals run about 75 ff per person, and the food is good, if not superior. What is truly spectacular, though, is the view of the bay and the ocean below. One last piece of advice: stay away from the best-known restaurant in Pyla, **La Guitoune**. For a spot advertising *haute cuisine*, it's below par.

The northern half of France does not offer the sparkling weather of Pyla and other beaches in the south. But it does offer the advantage of being within a two- or three-hour drive from the center of Paris. A trip to the beach in Normandy is an easy one for a two-day affair, perfect as a respite from heavy sightseeing in the capital. Perhaps the most spectacular spot on the Channel coast is at **Etretat**. Here a charming little Norman town is wedged between two magnificent white cliffs. One of the cliffs looks like an elephant leaning over into the sea to take a drink, and the beauty of this image moved writer Guy de Maupassant to write glowingly about it.

On either side of the "elephant" are the beaches. While their setting is unbeatable, the beaches themselves are made up of hard stones. At least this lack of sand keeps Etretat from being overrun in the summer like Deauville, Houlgate, and Cabourg to the south.

But if the beach has its drawback, the walks around the cliffs and the verdant green fields around town make up for it. Bring a picnic and enjoy the fabulous scenery. And even if it is overcast and rainy — and this happens all too often on the Norman coast — it is still possible to take an invigorating walk, right out of a scene from *Wuthering Heights*.

Low-price accomodations abound in Etretat. But many of the hotels ask that visitors take dinner and breakfast with their room, and this practice brings the price up to 80 to 100 ff per person. So the cheapest solution is to go to the Tourist Bureau in the center of town and ask to rent a room in an apartment or a house. If that doesn't please, the lowest priced hotels are the **Hotel de la Poste**, **Hotel l'Escale**, **Hotel Angleterre**, and **Hotel la Residence**. For a special treat, there is the **Hotel Dormy House**. A room here runs about 175-200 ff a person per night and offers a breathtaking view from the top of the cliffs.

Etretat's culinary specialty is *fruits de mer* (seafood). But they are as expensive as they are delicious. For budget-minded travelers, then, it's better to stick to the numerous inexpensive creperies and pizzerias in town. For cheap French food, try the **Windsor** restaurant. It offers three course meals starting at 30 ff, service included. Locals bring their families here for Sunday lunches, and that's the best proof that the food is authentic.

*At the Fastnet, a
long stare is almost as
good as a written invitation*

The Algarve
Portugal

Everyone from the Phoenicians to the Moors has tried to grab the riches of the Algarve at one time or another, and the continual waves of European tourists (far more lucrative than past invasions) confirm that the warm weather and golden sand make Portugal's southern coast one of the most alluring — and cheapest — vacation spots in Europe.

Besides the beautiful beaches and the unusually long summer season (it simmers here April through September), variety is the key to the Algarve's success. Sun worshippers of all types find their niche here, whether it be a secluded beach on the Sagres peninsula or the steamy nightlife of Albufeira. Between the small towns and cities, and the long beaches and hidden coves, there's a place to fit all budgets and tastes — as evidenced by the amazing international mix of tourists, young and old, rich and not so rich.

Albufeira is the jetset gem of the Algarve. There are finer beaches in the 170 kilometers of sand stretching from Vila Real de Santo Antonio to the Cabo de Sao Vicente, but nowhere is there better or wilder partying. By day Albufeira is a typical Moorish-style coastal town, with a jumble of stark white buildings stacked on its hills and piles of bronzed bodies (many still recovering from the previous night's debauchery) strewn on its beaches. But by night the narrow streets of the little town ignite with crowds of young Swedes, Brits, Danes, Italians, Frenchmen, Germans, etc., in hot pursuit of a good time. (English is fairly universal among the tourists, but Portuguese — or Spanish, in a pinch — is useful with the locals, as well as polite.)

At one time the town's nightlife centered on **Sir Harry's Bar**, a landmark English pub on the main square and now an eclectic gathering place for mods and the middle-aged alike. Locals and fishermen

35

gather on the **Cais Herculano** (the wharf) and in nearby cafes, while the vacationers sip drinks on the terrace at the end of the tunnel leading to the beach. But the real heart of the action is the **Rua Candido dos Reis**, a cobblestone pedestrian street stretching from the plaza down almost to the beach. Around nine o'clock the bars at the upper end of the street begin to fill with people, and seats at the outdoor tables (the best vantage point to people-watch or scout the prospects) get scarce. None of the bars have street numbers and few have telephones — "we're too busy to answer anyway" — but they're lined up on the same narrow street and easy to find.

The biggest knot of people forms where the alley Travessa Candido dos Reis feeds into the Rua — which is also the location of the two hottest pickup bars in Albufeira. It's the best place (beside the beach) to meet someone before hitting the discos, if that's your object. **The Fastnet**, very popular with Brits, is a hot and noisy wooden bar where a long stare is often as good as a written invitation. **Twist**, across the street and more popular with Scandinavians and Germans, is a bit more elegant and specializes in coffee drinks and cocktails. The vintage erotic art gracing some of the walls doesn't compare with the ladies in the locale. The two bars next door, **Isca** and **Jota Ce**, are quieter, and it's easier there to talk without shouting and drink without getting propositioned. The owner and bartenders at the Jota Ce love to play the guitar and sing — and encourage the customers to do the same. If a good crowd of singers and drinkers is still around at the 2:00 a.m. closing time, the owner occasionally locks the doors and continues the fun as a "private party" till dawn.

Most partiers move to the discos sometime after midnight. (Bars close at 2:00, but discos stay open until 4:00.) They don't have far to go — three good ones are within a cobblestone's throw. **Sylvia's** is unquestionably the best — slick and beautiful, like its clients, with a reputation for the best-looking men. Very popular with Scandinavian women looking for summer romances, most any blond woman or dark man should have luck here. Although the main dance floor is big enough for good dancers to showcase their best moves, the aim of most dancers isn't to outdo John Travolta but rather to look as sensual as possible. Two prowling Swedish girls gave us an outrageous floor show sexier than anything in *Flashdance*.

Across the street, **7½** also has a reputation for Scandinavian women, but pales in comparison to Sylvia's. The two dance floors are too small and the decor's boring, but it's a still a great place to meet the international set that packs in there every night. **Silver Screen**, a converted movie theater, bills itself as "the biggest disco in Portugal" and probably is. Dancers will like the huge dance floor, but the second floor also offers a balcony overlooking the dancers and a video bar, while the third has a quiet rooftop bar with a good view of the street and the town. The crowd is younger and more informal, and while most discos have 500-escudo (500$00) minimums, Silver Screen charges only 200$00.

Most Algarve discos charge only males the minimum. When you arrive at a disco, don't fork over the minimum immediately — let them ask for it. They don't always charge the minimum — if it's after 2:00 or there are few people, you stand a chance of getting in free. The minimum is usually worth two drinks but ask at the door — the number of drinks varies, and often you can get more beers than liquor drinks.

Two other busy discos are about two kilometers east of Albufeira, just off the small coastal highway near the Praia de Oura. The main problem is getting there, since taxis are scarce. It's possible to walk, but you can probably hitch a ride with someone else headed that way if you haven't got a car. **Kiss**, which also houses a restaurant and bar, is probably the fanciest disco in town (a multi-level retreat of suede, mirrors, and elaborate lights), but it falls short of Sylvia's as a pickup spot. It's one of the better spots to find handsome dark-haired Portuguese women, who are drawn by the number of foreign men at Kiss. (Portuguese men often complain that the summer months are the loneliest time of the year because Portuguese women only have eyes for the "exotic" foreign men. No one feels too sorry for them, however, since they get plenty of consolation from the flocks of blonds that fly down from the frozen North in search of warmer climes and dark-haired Romeos.) Although it's just up the hill from Kiss, **Summertime** is more difficult to find. It's buried in the basement of the Vila Magna, an apartment/shopping complex, with its name painted on an unlit window. Locals say it's an "American-style" disco: a large dance floor, an entire wall of neon, and a mass of spinning and flashing lights that could blind you. The music is loud, and the crowd young and informal.

Renting a car is a great idea in the Algarve. With the limited routes and timetables of the buses and trains, it's worth the expense. The more remote beaches become accessible, and nightlife options improve. (If you really can't afford it, don't despair. But resign yourself to long walks and waiting for the first morning bus out of Albufeira.) The age minimum is 23 at most agencies, although a few say 25. Small cars can go for as little as $25 a day, although bigger cars can cost three to four times that. Shop around; there's a big difference between agencies.

Albufeira's one drawback is cost. As the town has become more popular, the demand for apartments and hotel rooms has increased — as have the prices. Reasonably-priced rooms have become scarce, especially for late arrivals in the peak months of July and August. Many budget travelers stay in the campground just north of town, and informal camping is tolerated a few kilometers out from Albufeira. If you want to stay a while, plan ahead and rent an apartment with friends. The Portuguese National Tourist Office in New York,

Chicago, or Los Angeles can put you in touch with rental agents handling apartments in the Albufeira area. (Expect to pay $300 a week or more — and prices are rising sharply.)

Buying food in a market is still the cheapest way to eat, and the biggest market is on Saturday mornings, when neighboring townsfolk bring their wares to Albufeira. But despite the other high prices in Albufeira, most restaurants are reasonable. The best inexpensive restaurant is new, chic, and a welcome break from the steady seafood fare: **Liza's Pizza Place**. This wood-and-stucco eatery offers pizza, pasta, a good view of the water, and unbeatable prices: as little as $3 for a meal.

Still, no one should visit the Algarve without sampling the local cuisine, predictably dominated by seafood. In spite of calling itself a *restaurante típico,* **A Ruina** is one of the best places to try out a new Portuguese dish or simply load up on fresh fish. (You can eat for less, but expect to spend at least 1000$00 to do it right.) The five-story restaurant, which includes a small bar and a beach-level outdoor grill, is built on the side of a cliff next to the fish market on the Largo Cais Herculano. You have to order before they will seat you — but don't worry if you're confused by the wide selection. The multi-lingual chefs will show you the 15 kinds of fish and dozen different shellfish. (There are a few dishes for meatlovers, too.) The *linguados da casa* (sauteed sole) are good, but the *sopa de ameijoas* (baby clam soup) is exquisite. The fresh fish travels only a few meters from the boat through the market to the restaurant. The local white wine from Lagoa is good, and those with a sweet tooth should finish with the *morgado de amendoas*, made with marzipan and almond paste.

The most famous Algarve dish is *cataplana*, as unique and pretty as the paella of Valencia. The dish gets its name from the unusual copper pot it's made in, a sort of double-pot that clamps shut like a big metal clam. They're hanging as a decoration on walls all over the Algarve. A variety of fish, clams and other shellfish, pork, spices, and sometimes sausage is thrown into the pot and steamed in its own broth. Fans of local libations should try the *mendoa amarga* (an almond liqueur that, despite its name, is not bitter) or the *guardente de medronho* (a sweet brandy made from arbutus berries).

An off-season suggestion: As you may have guessed by now, there are a lot of almonds in the Algarve. If you happen to be traveling in Portugal in winter, consider passing through the Algarve in February when the hills are white not with snow but with blossoming almond trees.

A brief note on skin: topless sunbathing is now accepted all over the Algarve, but total nudity will not only get you hassled by the locals but also possibly by the police as well. Nude sunbathing is best done only in secluded spots.

The most beautiful and secluded beaches are in the west, nestled among the massive rocky cliffs of the sparsely-populated **Sagres** peninsula. Do not expect to find nightlife, however — the only beat you'll hear west of Lagos is the sound of the waves. Since the Algarve train line stops at Lagos, most of the beaches can only be reached by car or by bus. (There are frequent buses between Lagos and Sagres, but you still may have to walk a way from the bus stop on the highway to the more remote beaches. The same is true for beaches off the Sagres-Vila do Bispo-Aljezur highway.) Although the tourists near Lagos are mostly British, further west the company is mostly German and French.

Zavial is the best and the most remote beach between Lagos and Sagres. Get off the bus at the town of Raposeira (24 kilometers west of Lagos) and walk four kilometers along the small road to the beach. Take the left fork, through the little town of Hortas do Tabual. There's no official campground, but many young Germans camp by the beach. There are no townies to ogle the numerous topless bathers at Zavial or in the rocky coves to the south (just follow the road and look for paths leading to the water). Bring food and drink, since the only building at Zavial, a small cafe, is rarely open. The long beach at **Salema**, 18 kilometers west of Lagos, is second only to Zavial. While Zavial is completely isolated, Salema has a large campground, a hotel, and several bars in town. There are enough people to keep from getting bored, but the beach is still uncrowded and popular for topless bathing.

Many people will want to stay at the youth hostel in Sagres and trek from there to the various beaches. Although Sagres isn't very big, the town also has many rooms in private homes, for about 500$00 a night. Sagres has three good beaches of its own, **Mareta** and **Tonel** on either side of the fortress, and **Beliche** halfway to the Cabo de Sao Vicente, the site of Europe's most powerful lighthouse and some of its most beautiful sunsets. Nightlife is mellow in Sagres, centering on beer and good conversation. A favorite spot currently is the porch of the **Restaurant Mar a Vista**, overlooking Mareta beach.

There are numerous beaches north of Sagres, but most are extremely difficult to get to and all are buffeted by the Atlantic's strong winds and pounding surf. That makes them the most private, too. Two exquisite beaches are close to the tiny town of **Carrapateira**. A dirt road makes a loop from the town to mile-long Bordeira beach, south over massive multi-colored cliffs, down to superb **Amado** beach, and back to town. Many young French and German tourists set up camp by the expanse of dunes at **Bordeira**, one of the better places to work on an all-over tan. A four-kilometer walk from Vila do Bispo will get you to quiet **Castelejo** beach, and a few more kilometers on a dirt road north will take you to the even more remote beaches of **Cordama**, **Barriga**, and **Mouranitos**.

The beaches in the eastern Algarve — from Faro to the Spanish border on the Guadiana River — are long, flat expanses of golden sand. Many of the beaches are actually barrier islands and can only be reached by private boat or a ferry from the nearest town. Although some Brits come to the area, the majority of the people on the beaches are locals or tourists from other parts of Portugal. There are quiet sections on these beaches, but generally it means walking a few kilometers to get away from the crowd. Runners should think about putting in their miles barefoot down by the surf — the long beaches are firm and flat enough in most places for a beautiful workout.

Faro, the moderately-priced capital of the Algarve, has retained its national character far more than the tourist-flooded towns to the west. The Praia de Faro, accessible from the center of town by bus or ferry, is full of Portuguese families and singles. Everything from water skiing to windsurfing is offered there. Those looking for silent strands should walk a few kilometers away from the noisy and congested colony of beach houses, bars and restaurants, or head for the nearby fishing town of **Olhao**. Take a train or bus to Olhao, then walk down to the water, past the fish and fruit markets to catch a ferry for the Praia de Armona or the more remote Praia do Farol.

A stroll along the shopping district's Rua de Santo Antonio followed by coffee or ice cream at an outdoor cafe is still one of the favorite ways to spend the evening in Faro, but there are several good bars and discos hidden in the cobblestone streets. **Piper's Club** is probably the only place you'll hear French disco and German rock, and one of the few spots that's busy on weeknights. The **Olympus Bar** is a little gem of Moorish arches and white stucco tucked away on a dark alley. When the dance floor gets crowded, the people just dance in the aisles between the wrought-iron and marble cafe tables. **Sheherazade**, in the massive Hotel Eva, used to be the only disco in town and is still the fanciest. Welcome to Islamic disco: ceramic-tiled, grottoes with Moorish arches and flashing colored lights. If at night you're still at the beach or staying at the campground at the Praia de Faro, check out the packed discotheque **A Barracuda**.

*Costa del Sol is like
Ft. Lauderdale, but much
bigger and much more refined*

Costa del Sol
Spain

During Spring Break, American students go to Fort Lauderdale; on their break, European students head to the Costa del Sol. Scandinavians, French, Germans, and English all flock to this paradise by the sea, seeking sun, surf, sex, and sophistication. One verteran compares the two succintly: "The Costa del Sol is like Fort Lauderdale, but five times bigger and much more refined." And just like Fort Lauderdale, there are better beaches nearby, but people go to both resorts for the company of their peers and for the nightlife.

Europeans say that the summer weather on the Costa del Sol is the finest climate anywhere. Through June, July, and August, the temperature averages eighty-five degrees with next to no humidity and less than a full day of rain. In addition, low prices make keeping within a budget easy.

Two cities in the middle of the Costa del Sol, **Torremolinos** and **Fuengirola**, attract tens of thousands of young folk with their low prices and high-rise hotels. Here, people enjoy a fast-paced life of drinking, dancing, and playing. The days on the beach are long, but the nights in the discoteques are longer yet. Everyone comes here to relax and meet new people. This melting pot of vacationers explains why Torremolinos and nearby Fuengirola are so much fun. In one evening, you can dance with a Dane, flirt with a Finlander, and neck with a Norwegian.

Although Torremolinos and neighboring Fuengirola are good-sized cities, hotels on the beach fill up early. In-town hotels usually have rooms, though, or an American travel agent can help you book an apartment.

Days begin very late on the Costa del Sol because the beaches stay empty until 11:00. Some attribute this to the late-rising sun, but those with a keener eye note that no one is in bed before 5:00 a.m. On the beach, most rent a chaise chair and umbrella for the day at 200 pesetas (pts). While on the beach, natives enjoy a refreshing drink called *Vino Tinto y Cassera*, which roughly resembles a mixture of red wine and lemon soda. Other favorites include the white sangria (which packs a surprising punch), and San Miguel, the local Budweiser. All beaches have bars right on the sand, but shopping at a *supermercado* (supermarket) will save money. The **Calle San Miguel** is a shopping extravaganza of block-after-block of pedestrian streets, jammed with reasonably priced stores. Every Tuesday, a flea market takes place by the Fuengirola bullfighting ring. Vendors sell everything from matador underwear to clay pots.

Lunch runs from 2:00 to 3:30, and dinner starts at 9:30. Restaurants in these coastal cities dish up delightful seafood feasts with wine for less than 700 pts. Spaniards say the only place to eat is at **La Carihuela** in Torremolinos, the city's fishing village. This walkway, stretching a half mile along the water, is packed with fish restaurants. **El Roque**, **Los Remos**, and **Casa Juan** are three favorites, and all are good. In Fuengirola, the Calle de la Cruz feature two fine seafood restaurants — **Los Amigos** and **Rincon d'Cristobol**. These restaurants, in a narrow alley off the main beach road (Paseo Maritimo), are small gems — ask the waiter what fish is fresh that day. Local delicacies include *chanquetas* (tiny whitebait), *boqueronis* (akin to a cross between a herring and sardine), *calamares* (squid) and *coquinas* (small clams). For the sake of your stomach, avoid *libre buffets* (open buffets); they are guaranteed to put your Pepto-Bismol into action. But the hake in Basque sauce is delicious, as is the *dorado en als*, fish cooked in a large cube of salt to preserve the natural taste. *Paella*, the renowned Valencian dish, is best in the little lunch huts on the beach, and *Rioja Siglo* is an inexpensive and excellent dry white wine that goes well with any fish.

If you get tired of seafood, the three **Mamma Mia** restaurants serve excellent pasta and pizza in an Italian atmosphere. **Portofino**, on Fuengirola's Paseo Maritimo, is the city's best all-around reasonably priced restaurant. **The Beefeater** has good ribs and meats, though don't expect a thick New York steak. Or, to create your own romantic restaurant, buy a bottle of Rioja in the supermarket and some cooked shrimp or other shellfish by the kilo at a fish market. Nearly all the hotel rooms have a balcony overlooking the sunset on the horizon; you can take it from there.

Since most restaurants have outdoor tables, many people enjoy sitting and watching the people pass by. The Paseo Maritimo and La Carihuela are both popular post-dinner spots. The piano bars at the end of the Paseo Maritimo also make for a mellow but entertaining evening. Around midnight, the discos, the sites of the prime action, swing into action. Thousands of people crowd into the scores of discos on the Montemar road in Torremolinos. Two of the classier establishments are the **Gatsby** and **Borsalino**. In Fuengirola, the **Hotel Las Palmeras** draws the liveliest crowd. The **Discoteca Palmeras**, with its charismatic owner Paco, is a small, elegant place to meet nice-looking people. Most discos have cover charges that you can convert into drinks, but show this book to Paco, and he'll let you in for free.

Outside of town, **Tivoli World** replicates Disneyland, but on a smaller, Spanish style. The shows, such as flamenco dancing and singers like Jorge Felicano, are better than the rides. Its gardens are beautiful and worth the trip by themselves. Tivoli World opens at 6:00 p.m., closes at 2:00 a.m., and the entrance fee of 600 pts. covers all the rides.

Malaga and **Marbella** are Costa del Sol's two biggest cities. Malaga houses an international airport while Marbella is home to the jetsetters. Marbella and its port the Puerto Banus are fun to visit — Bjorn Borg and the King of Saudi Arabia have villas there — but you wouldn't want to spend too much time there, unless you have their kind of money. North of Fuengirola lies **Mijas**, an old village that has retained its old, white homes. Though touristy, it is scenic. For a more adventurous day, take a two-hour drive to Algeciras and hop on the hydrofoil or ferry to visit Tangiers.

> *Inlets and coves*
> *punctuate the rocky coast*
> *with sandy and gravelly beaches.*

Costa Brava
Spain

North and east of Barcelona, in a section known as the Costa Brava, inlets and coves known as *calas* punctuate the rocky coast with their sandy and gravelly beaches. This harsh, often unpopulated coastline, although not as popular as the Costa del Sol, attracts a set of people more intent on enjoying nature than playing with new-found friends.

Calas along the Costa Brava can be large and developed, or small and virtually deserted. **Tamariu** is one of the more intimate calas, wild and crowded in July and August, calm and collected in June and September. If the sun is out on Christmas day, you can tan or even swim in this protected strand of paradise. The village is about two hours from Barcelona, (off Exit 7 of *autopista* A-17 and through San Feliu, Palamos, and Palafrugell).

On the beach itself there are several places for sitting in the sun with a beer or a coffee. The best spot for lunch is **Es Dofi**, at the north end of the beach, near the boat ramp. Alfonso, Es Dofi's *maitre d'*, chief waiter, head chef, and owner, operates with a ready smile and few zingers in English, German, and other languages, as well as a very busy bar open twelve months a year. Es Dofi's terrace catches the late afternoon sun as plate after plate of locally caught seafood specialties emerge from the kitchen. The fishing boats, small skiffs with large spotlights attached to the stern for night fishing, bring in the produce at dawn. *Butifarra* (a Catalan sausage), bread with oil, garlic and tomato (*pan con tomate*), and wonderfully fresh seafood salad complete a memorable feast at about $5.00.

Es Got de Vi ("The drop of wine" in Catalan) is Tamariu's prime eating spot. Rabbit, duck, lamb, and especially seafood are all

44

specialities. Local white wine Blanc Pescador or reds from Torres (Tres Coronas) in the Penedes region or Falset in the Tarragona district are excellent choices.

For lodging in Tamariu, Sr. Enrique Corredor at the tourist information office, on the beach, has many different kinds of arrangements. Off-season lodging is easy to come by starting at about $7.00 per person per night. High season (July and August) lodging is hard to find at times and about double the normal price. Small apartments in Tamariu rent by the week and month.

The **Parador Nacional** at Aiguablava is just over the hill from Tamariu via the coastal route. Don't believe maps that do not show this Tamariu-Aiguablava connection; it's a lovely walk or drive. The Parador itself (a nationally administered inn) occupies a breathtaking position in some high crags over a deep water inlet. Lodging there should be arranged in advance. The **Hotel Aiguablava**, which many people actually prefer over the Parador, is an alternative. The rates are about the same at $15-$20 a head. A double at the parador is $35.

In case Tamariu is full, Palagrugell is the nearest town of any size. The Sunday morning market at Palagrugell is open until lunch time (about 2:00). Farmers bring fresh produce into town and set up stalls. Game (rabbit, partridge, duck) is abundant and the vegetables resemble Matisse still-lifes. Little cafes dispense cold draught beer or a *chato* of young red wine, with perhaps an olive or an anchovy.

For side trips, the Poble Iberico, Peratallada, Ullestret, and Pals are extraordinary visits to the architectural past, ranging from prehistory at the Iberian village to the 13th-century restoration of the town of Pals.

*The nightlife in
San Sebastian has gone
mad in the last five years*

San Sebastian
Spain

Sport and food are so important in the Basque country that many a
meal is spent talking about other meals, just as an eventful whaleboat
race or log-splitting contest remains a popular topic for years.

San Sebastian rests next to the Cantabrican Sea in northern Spain,
a fresh blast of wet beauty that produces lush green hillsides and
opulent beaches. At low tide, soccer games cover the Concha, the shell-
like beach around which San Sebastian is built. Every young boy plays
in one league or another, and those who rise to the top play for Real
Sociedad, the San Sebastian first division soccer club that has won
the national title two out of the last three years. Pick-up games are
always available.

On Sunday afternoon *Txistulari* (flutists) play in the plaza and little
children dance their first *jotas* under the portico. Young hikers come
in after a long day's outing and dance in circles in the twilight, prac-
ticing dances which have come down through dozens of generations.

In mid-September, San Sebastian's film festival is a big attraction.
There are whaleboat regattas concurrently.

All during the year, dozens of bars in the **Parte Vieja** (the old part
of the city) serve a lunchtime splash of wine in shallow glasses , or
shots of draft beer (*zurritos*) for a dime or so. The displays of hors
d'oeuvres are irresistable—eggs, anchovies, peppers, chunks of potato
omelette, *chistorra* (a spicy basque sausage), squid rings, and so on.
The system on "tapas" (hors d'oeuvres) is simply to help yourself and
later report in to the bar man who adds up the tab. *Raciones* are recommended for couples or groups, rather than individual hits or *pinchos*.

San Sebastian night life has gone totally mad in the last five years.
Attractive and numerous youths cruise the bars, the crowds often

overflowing into the streets until dawn all summer and on Friday and Saturday nights in the winter. **The Hollywood**, just around the corner from the Hotel Orly at Blas de Lezo, is a hot spot, as are **Twickenham Pub** and **Bowie**, next door to one another on Calle San Bartolome. **Bataplan** and **Kabuxia**, both on the Paseo de la Concha, deserve a visit. The **Guria**, in the Victoria Eugenia theatre on Paseo de Argentina, is filled with great looking people having a lot of fun. These are all drift-in, drift-out places, with no covers. Hard core disco lovers loiter at **Ku**, which is up in Igueldo, the peak overlooking the port of San Sebastian.

The two **Casa Valles**, one in the Parte Vieja and the other near the Amara Vieja railroad station, are two of the most famous saloons. **Ambrosio**, in Plaza de la Constitucion, is another excellent little *tasca* or tavern with an inspiring counter full of pinchos. The *pastel de pescado* at **Astelena** is a little seafood pastry which has become justly famous throughout San Sebastian. Astelena is in the northwest corner of the Plaza de la Constitucion across from **El Tamboril**, another fine spot for a shot of wine and a pincho.

Basque Nouvelle Cuisine is world famous. Pedro Subijana's **Akelarre** and Juan Mary Arzak's **Arzak** are probably the two best of a formidable fleet of culinary gems. Arzak is in its third generation, but Juan Mary Arzak, who won 1974's best chef prize national award, has taken it into the forefront of European cuisine. It is not cheap ($15 and up per person) but for the $5 or $10 difference between Arzak and a couple of cheeseburgers. . .it's just worth it.

Other choices for delicious dining in a less exalted culinary milieu would include **Aldanondo** for excellent ox steak which you order by the gram. A couple of ox steaks and a big lettuce, tomato and onion salad is about as close to gourmet nirvana as some of us might care care to get. Any good Rioja red will do justice to this fare, but you can't go far wrong with a pitcher of their house wine either.

Lodging in San Sebastian is varied. The **Hotel de Londres y de Inglaterra** is the grandest old-world hotel in San Sebastian. It runs $25 to $30 a night per person, depending on the season and the accomodations. On a slightly different note, rooms can be had for $5 to $10 per person at the the **Hostal Lasa** or for $12 at the **Hotel Bahia**.

*The grape harvest is
an incredible ceremony, sacred
and yet profane at the same time*

Cinque Terre
Italy

The person who hates crowded beaches, dislikes "worldly" places, and dreams of a simple vacation close to nature will realize his dream in Cinque Terre: fifteen miles of mountains covered with woods and small vineyards, perched high above the sea, overlooking countless inlets and coves. It is an austere area, of the purest beauty.

Until 1977, when the road was completed, you could reach Cinque Terre only by train or boat. Now, though the road runs nearby, the steep hillside defeated any plans to connect the villages directly to the outside world. The houses in the Cinque Terre are built on the very steep slopes of the mountain, practically one over the other, connected only by narrow paths.

The name *Cinque Terre* ("Five Lands") is derived from the five villages in the area: Monterosso, Vernazza, Corniglia, Manarola, Riomaggiore. Monterosso, with only 2,500 residents, is the largest village. This area has been inhabited for centuries, and people have sustained themselves by fishing and cultivating grapes, olive trees, and small vegetable gardens. Looking at the terraced mountainside, you can imagine what a very hard job it was to start a culture here.

In Cinque Terre there are only a few hotels and *pensioni*, but they are quite good. Monterosso has about a dozen small pensioni, including **Porta Roca** and **Palme**. Riomaggiore and Vernazza both have a couple pensioni, while Manarola has a *locanda* (a pensione with a restaurant open to the public) with only a few rooms. Affluent vacationers rent houses either for the full season (from May to October) or for the whole year. Manarola, probably the most beautiful and certainly the most austere of the towns, is the destination favored by intellectuals and artists from all over Europe.

If lodging sometimes poses problems, there's no dearth of excellent restaurants. The typical food consists of fresh seafood and vegetables from the local gardens. The best restaurants are **Il Gigante** in Monterosso, **Due Gemelli** and **Franzi del Sole** (with a wonderful location) in Riomaggiore, **Gambero Rosso** and **Franzi** in Vernazza, **Marina Piccola** (overlooking the sea), **Aristide**, and **Billy** (in the upper part of the village) in Manarola. Only Monterosso and Rio Maggiore have such frills as cinemas or discos; both have one of each.

Walking around is perhaps the best entertainment of all. Hiking through the woods at sunset, you can see the sun glimmering over the coast, smell the scent of the lemon and olive trees, and hear the sea crashing over the rocks. The most famous trail, the **Senriero dell'Amore** ("Love Trail"), leads to the Gulf of La Spezia. Also called the Gulf of Paradise, it so enchanted the English poet Shelley that he wanted his ashes scattered there after his death.

The wine production in Cinque Terre has been renowned since the days of the Roman Empire. An especially good and rare wine is *sciacchetra*, which comes from grapes sprayed by the ocean. This wine is difficult to produce because the grapes need constant care. Only a few bunches of grapes from each plant are considered worthy of the name. The bunches are chosen one at a time, as the harvesters seek grapes of the same size, color, and ripeness. Once ready, the grapes are dried in the sun until they shrink to half their original size, and are then pressed. With aging, *sciacchetra* darkens and reaches the high alcohol level (for a wine) of sixteen percent. Every family produces a small quantity and convincing them to sell even one bottle is very hard.

The grape harvest time involves all the people of each village, creating a truly magic period. The women pick the grapes and the men carry them in special large baskets to the valley. They deposit them in the square in front of the church for blessing, and then bring them to the wineries for processing. The men descend rapidly in long lines, almost as if they were dancing along the narrow paths. They sing bawdy songs to keep their rhythm and balance, trying hard not to hamper the others in line. When they reach the square, they put down their baskets quickly, make the sign of the cross, and silently return for another load. It's an incredible ceremony, sacred yet profane at the same time.

The town of
Hvar is pretty close to
being a beach bum's paradise

Yugoslavia

When you mention beaches, many Europeans think of Yugoslavia. Surprisingly, few Americans do. Maybe they mistakenly believe the country is a Russian satellite and therefore grim, or maybe they won't go because the Eurail pass isn't accepted. But whatever the reason, they're missing out on something special. Europeans know Yugoslavia for its rugged coastline, sophisticated nightlife, and well-planned resorts. Europeans also know Yugoslavia for something else: low prices. The country needs foreign currency and charges accordingly.

The coast of Yugoslavia runs from Italy to Albania; the farther south, the wilder the country, and usually, the rarer the tourist. Behind the coast lie rugged mountains that Yugoslavians say rival the Alps in Austria and Switzerland. To try to prove the point, the country hosted the 1984 Winter Olympics. We'll leave the hills for the more ambitious and head for the safe ground — the coast.

Yugoslavia has long been a crossroads, both north and south, and east and west. The Greeks, Romans, Venetians, Ottomans, and Austro-Hungarians each left their marks here, as did the Moslems. Churches and mosques, amphitheaters and bazaars, all co-exist along the coast. Farther north, the people tend to be more "European" — the Yugoslavians say "efficient" — and farther south, they are simpler and more reserved.

Germans and Austrians still dominate the summer tourist crowd, so don't be surprised to be greeted by a "*Bitte Schon*" from the waiter. The number of English-speaking tourists has been picking up, though, and they supposedly amuse the Yugoslavians with their enthusiasm to master a little Serbo-Croatian. Hotels fill up during the summer months, but private homes and campgrounds always have space. The coastal towns range from major resorts with sophisticated discos to fishing villages where the only nightlife will be the local wine tavern.

Yugoslavia may be a complex melting pot of peoples, but they agree on one thing: nudity is fine. For those who prefer total tans, Yugoslavia provides a welcome haven. Very few towns lack a nearby nudist beach. Of course, uncovered women's breasts are a common phenomena on "normal" beaches, but it's still against the law to be totally nude just anywhere So to acommodate the dedicated, the country has nudist campgrounds, hotels, and even an entire nudist island.

Yugoslavia has a well-developed system to cater to the low-budget or last-minute guest. Hotel rooms, when available, range from $9.00 to $20.00 for a single. But private rooms cost less and can be found easily: each coastal town has a tourist agency that lists all the people who offer rooms. Usually, you'll be staying with an old lady who needs the money because her pension is too small. But other more enterprising souls have developed entire motels with bars and television rooms. Prices shouldn't exceed $5.00 a night for stays longer than two nights, though a shorter stay may cost a little more.

Yugoslavia doesn't accept the Eurailpass, but don't panic: the trains are cheap, and, in any case, most of the coast is served only by bus. Buses get crowded, so seat reservations are a good idea. The whole coast can be travelled for no more than thirty dollars, counting trips for out-of-the-way places. Don't trust the schedules; double-check with the stationmaster. Comfortable ferries connect the islands to the mainland, and they also make trips to Greece and Italy. Hitch-hiking works better on the islands than the mainland. A final travel tip: change your money by buying checks denominated in *dinars*, and you will receive a ten percent discount at restaurants, hotels and other larger establishments.

Istria, the small peninsula that hangs between Italy and the rest of the coast, is Yugoslavia's "Little Italy." Signs are bilingual and most Istrians speak Italian. The problem is finding them. Tourists outnumber natives twenty-to-one in the summer. Besides its Italian touch, Istria is known for its wine, ritzy nightlife, and polished resorts.

The Slovenian "Riviera" starts at the Italian border and stretches for 22 miles down Istria's western coast. Izola, Piran, and Portoroz make up most of the Slovenian Rivera. Izola and Piran are nice old cities, modeled on Italian resorts, while Portoroz is a modern hotel town. Piran and Portoroz have everything possible as far as water sports and nightlife, though Portoroz is a bit snobbish.

A bit further down the coast is **Porec**, which is worth the longer trip. The town has a Mediterranean style, with people living a slower pace and things running not quite so smoothly. Nearby are some spectacular fjords. The modern hotels and beaches surrounding Porec make it Yugoslavia's biggest tourist center. But the town itself is a network of narrow cobblestone streets lined with red-roofed stone houses.

Medieval towers house galleries and artist studios open to the public. To make it short — the town is bustling, energetic, and picturesque. Private homes within the town and the nice old hotel, Riviera, keep the city reasonable.

Porec is a great old town to stroll around in, especially at dusk when everyone dresses up (or down) and walks the streets to be seen. Eating is fine at the fish restaurant in the harbor at the corner of Zagrebacka Ulica. When it gets a little darker there's a disco in the old town (at the end of Dekumanska Ul.), **Club No. 1** — it's small and chic with surrealistic decorations on the walls. For a more cosmopolitan nightlife, take the bus or walk to Zelena Laguna, home of the **International Club**, "a modern entertainment facility" with a disco, nightclub, bars, restaurants, and a stage for pageants. Closer to town, nearly every hotel on the coast has a band.

During the day, the rocky beach at Sv. Nikola, the little island a couple hundred yards from Porec, can be reached by boat. For a beach with sand, visit Plava and Zelena Laguna. You can take a boat, a bus, or just walk twenty minutes due south. The boats for both beaches stop in front of the Hotel Riviera. **Plava Laguna** has water skiing, para-sailing, scuba diving, horse-back riding and more at low prices (e.g., scuba equipment for $2.00 a day). The nearby fjords are best toured in a rental boat. Mussels are plentiful there. and many restaurants will cook any that you gather. A couple hours inland, the **Plitvice Lakes**, connected by waterfalls, are considered Yugoslavia's most beautiful scenery.

A giant nudist complex lies south of Porec at the entrance to the Lim Fjord — **FKK Koversada**. It has its own camp-site, hotels, and nightlife. The complex is open to day-visitors for less than $1.00, but males, or groups of males, may have a tough time getting in.

Rovinj, a bit south of Porec on the opposite side of the fjord, resembles its big brother, and serves as a good alternative for those intimidated by Porec's crowds. Built on a hill, it houses a church with a magnificent steeple. Rovinj has its own artist colony, located amidst its narrow, sloping streets. The harbor teems with outdoor cafes, restaurants, and ice cream parlors, great for people-watching. But for dinner, visit the **Monte Bar**, past the city arch in the old city, for good Istrian cuisine. Afterwards, stop by one of the *konobas* (wine bars) in the old town to sample the local vintage. For nightlife follow the signs to the **Hotel Eden** and the Monvi entertainment center. The hotel houses a relaxed casino and the center has a bevy of discos and bars.

A few other nearby cities make for interesting daytrips. **Pula**, at the tip of the peninsula, contains a well-preserved Roman amphitheater. On the east coast, **Opatija**, a 19th century resort, looks like Vienna-at-the-sea. The place has Cannes-like atmosphere, crowds, and prices.

Life on the islands is even more relaxed than on the mainland. But if you stop at **Rab**, the traditional starting point to the islands, you may never make it to the islands. Amidst lush, evergreen vegetation, Rab is yet another beautiful old town on a peninsula. The natives are exceptionally easy-going, and eager to help you enjoy your stay. All around Rab are hidden little coves that you can discover and declare your own for a day. The best restaurants are inside the city, not at the harbor. Live bands play on the terrace of the Hotel Imperial. From Rab you can take a boat to the island of **Pag**, which is for those who like spending their vacations in "untouched nature." Novalja and Pag (the town) are major villages with hotels, restaurants, and miles of beaches. Pag also has sports facilities and a scuba-diving school. The rest of the untouched island will be adored by nature lovers.

The **Middle Adriatic** is the heart of Dalmatia, stretching Zadar to just north of Dubrovnik. The people are loud, obnoxious, and warm.

Along the coast between Sibenik and Split are good beaches and resorts, but the place to see is **Trogir**. A town encircled by water, it's a monument to a glorious past. Over the years, the old palaces and houses have become cafes and restaurants, making it a tourist favorite. You won't need any directions and it's hard to miss anything in this small, lively town. The best way to describe it is to call it a miniature Dubrovnik.

The town of **Hvar** on the island of Hvar ("the island of sun") is pretty close to being a beach bum's paradise. The whole island smells of the flower "lavanda" and the sun shines more here than anywhere else in the Adriatic. The crowd is international, young, and beautiful and the nightlife trendy. Rental boats are big in Hvar. Split the cost ($15 a day) with a couple of acquaintances and go explore the beach. Or take the more conventional little boat services to the nearby nudist/normal beaches. For lunch or dinner, drop in at on one of the two "cute" little restaurants in the harbor directly opposite the old theater. They're both touristy — fish nets, life preservers, English-language menu, etc. — but they're good. Goat cheese and fresh seafood will taste just right with the "open" (not bottled), home-made wine.

At night, people leave Hvar's exotic little clubs and mingle on the streets. Later on, many grab new-found friends and head up for the castle. Lights flashing on top of the hill mark a disco housed in a castle that Dracula would appreciate. It's a bus ride or fifteen minute walk. The **Tvrdava Disko** has a huge outdoor dance floor but a steep entrance fee for Yugoslavia — $1.25. The castle also has a bar with a small dance floor, and plenty of turrets with romantic views of the city below. If it's raining, the **Hotel Amfora** is a good alternative even though it's only open until 2:00.

Korcula (on the island of Korcula) is a bit quieter than Hvar and uniquely Spanish. To soak in the atmosphere, walk up the steps (next to the market) to the old town, down the main street to the sea, hang a left on the shoreline and arrive at the **Hotel Korcula**. Sit in one of the wicker chairs on the terrace and enjoy the view. A good restaurant is the **Adio Mare**, located near the church in the town — just look for the sign. It's always crowded, but the owner never turns anyone away — he'll squeeze you in somewhere. For later on, there are disco-cafes and bars on the shore on the other side of the town from Hotel Korcula. For a great beach, take the boat to Orebic.

Mostar, a city two hours inland from Dubrovnik, retains much of its Middle Eastern heritage. The city, bright and picturesque, has stayed off the tourist route. Once a year, the city's young men still prove their manhood by jumping off a bridge arching high across the Neretva river.

"Those who seek Earthly Paradise should come and see **Dubrovnik**," George Bernard Shaw wrote in 1931. It hasn't changed much, so it still rates a trip. It reminds many of Venice. Walking the ancient walls around the city remains the best way to view the city. Most natives go to the beach on **Lokrum**, the island just out from the harbor. A shuttle boat runs back and forth. Prijeko Street has the best restaurants, with **Rozarij**, on the west end, offering a fine variety of dishes. **Raguza**, which has a sister establishment in New York, sets a fancier table. **Stonska Zadruga** on Gunduliceva Poljana provides a relaxed atmosphere and lots of mussels or shrimp. At night, the streets between Prijeko and Placa fill with young folk, sitting in front of the bars, cafes and ice cream parlors. Out the past west gate, **Disco Lazaret**, housed in a former palace, is the best disco.

*Passengers on
incoming boats can hear
the beat of Myconos miles away*

Greek Islands

The Greek islands are paradise. Well, if not perfect, we've yet to find out what's better. On one island, thousand-foot cliffs topped by ancient ruins tower over beaches of black sand; on another, the nightlife rivals that of any European capital's for decadence; on a third, dark pine forests create an atmosphere of rustic tranquility. All this, at low prices, in a lovely summer climate surrounded by the dark blue sea.

We've picked five islands that provide the "best" in Greek islands: **Corfu**, a cosmopolitan melange of cultures; **Myconos**, world famous for its nightlife; **Santorini**, with its beautiful cliffs and ruins reputed to be Atlantis; **Ios**, a less-crowded Myconos; and **Skiathos**, with its dark forests.

Athens

Unfortunately, Athens, the departure point for the islands, has left its glory mostly in the past. Of course, most want to see the Acropolis, the Agora, the Hephaesteum, the Parthenon, and the Archeologicical Museum. Visit the flea market, next to Monastiraki subway station, for the cheapest in sweaters, hats, cotton shirts, not to mention power tools, army surplus, and just plain junk. Nearly all these goods are manufactured in Athens, so you won't save by waiting to get to the islands. Argue down the prices 10 to 20 percent, at least; more if you're an attractive female.

Athenian night-life is mediocre. Avoid the badly imitated American-style bars, and visit **Plaka** with its genuine Greek tavernas with good food. The restaurants serve similar food at pretty much the same prices. Service can be slow, so sample the good barrelled wine as you wait.

Greece's appeal lies in its islands, so the sooner you leave Athens, the better. The ships serving the islands can be overcrowded and sometimes slow. But if you survived the trip from Brindisi, you'll cope. However, with a little extra money and some planning, you can double your pleasure by chartering your own boat. This will let you be your own captain, set your own schedule, and discover that almost every island has an unspoiled side, accessible only by boat. Also, what more irresistible pick-up line is there than "Would you like to have cocktails on my yacht?" For details, see the essay on sailboat chartering.

The Islands:

The islands come in a variety of shapes, sizes, and types. During the peak summer season, lots of islands like Corfu, Rhodes, Myconos and Santorini have more tourists than locals, while Greeks still dominate on others like Milos, Pholegandros, Thasos, and Kilos. For those who want a taste of both worlds, island-hopping provides the best solution.

Corfu

Corfu, in the Ionian Sea just off the northwestern coast of Greece, and on the path from Italy to Greece, mixes its Venetian, British, and Greek heritage with panache. For anyone taking the ship from Italy, the island is worth the free stopover. Your landing point, the city of **Kerkyra**, retains an aristocratic Italian atmosphere with its narrow intertwining streets and rich villas. This very air of aristocracy attracts wealth from all over the world and inflates prices, so shop carefully.

The island (along with the rest of the Ionian) belonged to the Venetians and the British before being turned over to the Greeks. Besides the architecture, Corfu contains other reminders of its past rulers. Greeks love this city because it seems so foreign to them. Cricket, for example, is still played on the town green — enjoy a cup of coffee at the cafe while watching a match. The city offers much to do and much more to see. If you're not too busy trying to disentangle yourself from the winding narrow streets, the **Museum of Asian and Byzantine Art** houses a quite haphazard collection of Japanese, Chinese, and Byzantine art — a hard combination to match!

Although Corfu's too big to "do" in a day, mopeds, at 500 drachmas a day, are the best way to discover the island. At dawn and dusk, the groves of olive trees merge into a beautiful swath of silvery-green haze. Unlike Kerkyra, the villages have stayed very Greek and much less sophisticated. The beaches, although rarely sandy, are almost all equipped with the tourist essentials: tavernas, bars, and fast food joints. Topless bathing is rather common, but nude bathing on this island can lead to arrest, unless the beach is totally empty. You should visit **Paleokastritsa**, one of the most popular and beautiful beachs, though not on Sundays and holidays. Stop by the nearby monastery while there. **Glyfada** beach has a half-mile stretch of fine sand, quite unusual for Greece. For compulsive nudists there is even another small bay within swimming (or wading) distance; or if you would rather walk, it's accessible via a small path over the right side of the mountain (when facing the ocean) After a day on the beach, relax by going to **Pelekas**, a spot on the hill directly behind Glyfada beach. From here you can watch the sun go down in all its glory. The best combination of swimming and sea food is found at **Benitses** and **Dassia**, towns where the tavernas are lined up one after the other.

Corfu is a gastronomic island; a recent survey found one taverna for every fifteen houses on the island. The island's vegetables, especially tomatoes, are perhaps the tastiest in Greece. Most restaurant owners and farmers attribute the good food to the Corfu water and delicious oil made from native olives (the only kind you can get there). A romantic Belgian described them best: "They taste of the sun," he warbled, as he downed one after the other.

The best taverna in Kerkyra town is **Orestes**. It not only has delicious Greek dishes, but also a fanastic choice of *mezedes* (hors d'oeuvres). Try some with a glass of *ouzo*, the unofficial Greek national drink. Greek custom dictates that the more macho mix less water in their ouzo. Skip the foreign (especially Chinese) food.

The nightlife sparkles in Corfu. If spending a few hundred dollars at the Apollo Casino is not your style, there are several relatively inexpensive discos, cafes, and bars to choose from. Two discos merit mentioning: **La Boom**, for a rather loud and crowded environment, and **Playboy**, for decent drinks. Most other small discos have interesting collections of vintage oldies, mixed with New Wave and Greek *bouzouki* (folk) music. Bars also abound, but the DJ's seem to have problems finding the right music. The **Magnet** and the **Yuka** are the better ones.

Myconos

Yes, all that you've heard and read about Myconos is true. Key West, Fort Lauderdale, Acapulco — all pale in comparison to it. Passengers on incoming boats can hear its beat miles away. Some call it the world's greatest "party island," and it surely is — there is virtually no place to escape the tourists, the noise, and the commotion. No resort can rival its concentration of homosexuals and transvestites. If you don't go for the fun of it, you may as well go to see what's causing all that commotion.

For those not up to the constant struggle of weaving through crowded streets and body-strewn beaches, late May/early June would be the best time to visit the island. Don't worry, though: even then you won't be alone. For those visiting in August on a boat, the main port is not sheltered from the early winds; anchoring in some other adjoining bay may be a better idea.

Mobs of home and hotel owners meet every incoming ferry. The island has as many rooms in village homes as hotel rooms (about 3000), so owners not at the pier are probably booked solid, especially in the case of hotels. If you haven't made reservations (far ahead of time) it would be wise to take up an offer at the pier — but never the first one. Ask around. Prices drop as owners see the visitors leaving. Rooms at homes are just as clean as those at hotels and most include hot showers. The going rate for two people for one night is 700 drs., but owners won't hesitate to ask for more. It doesn't really matter where the room is situated if it's in Myconos village, since you'll either have to walk to get the bus to the beach or walk downtown for the nightlife.

Clothing and souvenir stores line every street, but remember, prices in Athens are lower. Myconos has a great collection of new wave clothing stores and others that will give the proper Myconos look — at a price that will knock your Greek fisherman's hat off. Myconos is known for its linen articles; this is one of the few souvenirs worth buying since these items are not imported from Athens.

Plati Yalos is the island's first beach to visit. It can be reached by a 10-minute bus ride. The beach is usually rather crowded, and the water is filled with jet skis and windsurfers. Plati Yalos is, relatively speaking, the quietest place to stay on the island — any of the four beach-side restaurants will provide fairly cheap but mediocre meals. **Anna's Rooms To Let** will give you a good off-peak-season deal (1,000 drs./night for 2) but jacks the price up to 1,200 drs. during peak season.

Plati Yalos serves as the gateway to the **Paradise beaches**. Small boats connect the three beaches regularly. Paradise beach has been one of the best known and most decadent nudist beaches for a decade. Here was one of the world's wildest stretch of beaches — until everyone came to find out what it was all about. Now, over half the beach is far too dressed for the occasion! The fame also has brought in a decent, inexpensive camping site and a self-service restaurant with mediocre to bad food. There is a sense of community here since the beach boat service stops in the early evening and most campers stay at the site (taxis are too expensive) and enjoy themselves with the night-time festivities that the restaurant sponsors.

Super Paradise is the next beach along the coast and has become the hard-core nudist beach, especially for homosexuals. Before long, this beach too will turn into a commercialized Paradise and those seeking some quiet will move on down the coast. For those less interested in fame or flesh, **Korfos** beach is a large, sandy, unspoiled and uncrowded beach right outside of Myconos village.

Back in Myconos village, restaurants cook up every type of food imaginable. For excellent sea food, try **Maetopoulou Square**. **Fisherman** and **Marco Polo** tavernas serve fresh seafood cooked in the Greek traditional ways (great lobster and crab). You may wait a while to be seated, but just the smell of fresh fish and squid make the wait worthwhile. **Spiro's** and **Ta Kymata**, by the windmills, offer a picturesque view of the sea. **Alefkandros** serves good, fresh swordfish. The most picturesque, secluded and romantic of them all is the **Sundown** restaurant, on the coast. **Maky's**, **Niko's**, and **Paraportyani**, all a block from the police station, are inexpensive reliables.

In the evening, everyone joins in the village's unending round of nightlife. Crowds overflow the bars and and pack the streets. The chain of four homosexual bars (**Christina**, **Pierro's**, **Manto**, **Nefeli**) make Adronikis St. look like a huge frat party. Everyone from punks to preppies comes to show off their clothes and bodies. Homosexuals and transvestites are always the best dressed (and often the best looking). Whether you go there to drink or dance, or just to be there, you must see Pierrro's nightly transvestite show at 1:00. Chances are that you won't be able to get through the crowd into the bar from the front entrance, so go to the next parallel street and get in through the bathroom entrance.

The Irish Pub, about 60 feet from Pierro's, gives you a chance to drink cheap beer, flirt, and listen to drunk Irishmen sing patriotic songs. **Apollo 2001 Disco** (by the Taxi square) tries to attract customers by employing its own friendly transvestites, but fails with its mix of underaged locals, average drinks, and repetitous disco songs. The **Sempre Viva** piano bar is crowded, but a bit more quiet and relaxing than other places.

Most of Myconos' visitors are more interested in continuous spectacles than sightseeing and relaxation. And for entertainment, no other island even comes close. But after a few days there, you'll be ready for peace and quiet somewhere else.

Santorini

Santorini landscapes: volcanoes, cliffs, beautiful sunsets, and panoramic views. It's the island with allegedly "more donkeys than people, more churches than houses, and more wine than water." If you arrive at the port of **Fira**, take the donkey ride up the steep 580-step hike: it's just as fast as the cable car on more crowded days, and definitely more fun. Santorini also provides the homeowner/hotel reception, but ask where the lodging is located, or the hotelkeeper may take you two or three miles out of town. Anything under a half mile away is still in Fira village. Rooms in Santorini are as cheap as you'll find anywhere in Greece (600 drs./night for two). There's also a youth hostel in Kantohori (which is close to Fira) with two single-sex dorms and a crowded snack bar for 210 drs. per person per night. At such close quarters, you can't help but meet interesting young people.

Fira has the usual popular island souvenir and gold shops that offer Athenian products at higher prices. You may, however, find some interesting things at some of the antique stores. For those interested in lost Atlantis, the museum down the street from the cable car station, with its great collection of vases from Santorini's ancient civilization, suggests that Atlantis has been found. An ancient city has recently been discovered at **Akrotiri**, and daily tours to the site are scheduled by various travel agents. The boat trips to the live volcano, **Nea Kameni**, give you the unforgetable chance to swim in the warm, yellow water surrounding the volcano.

The popular **Kamari** beach (twenty minutes in a jammed bus) lurks under dark cliffs topped by ancient ruins. Kamari drops off quickly to the deep ocean. **Perissa** beach on the southern end of the island doesn't have Kamari's selection of medicore restaurants, but does offer a much larger beach and a chance to get rid of those tan lines (only topless at Kamari). Part of the beach is reserved for the more conservative bunch. Both beaches have something unique: black sand (very fine in Perissa, and more like small pebbles in Kamari) that burns feet very quickly. Camping and a few rooms are available at Perissa.

Santorini is known for its delicious tiny tomatoes, its watermelons, and especially its wines. For a fairly good meal with a great panoramic view of Santorini and the volcano, visit **Babis** or **Santorini** restaurants in Fira. **Dionysos Taverna** and **Taverna Nicholas** are more quiet restaurants on Stavrou St. with less of a view but slightly better food. And if you've been searching everywhere for homemade octopus — Greek style — **Taverna Paradise** on the main road to Perissa is the place to go. Octopus takes about one hour to cook on charcoal, so don't hesitate to order an extra bottle of that great Santorini wine.

Santorini doesn't erupt at night like Myconos does. The pubs on Stavrou St. combine mediocre drinks with a pretty unfriendly crowd. It's probably better to spend more for the relaxed atmosphere, reclining chairs, and excellent view at **Franco's**.

Santorini deserves to be explored. A day is more than enough to see the whole island. **Oia** on the north end and **Pyrgos** on the highest mountain are small but memorable villages. The vineyards, the landscape, and the small churches along the way will make it all worthwhile.

Ios

Myconos may soon face competition from **Ios**, so get there soon. Ios has a young tourist population — almost all in their 20's. Its nightlife tries desperately to resemble that of Myconos (and does a pretty good job), but the type of people that visit are quite different. Ios attracts a less snobby, more punk, more heterosexual group. There is a surprisingly large number of singles, or groups of singles, that immediately make the environment more friendly. Scandinavians and British swarm over the island, with a few Americans scattered here and there, usually on their way to Santorini. The island has a high percentage of really good-looking people.

Ios is completely barren, with only one road connecting the port, the village, and the beach. The ship lets everyone off at the port village. Most get rooms there, but the main village is actually cheaper (500 drs. per night for 2) and closer to the action — only a five minutes away by bus. Rooms in homes on Ios are pretty bad, so make sure that the beds are clean, that the shower is included in the price and has hot water, and that the toilet works. Often the owners are so stingy with their toilet paper that you have to buy your own.

The main village makes up for the Greek architecture that the port village lacks. Only one beach, **Milopotas** can be reached by bus; it's large enough to fit everyone comfortably. This lovely beach is one of the longest in Greece and one of the favorite nudist bathing spots in the Aegean. There are camping grounds down at the beach, as well as wind-surfing. For a change of scene, a boat will take you from the port to **Maganari** beach, secluded and beautiful.

The food in Ios ranges from mediocre to bad. Restaurants down in the port village are overpriced, and the customer is often ignored; if you have to eat there, don't hesitate to go in and grab your own silverware and food. They are a little more organized in the village, but the food is still middling.

Pubs and bars abound everywhere. They do their best to be as Western as possible, including the traditional happy hours. The **Fanari Club** (on the road to Melopotas) sells cocktails for as low as 50 drs. **The Friend** is a favorite for the hippie group that usually goes and hangs out on the pavement, while the **Club 69** attracts all the "real partiers" that go and sit on the wall right outside (probably just to imitate Pierro's in Myconos, since the bar inside is usually fairly empty). For a quieter environment with jazz music and lots of British accents, try the **Kalimera Pub** and some of its cocktail specialties, the Orgasm and the Impossible.

The Sporades

The Greek islands cannot be placed in one single category; those in the Ionian Sea don't resemble those in the Aegean, and those in the western Aegean differ from those in the east. Each section has its own character and beauty. But one group of islands brings all the beauty of the rest together: the Sporades (Skiathos, Skopelos, Alonissos and Skiros).

Of the four, **Skiathos** is closest to the mainland; nature lovers and excitement seekers alike are discovering it. The island combines some of Corfu's luxuries, Myconos's nightlife, Ios's beautiful beaches, and Santorini's natural beauty, and adds to all of that a special Sporades touch: endless acres of pine forests. For Greeks it's an exotic paradise — they've never seen that much green in their life. The island attracts the young and the old, families, lots of couples, and relatively few singles, and can be enjoyed as either cosmopolitan or pastoral. Skiathos' sole drawback may be its mixture of traditional Greek buildings with ugly modern structures, but the island's natural beauty makes up for any of man's errors.

The beaches are Skiathos' greatest asset; not only are there many accessible by bus, but boat excursions can help you discover the rest. Many Greeks think of **Koukonaries** beach as their country's most beautiful. They know how to appreciate the fine sand and pine-tree shade right by the shore (most tourists, on the other hand, complain about the insects that also seem to enjoy the shade). **Agia Eleni** and **Troulos** beaches in adjacent bays are always the best alternative if Koukonaries is crowded. And you really shouldn't miss two boat excursions: Take a 20-minute ride to to the virtually unspoiled island **Tsougria**, with its one small farm surrounded by the forest. Goat trails connect the island's three beaches; most visitors stay at the middle beach (where the boat lets everyone off) while the rest go to the one facing Skiathos for nude sunbathing. The third beach usually remains deserted. The other boat excursion is to **Lalaria**, which is often combined with a hike up to Kiathos' castle, on the cliffs overlooking the sea.

Almost every restaurant in Skiathos has good food; you can get anything from a three-course dinner to a simple souvlaki in pita bread. But for those who would like to try a little bit of everything at a low price, Skiathos is home to some of the greatest *meze* (Greek snack) places. The **Mezetzidikoe** on the waterfront offers great boiled octopus, Greek salads, small cheese pies, fried eggplant, stuffed grape leaves (*dolmadakia*), and a few dozen other Greek specialties. Of course, you should enjoy it all with *tsipouro*, the best and strongest type of ouzo, and a specialty of central Greece. To escape people for a while, a twenty minute walk to **Megali Ammos** beach will take you to a very small and cozy taverna right on the beach, which serves excellent fresh squid and ground beef steak. For dessert don't miss **Neos Kosmos Coffee Shop's** *loukomades* (deep fried donut holes in honey is the best western description for it); they are worth postponing any diet until you leave the island.

It seems that people who go to Skiathos like to dance — perhaps that explains why discos get crowded much quicker than bars do (just the opposite of other islands). The large number of discos and bars aren't that distinctive, except that their drinks are a bit overpriced.

When you go abroad
send us a postcard!

Let us know if we got something wrong, or something right. And tell us how we can improve the book for future editions. If we use your contribution, we'll send you a free copy of the next edition. Mail your postcards to:

Mustang Publishing
4651 Yale Station
New Haven, CT 06520

*Two or three days
in Berlin can have the impact
of a week spent someplace else.*

Berlin

Long after you leave, Berlin will haunt you. The booby-trapped Wall,
the frantic nightlife, the anarchic squatters — all these images blend
together for a chaotic and sometimes frightening vision. This Prus-
sian city, once famous for its order, now contains thousands of squatters who live illegally in vacant buildings. This "island of freedom"
houses tens of thousands of university students who go there to avoid
their country's military draft. Isolated as an oasis of democracy amid
Communist tyranny, the city forges ahead, trampling over its own
contradictions. Berlin just doesn't add up — for outsiders or for
Berliners — but it's worth the try.

Like New York, Berlin never sleeps, so a visit there of two or three
days can have the impact of a week spent elsewhere. Alone among
German cities, Berlin has no curfew on alcohol, so nightspots stay open
until daylight. But although the strains of the decadence made famous
by the movie "Cabaret" remain, expect to see more than smokey
nightclubs and slinky singers. Berlin surprises the newcomer with its
expanse of parks and lakes — about a third of the city is park or water.

Nightlife

How do you follow the "When in Rome..." maxim in Berlin? Well,
when they're not demonstrating (no minor restriction), Berliners are
likely to be found hanging out at their favorite *Kneipe*, a word that
has no better English equivalent than "joint" or "hangout." A Kneipe
(pronounced "k'NYE-puh") can be a bar, a cafe, a restaurant, or

an indefinable combination of all of the above. If it serves alcohol and is open late, you can call it a Kneipe with a high degree of security — unless it's clearly a nightclub.

The prototypical Kneipe is pub-like in decor and patronage, with lots of wood paneling, hearty laughter, malt beverages, and maybe a dart game or a chess match to complete the image. But there are also hi-tech Kneipes (with floor-to-ceiling windows, neon lights, and waitresses with electric-blue hair) and everything in between. What these places all have in common are late hours and good conversation. The Kneipe is a home away from home, and the talk, ranging from politics to art, from sports to just plain gossip, is appropriately uninhibited.

While Berliners by nature may not be the most tourist-loving folks on earth, the Kneipe atmosphere will bring out the best in them. Once you get away from the center of the city, the number of out-of-towners in a Kneipe will diminish drastically. The neighborhood itself will be a pretty good guide as to whether the people who are there will be to your liking. If you're looking to meet students, try the Charlottenburg or Dahlem districts (near the two big universities); if you want to make contact with the local radicals, try Kreuzberg.

One good place that never shuts down is **Loretta**. With its strings of lights, the place looks like a cross between a county fair and a circus. Loretta combines a huge beer garden with a second bar in the back and lighted dance floor. It's self-serve, which is often self-serving (lots of singles here). The place has a cover charge only on Fridays and Saturdays, which is when it has live tunes.

Beiz has the atmosphere of a country tavern in the middle of the city, except the wine cellar is now the first floor. Beiz serves a smorgasbord of seven German wines for 15 deutsche marks (DM), which is a great way to look like a connoisseur while you're getting loaded. There are always at least a few tourists around, but Beiz is also popular with Berlin's young professional set. The big tables throw different groups together, which makes this spot a natural for getting to know the natives, who, after a glass or two, are bound to be friendly. To keep you from floating away, they offer cheese and meat platters for DM 10-15.

A third kneipe, **Slumberland**, looks like a former mattress outlet. It's one of the places where people go after everything else has shut down and caters mostly to punks and other trendy types. **Die Dicke Wirtin** (The Fat Innkeeper) draws many students with its inexpensive yet tasty fare. The atmosphere is cozy, loud, and friendly.

For bars, the Savignyplatz district, just north of the Ku'Damm, is lined with joints of every size and type. **Bogen**, with its brick walls and location under train tracks, is a classic. Bars also cluster around the two big universities, the Free University in southwest suburban Dahlen, and the downtown Technical University.

The musical nightlife in Berlin is lively as well. The jazz clubs of the 50's and 60's have been augmented by a new generation of reggae, punk, and new wave clubs, mostly in the same mold: not too expensive, but small, smokey, and usually very crowded. They draw a heterogeneous audience with a common interest in music and a common lack of concern for their eardrums. The shows usually start rather late, but that will give you time to case the joint, grab a beer, and maybe meet some of the regulars. And if the club is one of the very small ones, it's a good idea to arrive early just so you can find a decent place to sit. Though tough to get into after 10:00, **Floz** is worth the effort for its great jazz. **Eierschale**, with its smorgasbord of music, nice garden and dance floor, is popular with students from the Free University.

Quasimodo plays everything from R & B to *chansons* to *salsa* to new wave. It's great, but get there before they go on vacation (most of July and August). **Metropol**, formerly a huge, old art deco theater, has been converted into a combination cafe/disco/cabaret. Popular with the young innocents, it thus attracts its share of old degenerates.

In the summer, there are outdoor rock and jazz concerts at the **Tempodrom**, the **Waldbuehne** (also crowded but at least not so claustrophobic), and in the garden of the National Gallery.

Some cafes can entertain you as much as the nightclubs and Kneipes. On weekends, **Das Schwarze Cafe** never closes, and it only closes on weekdays if the action slows. Street musicians wander in for short sets. The crowd gravitates toward New Wave, but you can always pick up a game of pool. Breakfasts start at DM 3.50, and run to an extravagant DM 19.50. For a late-night snack, sample their ice cream, hot chocolate, or coffee with liqueur.

The **Cafe Einstein** took over an old gray house, with a nice garden out back. Intellectuals (pseudo and real) gather at the tables from 10:00 a.m. to 2:00 a.m. Berliners enjoy the Vienesse accent of the staff (they consider it romantic). The Cafe Einstein sports a more interesting menu than most cafes, including such dishes as *plataschinken* (crepes) filled with meat spinach, deep-fried mushrooms or Camembert.

Berlin's nightclubs are as varied as they are numerous. Along the Lietzenburger Strasse is a string of girly clubs featuring such exotica as a "bathtub act" and some of the biggest mammaries in captivity. (There's always a lot of action available on the street, too, for a price.) Then there are the fancy clubs which rival the Folies Bergere for ingenuity in the face of years of the same kind of show. These places run the entire gamut from the extremely vulgar to the boringly conventional to the highly entertaining. You should be able to tell what's up by the ads posted out front.

Many cabarets may not have much in common with Liza Minelli's movie set: they're more likely to be a forums for political satire that may be inexplicable unless you're up on your German and your Berlin current events. But **Chez Romy Haag** retains the old-time decadence. Even if your German is restricted to *"bier"* and *"Wiener schnitzel,"* you can understand the action at this popular transvestite show. Just DM 5 to get in, but you'll have to spend another DM 20 on drinks to get out.

Summer in Berlin is never as lively as the other seasons, primarily because the student population, which hovers at about 75,000, goes home. Many interesting places are closed during July or August for vacation, but there will always be plenty of others open. To keep track of what is available, German speakers can assure themselves of a thorough sampling of the city's delights by consulting one of the bi-weekly magazines. Either *Tip* or *Zitty* is a treasure-trove of places and events. Berliners read them religiously for theater, concert, and film calendars and reviews and restaurant listings. Non-German speakers can at least check for the hours of shows and clubs.

Restaurants

Unless you're very unusual, somewhere along the line you're going to get hungry for more than bands and booze. A few general remarks about eating in Berlin. Many restaurants don't open during the day at all, so the main meal will probably have to be during the evening. It may also set you up for the charming late-breakfast custom that's the rule in Holland but still the exception in the rest of Germany. Many Kneipes open up at 10:00 or so for breakfast, usually offering a basic continental breakfast plus a la carte extras. If this kind of schedule appeals to you, you can survive very nicely in Berlin on what amounts to brunch and a late dinner.

Few Berliners eat German food. The plethora of Greek and Italian restaurants, with their low prices and good food, attract most of the natives. But for those who want very traditional fare, visit **Tafelrunde**, which bills itself as a typical Medieval hostelry and manages to be pretty convincing. It serves more German specialties than you could shake a fork at. (That is, if you had one. They don't offer untensils, but don't treat it as an invitation to a food fight.) All the food you can grab costs DM 40. **Schoneberger Weltlaterne** is a more traditional restaurant, but still encourages the use of fingers. Smoke tends to hide the candles and fresh flowers on the tables. Spareribs, fish, and paella all look good, but the chicken in garlic sauce is the big attraction (DM 8.50 and you're *expected* to eat with your fingers). The place has a nice selection of wine, beer, and liquor. Or, for the best of the *wurst*, go to **Hardtke**. Although in the middle of the tourist district, this place still draws a lot of Berliners. You can stuff yourself for DM 12-14. **Lusiada**, at the west end of the Ku'Damm, dishes up good, inexpensive portions of Portugese food. Or **Litfass**, in Charlottenberg, is another inexpensive standard.

Daytime

Wandering the streets of the city isn't something most natives do, but it's a great way for tourists to get a feel for Berlin's multiple personalities. Unless you make the effort, you'll probably spend most of your time meandering along Berlin's main street, the Ku'damm. (Forget the myth, Prussians are as lazy as the rest of us; *nobody* bothers to say "Kurfurstendamm.") Although there's plenty to see and do there, it's just scratching the surface, and you won't get to know Berlin any better than you would New York if you stuck to Fifth Avenue and Times Square. Straying from the beaten path will yield a vision of Berlin most tourists never dream of.

For example, there's a quiet little courtyard just off the Hagelberger Strasse (in Kreuzberg) that's like a stock movie set for late 19th-century Europe: several gracious buildings surrounded by tall trees. Then there are the private villas in the Dahlem district — testimonials to the capitalist spirit that still reigns supreme here and the comforts it makes possible for some. In the opposite end of town are the neighborhoods populated by Turkish "guest workers," in such areas as along the Kottbusser Damm near the Landwehrkanal.

In the Kreuzberg neighborhood and in the Schoneberg district, there are interesting old buildings now inhabited by interesting new people. After the landlords abandoned them in an effort to demolish and replace them, squatters took the buildings over and renovated them. These squatters are not just derelicts — many of them are engineers, professors, and artists. Representing one of the phenomena that separates Berlin from West Germany just as effectively as the geographical barriers, these people are living their anti-establishment philosophies, and their homes serve as pointed reminders of alternative solutions in this enclosed city where housing is always hard to find, and by European standards, expensive. Although you shouldn't expect anyone to offer you a guided tour — remember, many of the residents are anarchists — this, like Checkpoint Charlie, is a slice of Berlin you should not miss. The houses can often be recognized by slogan-bearing banners hanging from the windows, graffitti, and wall murals, and those who want to meet real, live anarchists should frequent the neighborhood hangouts.

You can always head back to the Ku'damm if you get a sudden irrepressible urge for a Big Mac or Baskin-Robbins (actually, B-R is on Budapester Strasse, right across the street from the Europa-Center), but you'll generally get more for both your time and money in the outer districts. And since Berlin is like an island in the middle of East Germany, the outer districts are not too far out — you can get all the way across the city by subway in 45 minutes.

If the weather's halfway decent, you can almost do as well on a bicycle, and Berlin is an urban bicyclist's heaven. Almost every large street has bike lanes, and exhaust fumes are minimal. Although Berlin is quite flat, there are even provisions for tired cyclists: you can take a bike on the subway (except during rush hour) for a slight surcharge. Two places to rent: **Fahr-Rad-Mobil**, in the Charlottenburg district, and **Radhaus Wedding**, Liebenwalder Strasse 1, near the Nauenerplatz subway (U-Bahn) station in the northern part of town.

For fresh air, visit the **Tiergarten**. It means "zoo," but there's a lot more than just lions and tigers and bears. The nocturnal animal house is interesting if somewhat fragrant, and the aquarium has some real rarities. The surrounding park is one of the nicest inner-city parks anywhere (you can sunbathe on the grass, row on the lake, or just escape the city sounds in civilized green safety). If you weren't impressed by the park in the middle of the city, go out to the forest in the suburbs. The Grunewald has great bicycle paths, lakes where you can swim or sunbathe in whatever costume suits you, and many acres of pine and birch trees. Berliners love to rendezvous at **Schloss Glieriche**, at the Wannsee lake. Built by the Prussians' favorite architect, Karl Friedrich Schinkel, it serves great snacks.

For a walk to the other side of the world, visit **East Berlin**. A stroll through the center of East Berlin will tell you more about the city than any book could. Since Berlin grew westward in the 19th-century, the oldest part of the city lies in the eastern Soviet sector; the newer, more commercial region is in the west, under Allied control. The beautiful old buildings along the main street, Unter den Linden, stand next to enormous palaces dedicated to the people of the new Socialist state, and they symbolize perfectly the differences between then and now. And the experience of looking at the Brandenburg Gate from both sides of the Wall may shock: you might as well be viewing the same structure from two different worlds.

There are two ways for tourists to go from West to East (and, we hope, back again). You can take the subway and get out at the Friedrichstrasse station (the only stop in East Berlin still serviced by West Berlin's system) and run the visa and customs gauntlet before emerging onto the street in East Berlin, or you can walk across and do it all above ground at **Checkpoint Charlie**. Either way you should count on spending an hour or so getting across the border. Though you may be reminded of "Hogan's Heroes," the guards are not related to Sergeant Schulz: they are bureaucrats who take their jobs very seriously, and they have no sense of humor.

Once over, relax and enjoy it. You'll have to find someplace to spend the DM 25 they make you change, and though the restaurants are cheaper than in West Berlin, the food is proportionately worse, so it's a good idea to plan on either shopping or going to the theater. Foreign language books, music, and records are good buys, or you might want to pick up a cheap (in price and quality) camera or tape recorder. Most of the other stuff isn't worth carrying.

Shopping

At the flea markets, shopping is always entertaining, if nothing else. Perhaps because Berliners can't just drive out and dump their junk in the country, their city has countless flea markets and "antique" stores. The most established flea market is upstairs in the subway station at **Nollendorfplatz** (open daily 11:00-7:30, except Tuesdays). Old subway cars house glassware, lamps, jewelry, and books. The items are neither junk nor cheap. On Sundays there's Dixieland music in the cafe. A second flea market, open Saturdays and Sundays from 8:00 to about 3:00, is located on the Strasse des 17. The prices and quality of the goods are lower and include second-hand clothes, books, and bric-a-brac. The most innovative flea market takes place outdoors at the **Tempodron**, near Potsdamerplatz, on weekends.

Berlin also abounds in *troedelmarkt* (second-hand shops). A couple of neighborhoods specialize in them: Kreuzberg, along Bermannstrasse near Mehringdamm, has cheap things; Charlottenburg, along Pestalozzi Strasse, has more real antique stores. They're open afternoons from 3:00-6:30 and Saturdays 10:00-1:00.

LISTINGS

Nightspots, Kneipes, and Cafes

Mentioned in the text:
Loretta, Lietzenburgerstrasse 89, phone 881-6884.
Beiz, Schluter Strasse 38, phone 883-8957.
Floz, Nassauische Strasse 37, phone 861-1000.
Eierschale, Podbielskiallee right by the subway, phone 832-7097.
Das Schwarze Cafe, Kantstrasse 148, phone 313-8038.
Cafe Einstein, Kurfurstenstrasse 58, phone 261-5096.
Slumberland, Winterfeldtplatz and Maassen Strasse, phone 216-5349.
Quasimodo, Kantstrasse 12a, phone 312-8086.
Metropol, Nollendorfplatz 5, phone 216-4122.

Not mentioned:
Cafetarium, Knesebeckstrasse 76, phone 883-7878. Small, old-fashioned European-cafe style, with little round marble-topped tables, heavy glass windows, background music. Breakfast 11-2, DM 4.50-12.00. Lots of rare alcoholic treats in stock.

Cafe April Lausitzerplatz 12, phone 612-4505. Cooperatively run natural food cafe populated with the appropriate customers, funky music on the stereo. Breakfast (until 1:00), DM 3.50-8.50. Try the *muesli*, a Swiss dish, or the onion soup.

Galerie Garten, Tempelhofer Ufer 6a, phone 251-6730. A cafe making the transition to Kneipe. Pool and poetry readings. Beer DM 2.50, wine DM 3.50.

Mawi, Maasen Strasse at the corner of Winterfeldtplatz. Kneipe with bright, hi-tech decor. Big windows, cathedral ceiling. Pool table upstairs, pinball and video below. All kinds of people, but all of them under 30 or so. Beer DM 3.50, highballs DM 4.50.

Weinstube am Savignyplatz, Savignyplatz 11. Cozy Kneipe with a few tables outside in the summer. German wines only (about DM 4). Menu includes soups, salads, and quiche, as well as more substantial fare (steak, frog legs), all at very stiff prices.

Joe's Bierhaus, Theodor-Heuss-Platz 12, phone 301-7092. Not to be confused with Joe's on the Kudamm, this one in the suburbs is okay. Lots of space out there in the suburbs and the music is usually good for dancing.

Quartier Latin, Potsdamer Strasse 96, phone 261-3707. A converted theater — the hard-backed pews make for concerts that feel even longer than they are, but the artists, from jazz to Chilean folk rock, are first-class.

Wuhlmause, Nurnberger Strasse at the corner of Lietzenburger Strasse, phone 213-7047. Performance at 8:30 pm, closed Mondays. Cabaret. Mostly political, mostly left-wing.

Go-In, Bleibtreu Strasse 17, phone 881-7218. Loaded with nostalgia: a lot of people got their European start here. Music is mostly folk now. Occasional cabaret program, heavy on the literary side.

Restaurants

Mentioned in text:
Tafelrunde, Nachodstrasse 21, phone 211-2141.
Hardtke, MeineKestrasse 27, phone 881-9827.
Schoneberger Weltlaterne, Motzstrasse 61, phone 211-6247.

Not mentioned:
Midgard, Kopenicker Strasse 174, phone 612-5202. Vegetarian. Organic tempura, great salads and cheeses. Dinner about DM 13.

Plundervogel, Pestalozzi Strasse 8. Very small, plush decor but nostalgic. Not too expensive: DM 15-24 for an a la carte steak or filet with five sauces. Good wines and beer.

Kurdistan, Kaiser-Friedrich Strasse 41, phone 317-021. Cuisine from Iran: pilafs, stuffed grape leaves, shish kebab, served by waiters in nifty native costume. Main courses run from DM 8.50 to 22.

Gottlieb, Grossgorschen Strasse 4, phone 782-3943. High windows, long tables, a friendly atmosphere, and a big menu that has attracted a big following. Main dishes with meat about DM 15, vegetables (in casserole with cheese) DM 9.50.

Ernst August, Motzstrasse 30, phone 213-2715. Classical decor, delicious food, not the cheapest around but a comfortable splurge. Try the steak with 15 herbs (DM 17).

Schmargendorfer Wagenrad, Berkaerstrasse 39, phone 826-3927. A bit off the tourist-beaten path, this is a nice place to end a day at the Dahlem Museum or in the nearby Grunewald (if you didn't get too dirty). DM 20 should do it from beginning to end.

Comment Ca Va, Pariser Strasse 15, phone 881-8751. Stands to reason that a French restaurant would be on Pariser Strasse, *n'est-ce pas?* This one serves prime steaks and other goodies at low prices, considering that it's only minutes from the Ku'damm.

Shops

Elefanten Press Galerie, Zossener Strasse 32, phone 693-7026. Clever exhibits, books with a counter-culture emphasis.

Boutique Lakshmi, Pestalozzi Strasse 106, phone 313-7239. Trendy, but not too. European and Asian imports. Lots of Indian cotton, nice accessories (scarves, earrings), friendly owner.

Pop Shop, Budapester Strasse 48, phone 262-3799. This is just one of a string of shops near the Europa Center. They all have very low sale prices. Everything from water pipes to the latest in leather.

Kaufhaus des Westens (KaDeWe), opposite the Wittengergplatz subway station. Why include Berlin's biggest department store in this exclusive listing? For one thing, the grocery store on the top floor will satisfy your wildest cravings. Exotic fruits and vegetables, cheeses, canned delicacies, a good French bakery, a very good selection of wines and liquors.

Rapunzel, Hagelberger Strasse 52, phone 786-4047. This is the opposite of KaDeWe, but equally enticing. A little natural foods store with wonderful herbs, teas, and other things to make you feel good (massage rollers, all-wood combs, etc.).

Take Off, Langenscheidt Strasse 7. American Kitsch. Need a little something for your *hausfrau?* You can find a Marilyn Monroe make-up mirror or a Mickey Mouse lunch box here.

Antiquariat Robert Hartwig, Pestalozzi Strasse 23, phone 312-9124. Old books, sheet music, etc.

You can drink your
way through Burgundy
on the Canal de Bourgogne

Chartering Canal Boats

Your feet are blistered from walking through Rome and dancing through Paris. Your head still throbs from Munich, and you got the sniffles in Amsterdam. You've done all the major cities in Europe and they've just about done you in. The answer is obvious: you need a vacation.

A canal boat may be the solution to your problems. The slow passage through the friendly, relaxed back-country of Europe will refresh and reinvigorate you. You can drink your way through the hills and vineyards of Burgundy on the Canal de Bourgogne or come down from the foothills of the Pyrenees to the Mediterranean on the Canal du Midi, stopping off to visit the fortified village of Carcassone.

All it takes is a few friends, a little planning, and surprisingly little money. Prices range between 250-300 British pounds or 4,000-5,000 French francs per week for the typical six-person boat. Fares vary more with the season than the location and are highest during July and August. Unfortunately, many find the weather too cold during the other months. Though this may sound expensive, divide by six people, calculate what you are paying elsewhere for lodging, and subtract all your restaurant tabs (you can conveniently cook all your meals on the boat). Then add the intangible value of being able to ask that attractive blond at the cafe back for "cocktails on my boat."

Renting a canal boat is really quite simple. **Blake's Holidays** seems to have a monopoly on chartering European canal boats. Companies with different names always seem to end up as some operating division of Blake's. In any case, Blake's does a fine job, both on the Continent and in Great Britain. Running the boat poses few problems, too. They are comfortable and fully insured against your running them over a waterfall. This, however, shouldn't occur, since the canals are well-marked and the boats very easy to maneuver. If you can drive a car you will have no problem with a canal boat. The companies supply everything from linen to a refrigerator, and most places will rent bicycles that you can take on board and use to explore the country. Added expenses are tips for lock-keepers (about 1 ff.), gas, water, food and the occasional mooring space. Most nights you can just tie up to a tree — no parking meters, no hotel fees.

Language shouldn't be a real barrier, either. By the end of the trip your sign language should be pretty good, your French, Dutch, or Irish a little better, and you will have some great stories about trying to convince a *gendarme* that all those empty bottles near the boat really aren't yours.

France has some of the most beautiful and most efficient canals, often with train tracks near enough to make connections easy. As already mentioned, the Burgundy and Midi routes are spectacular. Brittany's canals are a bit less beautiful but are closer to civilization. Most canals date back to the seventeenth and eighteenth centuries, when extensive canal systems were built all through Europe; many of them remain virtually unchanged. They run mainly through farm lands and small towns. A few of the bigger canals still carry a good deal of commercial traffic through industrial towns. The rest (especially the Canal du Midi and the Canal de Bourgogne) cut across rural countryside and cater to charter pleasure boats and small family-owned barges. Floating along only a little faster than the former mule-trot pace gives you a chance to explore the countryside while lounging in a deck chair. The more energetic can explore ahead by biking to the local chateau or cathedral. The charter company will tell you what points of interest are along your way, but, for the most part, the country is yours to discover.

Most canals run through land that is primarily agricultural, and in France, this often means vineyards. The farmers are very possessive about their vines, and they can shake some pretty sharp hoes if they find strangers tramping through them. However, if you ask them about their vines or their presses, they usually will cheer up, show you around, and offer you a glass of their best vintage. Cattle and sheep also prowl near the canals. Beware trespassing too near them, lest your picnic be trampled. It is a good idea to have at least a pocket-size French dictionary around to help you out if you get lost biking or need to find directions to the nearest store — which is often several miles inland from the canal. Americans are usually well-regarded, especially in the northwest, where many of the villagers fondly remember the American troops coming through during the World War II.

Sadly, lock-keepers are a vanishing species, since many of the locks have become completely mechanized. Those who remain usually have lived beside the canal all their lives and know the rest of the world only from the boats which pass by. They live off the tips they get for catching lines and opening the gates and whatever grows in the small garden around their houses or whatever they catch in the canal. Many will sell you fresh fruit and vegetables for much cheaper than the markets in town, and they'll try you keep you there talking for as long as possible — even if it's only in sign language.

For a full list of boats available, prices, and places you can rent boats, check with your local travel agent, or, in the U.S., call or write:

> Morgantown Travel Service
> 127 High Street
> Morgantown, West Virginia 26505
> phone: (304) 292-8471

In England, contact:

> Blakes Holidays
> Wroxam, Norwich
> NR21 8DH England
> phone: 06053-3221-3224

In France only, contact:

> Jean-Marie Bouvry
> 67, rue Condorcet
> Paris 75009, France
> phone: 878-46-21

Or, for a list of other companies in France and Europe, try:

> Syndicat National de Loueurs de Bateaux
> Port de la Bourdonnais
> Paris 75007, France
> phone: 556-10-49.

Renting a Sailboat

If the hotels at Cannes are booked, if the ferry to Greece is too slow, there's an easy solution: rent your own sailboat. You can then cruise from resort to resort in your own floating hotel/cocktail bar.

Both expert sailors and nautical novices can enjoy the benefits of renting a yacht. Those with experience can use "bare boat" charters, while the less experienced can sail in "flotillas." Bare boats come equipped with sails, life jackets, cooking gear, and maps. You provide food, linen, and proof of your sailing expertise. Flotillas require only modest sailing skills. If you can handle a Sailfish, Laser, or other small craft, you can join the group of about ten other boats.

Blake's, mentioned in the chapter on canal boats, rents sailboats in the Greek Islands and off the coast of France. For three people, a two-week flotilla cruise off the Greek Islands costs about 225 British pounds per person. Off the Cote D'Azur, a bare boat that can sleep six costs 450 pounds during July and August, and 320 pounds during June and September. Blake's also rents larger boats and for longer periods of time. See the chapter on canal boats for the methods of contacting Blake's.

*By the end of your
trek, you'll find yourself
speaking with a Scottish lilt*

Hiking

At least half the Americans going over to Europe carry backpacks and sleeping bags, but few use them for what they're designed — hiking — and that's a shame. Europe has some of the most spectacular and accessible hiking in the world. Well-marked trails climb ridges thousands of feet above Norwegian fjords, or wander through Alpine valleys below the Matterhorn. The beautiful trails are complemented by huts that make most youth hostels look shabby. Most huts provide sturdy beds, warm covers, and lots of hearty, country food. Local hiking associations have placed some of these huts in spectacular sites: one hut in Switzerland, for example, is bolted halfway up a cliff and is accessible only by a technical rock climb. A helicopter flies in daily to bring fresh food and take out the garbage.

European trails cater to both the novice hiker and the "rock-jock." Frequent huts and gentle, well-marked paths make for easy hiking, since hikers need not carry food or tents. Any beginner may get blisters or learn half-way through the day that his knapsack is on upside down, but in Europe, the chances of starving, freezing, or getting lost are very low. Just start the first few days with short hikes between the huts. Experienced alpinists will find excellent rock and snow slimbing; they should consult the appropriate climbing guides.

Hiking helps to stretch any budget. There's not much to spend money on out there, except food and lodging in huts, which are cheap. In countries with extensive hut systems, a traveler with a backpack and a sleeping bag need not purchase much more equipment, excluding a sturdy pair of shoes and a warm sweater or two. In fact, the sleeping bag may be optional. The appropriate equipment for the various countries and various seasons will be discussed at the end of the chapter.

Besides being a low-cost break from the hectic pace of the cities, hiking gives the traveler a chance to meet some friendly people, namely, other hikers. An international set frequents the trails: you'll find Scotsmen hiking Norways's trails, and Norwegians hiking Scotland's. And they're all fairly sociable — sharing a stove makes for quick friends.

This chapter will discuss hiking in five areas: Scotland, England (very briefly), Norway, Switzerland, and Austria. Britain's hills are very easily reached, and of course, English is spoken; Scotland has beautiful terrain; but the latter three countries have the best huts.

Scotland: Unlike the Alps, Scotland's peaks will neither intimidate nor awe you; they rarely top 4,000 feet. Rather, they will seduce you with their bare-topped beauty and craggy passes, so that by the end of your trek, you'll find yourself speaking with a Scottish lilt to your voice, and wondering when you can move your clan over. Although the country is rugged, civilization is always nearby. Even northern Scotland has enough roads and villages that it's pretty rare to go more than two or three days without seeing some sign of civilization. Whether that's good or bad is up to you.

Scotland hasn't worked as hard as other countries to "domesticate" its hills with huts and trails. The huts are like the country: simple and sometimes bleak. They do *not* have stoves, so you must bring your own. Unlike some other regions, tents are well accepted here. Some Scottish trails are well marked, while others have occasional unmarked intersections. Buy ordinance maps (1:25,000 scale) in the Army and Navy store in London, or in hiking stores in larger Scottish towns. If you want to learn a new skill and better understand the maps, purchase *Be Expert With Map and Compass* by Bjorn Kjellstrom before you leave. (A warning: not all sites marked on maps as "lodges" are public; check first.)

Perhaps the most famous trail in Scotland is the **Lairig Ghru**, a remarkably flat pass that runs between three thousand foot hills. It is located in the Cairngorms, a range with some of Scotland's tallest mountains, near Aviemore. The trail is very well-used, well-marked, and has frequent huts. A fast hiker could make the loop we suggest in two-and-a-half days, but there are plenty of side-trips to scenic spots to prolong the trip. In short, this is a great place for the beginner to start: it's beautiful, popular and accessible.

The Lairig Ghru is easily reached by an inexpensive overnight train from London to Aviemore. Ask the conductor to wake you when you reach Aviemore, where you will find some expensive hotels and B & B's, and hiking supplies. From Aviemore, walk along the road in the direction the train came from, take your first left on the bridge, then go right on the footpath at the camping site, and you're on the trail.

Follow the path, climbing gently out of the trees and valleys and into the pass. A short day hike will take you to the **Sinclair Hut.** The water is potable at all locations. There's an easy hike to the top of Creag an Leth-cholin from here, with a good view of the neighboring peaks. The next day, walk down to Derry Lodge, where there's great camping. From here, you could hitch back to civilization, but much better is to loop up the back side of **Ben MacDui**, the tallest local peak.

If you were a very fast walker, you could do the Lairig Ghru in one day, hitch back, and not need the camping gear, though this haste seems to defeat the purpose of hiking.

To continue the loop, follow the path north up Glen Derry, toward the Cairn Gorm. It passes through a broad, grassy valley, populated by wandering deer herds. Go left up the hill to the **Hutchison Hut**, not straight to the Fords of Avon, and you'll find a hut with a spectacular view next to a tumbling stream. Hikers with tents can hike another half hour and be rewarded by the tranquility of the snow-fed **Loch Etchachan**, nestled on the back-side of MacDui. For our money, this is the prettiest location on the hike. For the last, somewhat longer day, hike up to the top of Ben MacDui and along the ridge for a couple miles, then descend back to the Lairig Ghru toward Aviemore.

For those who want a little rougher terrain and less company, take the train from Inverness to **Achnashellach.** Achnallshellach consists of three houses; on some trains, you have to ask to stop there. The hiking starts with a walk up a lovely pass, then back down to Liatach, a spectacular mountain bordering the ocean. But the trails are *not* well-marked, so bring a map. You won't lose the trail, but you just won't know which one you're on. Furthermore, there are no public huts, and the only public housing is the youth hostel at Torridon, a very long day hike from the train station. Again, you can drink the water anywhere.

Start the hike by walking about a hundred feet along the tracks in the direction the train is going. Take a right up the trail after the stationmaster's house. The ground around here is very boggy, so if you've arrived late, your best bet may be to camp in the dingy hut at the station. The trails fork shortly after you start. Make sure that you are not confusing the earlier trails that double back with the more major trails that fork off left and right. Continue climbing until you reach the pass with its lovely lake, cliffs, and view. Keep an eye out for deer. On the way down, the trails again become a little confusing. Fortunately, you have a large mountain and a road as reference points, unless it's foggy. If you pitch a tent up from the road (beware the small insects known as midges), take a day-hike around the back of Liatach to the ocean. Torridon has a general store. To continue your hike, explore the country around the National Trust at Liatach. For a much easier hike back to the train, take the road away from the ocean, and then follow the dirt road to Achnashellach; this will cut your hiking time in half.

There is no good book on hiking in Scotland. The standard is *The Scottish Peaks* by W.A. Poucher, but he only is concerned about getting to the top of each mountain. His directions start by telling you how to drive in as far as possible. However, his book can be amusing, as he tells you exactly how pretty each mountain is, or gives advice like "wear red socks in case you get lost." If you want to hike further in regions like the Isle of Skye, an ordinance map should give you a good idea of the nature of the country.

England's Lake District: This region, a few hours from London, justly draws loads of tourists to its steep hills, deep lakes, and stone walls. It manages to accomodate the tourists without being contaminated by them — a real testimony to British good taste. The hills here probably equal Scotland's in beauty, but this is *not* backpacking country. You will walk up one valley, with its sheep pastures, over the pass, and into the next pasture. With a little creativity, you could conceal your tent, but camping violates the spirit of the place. Instead, camp at one of the public campsites and take day hikes. You won't be escaping civilization, but you will be wandering through beautiful countryside. If you don't have the time or the desire to go to the mountains farther away, the Lake District makes an easy alternative.

One lovely and accessible spot is **Windermere**, just one train connection away from London. You can then take the Mountain Goat Bus to any of the campsites. If you don't like the razzle-dazzle of the more established campsites, ask the driver if he knows any farmers who will permit camping for a small fee. Don't believe what any guidebook says about Mountain Goat's schedule; its times and stops change according to its drivers' social habits. There's pretty hiking from Brother Water to the west, especially up "The Step." Beware the water: local custom has it that above 2,000 feet its safe, but no one seems to have told this to the numerous sheep.

Norway: The land of trolls and Vikings, fjords and waterfalls, contains perhaps the most stunning scenery in Europe. Mountain ranges cover three-quarters of the land, their peaks rising thousands of feet from the ocean. The Norwegians, who love the pristine beauty of their land, have worked hard to preserve it yet keep it accessible. Ninety-six percent of the land is open to camping: only four percent, farmland, is off limits. Fourteen parks house hundreds of thousands of acres of wild land and shimmering lakes full of salmon. It's a tribute to the Norwegian character that some huts work on a self-service, honor basis: they give you the key to the place, which you then return. If you're looking for Europe's wildest countryside, come to Norway.

Norway's touring association manages over 200 huts, ranging from unstaffed huts of four beds to 100-bed lodges. Staffed huts serve meals, self-service huts have provisions, kitchen equipment and bed linen, and unstaffed huts have everything but provisions. You may pitch a tent where you like, but if it's near a farm, it's a courtesy to ask first. No open fires are permitted during the summer months. Two traditional Norwegian foods are *knekkebrod*, a bread that keeps for weeks, and *gjetost*, Norwegian goat cheese, also with long staying power. Both may take a little getting used to.

Language poses few barriers in Norway. Many Norwegians speak English, and most youths speak it relatively well. The Norway Travel Association publishes a superb book called *Mountain Touring Holidays in Norway*. The manual is packed with suggested tours, a glossary of terms found on Norwegian maps, and the like. It can be purchased from The Traveller's Bookstore, 22 West 52nd Street, New York, NY, 10019. Maps can be purchased in Oslo at the Norwegian Mountain Touring Association (DNT), Stortingsgst. 28, Oslo 1. Or they can be purchased in London at Edward Stanford, Ltd., 12-14 Long Acre, London, WC 2. The DNT also has produced its own maps of hiking regions.

Few tourists realize that the southern tip of Norway is closer to Rome than it is to the country's northern tip. In other words, you have a lot of area to explore. Probably the best and certainly the most famous countryside lies roughly between Bergen and Oslo in a region called **Jotunheim**. Home to 60 glaciers and over 250 peaks of 6,000-feet or better, the land earns its title, "Home of the Giants."

Following the travel association's suggested route, start at Gjendesheim, which can be reached from Oslo by a combination of train and bus. Follow the path, marked by cairns, up to Memurubu, a five to six hour hike. The route runs up a ridge to the Glitterheim junction. Go west up the steep gorge (try the echoes), then up an even ridge. Descend toward the Besseggen arrete, a famous ridge. Ibsen had his anti-hero, Peer Gynt, madly ride a reindeer down it, plunging off it a thousand feet into the lake below. According to the guidebook, no one else has taken the plunge since. We weren't entirely reassured. Then up another slope, and on to the Glitterheim trail to Memurubu and the private hut there.

The next day, hike to the hut at Gjendebu. Follow the trail up the south bank of the turbulent river to the Memurutunga ridge. Or follow the even more spectacular trail that heads directly up the steep gorge. From here must be some of Norway's most spectacular views. The route passes several small lakes and joins the cairns coming from Memurudalen. Walk southwest to the big cairn above Bukkelaegret, and take the branch of the trail down Bukkelaegret to Lake Gjende. This part of the trail is a tad bit treacherous, with railings in the worst areas. From here, follow the lake to the DNT hut. At this point, we leave you to your creativity. A boat stops at the hut and can take you back, or you can continue your trek. Some of the huts, like Leirvassbu, provide guided trips across the glaciers. Near Vetti is Norway's highest waterfall, with a vertical fall of about 900 feet.

Switzerland: When most people think of the Alps, they think of Switzerland. The Alps, with their high snow-covered peaks and narrow, twisting valleys provide great hiking for all. Somehow, the Alps seem more civilized than American mountains: there's so often a quaint village in sight; or a hiker, after a steep two-hour hike, can find himself at a herder's summer hut, thousands of feet above the valley floor. Few can avoid thinking of Heidi at such times. Hikers can practice their French, German, or even Italian in Switzerland, depending on what region they choose. Beware: Swiss-German is quite different from the German spoken in Austria or Germany, though most Swiss-Germans can handle both languages.

Surprisingly, the hut system in Switzerland is a little less organized than in Norway. The huts are usually accessible by good trails, but hut-to-hut hikes can involve glacier crossings or some stiff scrambles. Furthermore, Swiss huts do not always provide food. As a substitute, there are many mountain inns near the trails that can be as inexpensive as the huts. Finally, a farmer's hay loft can provide a pleasant alternative.

A Sierra Club book, *Footloose in the Swiss Alps*, also available from The Traveller's Bookstore, helps sort out this mess. The book covers trails in six different sections of the country. *On Foot Through Switzerland*, published by the Swiss National Tourist Office, 608 Fifth Avenue, New York, NY, 10020, gives an overview and description of six routes. They also can supply maps. The 1:50,000 is probably the most helpful; maps are easily procured while in Switzerland.

While in Switzerland, most people want to go to the Matterhorn and Zermatt. Well, the Matterhorn is pretty, but you're going to have company. With some skills and a guide, you can even conquer the peaks yourself (at a healthy cost).

Another climbing region is Arolla, accessible by bus. Near the Matterhorn and Italy, the village lies in the French-speaking part of the country. Arolla houses a climbing school for Swiss youths, and is home to many guides. The country is strongly Catholic, so plastic Virgin Mary's top the ridges where trails pass along treacherous sections. They are supposed to be reassuring.

One short but spectacular hike leads from the **Arolla** to the **Cabane des Aigulles Rouges d'Arolla**. The hut overlooks a glacier that descends from the "red pinnacles" of Arolla. The route starts in the village, and follows a road until it meets a junction of three trails. The path to the hut heads northwest, up the slope. It climbs steadily, passing a group of buildings, and then heads north. In theory, the hut sleeps a couple dozen, but often twice that number stay there. Room and board run less than 20 Swiss francs. You can then retrace your footsteps back to Arolla, or head to Les Hauderes with its youth hostel. The hike, one way, is just three hours.

Austria: The question is, what will you remember more, the Alps or the huts? The German and Austrian Alpine Clubs operate about 500 huts, with 200 more operated by other hiking organizations, not to mention the private ones, accessible only by trail. They come in all shapes and sizes, ranging from primitive to elegant. All serve hot food, and all supply beds with a pillow and blankets. Nearly all have common rooms for talk and revelry; many have drying rooms for wet gear. Conveniences range from hot showers and electricity to outhouses and cold water.

The food, served a la carte, is wonderful: hot soups, veal cutlets, baked meat loaf, goulash. Breakfast is usually Continental, although a few places will cook you bacon and eggs or Austrian pancakes. Beds are on a first-come, first-serve basis, although some establishments wait until 6:00 or 7:00 to serve club members first. Do not wear your hiking boots into the huts, and although they will sell you food at the hut, it's best to bring along your own lunch. Postcards can be purchased, and it's a tradition for hikers to get their diaries stamped with the identifying mark of each hut.

The trails have frequent signs and good blazing marks. The signs often mention distances (in kilometers) and time (in hours) to the next point. Especially by American standards, a few of the trails may seem a little treacherous: crossing boulder fields or providing a steel cable or pitons as hand-holds over narrow sections. These man-made hand-holds are more for psychological reassurance than anything else, but if heights make you nervous, ask ahead about the trails. Finally, avoid glaciers, unless you possess ropes, ice axes, crampons, and the skills to use them.

You can buy maps in a variety of convenient shapes and sizes. Government maps are excellent, but are arbitrarily arranged. Better are the maps published by the Austrian and German Alpine Clubs that are designed to cover regions, not just grid points. Several commercial cartographers sell hiking maps, with legends printed in English. For those who speak German, there's the *Taschenbuch der Alpenvereins-Mitglieder*, the official guidebook to the huts. In English, there is the Sierra Club Totebook, *Hut Hopping in the Austrian Alps* (also available from the Traveller's Bookstore), or the 92-page *Mountain Rambles in Austria*, available free from the Austrian National Tourist Office, 545 Fifth Avenue, New York, NY, 10017.

The Austrian Alps need less recommendations than Scotland because there are so many huts and trails that it's hard to go wrong. East of Innsbruck, the Alps are more accessible; the Stubai Alps are more rugged and more spectacular.

Your Gear: A sign at a Scottish hut summed it all up: "Too Many People Have Died In The Hills." Be cautious, think ahead, and bring adequate gear. It takes but a few minutes for a mountain storm to move in and surround you with fog and cold rain. At that point, if you're ready, you'll put on some rain gear, an extra sweater, and sit tight until the fog lifts. Otherwise, you'll start to get hypothermia as your body temperature drops, and start to lose control of your mental faculties. Your prospects don't improve.

The first rule is to know the country. Decide what your route will be, and survey the country ahead. Ask natives what they would bring for clothing. If you can't read a map well, or if the map isn't very detailed, ask someone else for advice. Finding out late that a ridge that looked passable is actually a sheer cliff, or that blue lines denote glaciers, can have nasty consequences. If you are't sure, go another way.

The second rule is to bring warm clothes and sufficient food. Always, even on an afternoon hike, bring a spare wool sweater and some rain gear. A sample set of clothes for a trip would include two pairs of pants, a rain coat, a couple of shirts and sweaters, and a wool hat (if your feet are cold, put on a hat — your head loses the majority of your body heat). Break in a heavy pair of shoes before you start. If you'll be hiking in terrain with no huts, bring enough high-calorie food to sustain you. A dinner of sunflower seeds after a long day's hike won't do much to restore you. A rough guideline is to bring fifty percent more food than you normally eat. Mix your foods: take fats (butter, sausage, etc.), proteins (cheese, dried milk), and carbohydrates (noodles, flour).

The final rule is, plan for problems. If someone sprains an ankle, is there an easy route out? If it drops to forty degrees and rains, will you survive? What if your down sleeping bag gets wet? Think about a route that will keep you near civilization for the first few days, so you can pick up any supplies you forgot. A little planning would have prevented most of the tragedies noted on that sign.

In the summer,
young Europeans flood Lisbon,
attracted by the 'exotic' culture

Lisbon

Like several other European capitals, Lisbon had its turn to rule the world, dominating both its hungry colonial rivals and a far-flung empire. But while London, Paris, and now even Madrid have moved on to international finance and multinational markets, Lisbon seems to have stayed centuries behind — often in the same old buildings. The newer sections of the city are quite flashy, but many older ones show the effects of time and the weak Portuguese economy. A visiting businessman sniffed that Lisbon was "a second-rate city" for its lack of cosmopolitan hotels and restaurants — but perhaps that social and economic backwardness is why Lisbon, which sometimes seems a throwback to another era, retains so much of its old-world hospitality and character.

Unlike other European powers, Lisbon ("Lisboa" in Portuguese) brought its colonists home when its empire fell apart — and the former colonials keep coming. The city today is home to a human potpourri of Africans from Angola and Mozambique, Asians from Macao, multiracial Brasilians, and others. In the summer months, young Europeans from north of the Pyrenees flood the country, attracted by an "exotic" Iberian culture, the warm clime, and outrageously low prices. One of the few peoples seldom seen in Lisbon are Americans, perhaps because Portugal is neither in the usual tourist path (France-Italy-Germany), nor on the most direct route to Morocco.

Some Lisboans speak English or French, but most of the time travelers have to resort to phrase books and hand signals. The Portuguese understand Spanish easily — with the thick Portuguese accent, they'll understand you much better than you'll understand them — but it pays to throw in as much Portuguese as you can.

Daytime

Although Lisboans are basically nightowls, the city has more than enough monuments, museums, and shopping to keep tourists busy for several days. The 1755 earthquake destroyed two-thirds of the city and scores of palaces, monasteries, and other buildings, but fortunately spared the area called **Belem**. Take the trolley there from the Praca de Comercio (also called Black Horse Square) and see two great works of Manueline (Portugese Gothic) architecture, the cloister of the **Mosteiro dos Jeronimos** with its lacy facade, and the **Torre de Belem**, which looks more like a stone boat than the fortress that dominated the region for centuries. The **Se**, Lisbon's largest cathedral, is dour and boring by European standards, but don't miss the **Igreja de Sao Roque**. Though decidedly homely on the outside, this Jesuit church houses the chapel of **Sao Joao Baptista**, which is lavishly decorated with amethyst, agate, various marbles, and entire columns of Chilean lapis lazuli.

The **Castelo de Sao Jorge** has the best views of the city and the river. A trolley will haul you up to the old Moorish stronghold, but it's more fun to go on foot. Plan on getting lost and then picking your way up through the twisting cobblestone streets of the **Alfama**. Parts of this old fisherman's quarter date back past the Moors to the fifth-century Visigoths. Fishermen still repair their nets among the tiled houses, while fishwives hawk everything from lamprey to *sardinhas assadas* (sardines roasted over coals). For the hungry, there are dozens of small, cheap working-men's restaurants scattered in the narrow streets — but if you don't like the simple fare or are nervous about rubbing elbows with an ordinary Joao, head for **Malmequer Bemmequer** (if you can find it). The owners speak six languages, including English, and serve great food with real style. Despite the elegance and few tables, a meal runs only 500 to 1,000 escudo (500$00 to 1,000$00).

The city has two main shopping areas: around the **Rua Garrett**, and the area called **Baixa**, a grid of streets between the river and the Praca. (The Rua Garrett is popularly known as the "Chiado," and the Praca de D. Pedro IV is always called the "Rossio" — Lisboans are big on nicknames). Old book shops and antique stores pepper the Bairro Alto from the Rua da Misericordia to the Rua do Alecrim. Several names on the books and engravings in the O Mundo do Livro bookstore appear on Lisbon's streets as well. Ceramics and *azulejos* (tiles) are also good buys, and you'll find everything from vases to chandeliers to a complete tiled fountain (only $600 — plus another $250 to ship it back to the States) at the showroom of the **Fabrica de Sant'Anna** on Rua do Alecrim. Tours of the factory are also available, but call before you go and have the English-speaking staff at the store arrange it for you. Jewelry stores dot old Lisbon's streets

— see the gold and silver filigree at **Sarmento** in the Baixa (at the foot of Gustave Eiffel's Santa Justa elevator), and check out the ceiling as well as the silver at the **Ouriversaria Alianca** on Rua Garrett. Shoe stores, leather goods shops, and clothing boutiques fill the Baixa. **Phoebus** and tiny **Coco Loco** sell the latest disco wear and you also can pick up the slimmest of bikinis — for men and women — at **Por-fi-ri-os Contraste**. Most stores are open 9:00-1:00 and 3:00-7:00, and many have sales (*saldos*) in August and September.

If your feet get sore while tromping the Bairro Alto, head for the **Solar do Vinho do Porto**. The Port Wine Institute serves almost 300 different ports from 60 vintners in its comfortable lounge. In the Chiado, try coffee or beer at **A Brasileira**, where intellectuals hang out in a Victorian wood-and-mirror cafe and lots of Baixa shoppers take a break with coffee and pastries at the 155-year-old **Confeiteria Nacional**. Also keep your eyes open for the tiny, nameless bars that sell shots of *ginja* (or *ginjinha*), a sweet brandy made from morello cherries, a Lisbon specialty. A good one is hidden at Rua das Portas de Santo Antao, 7.

Locals and tourists alike gather in the evening to chat and people-watch at the cafes on the Rossio. Getting a table at the **Pastelaria Suica**, the most popular cafe, requires sheer luck. Try across the square at the **Cafe Gelo**, also a good breakfast spot. (A note on coffee: it also has nicknames. *Uma bica* is straight espresso, while *um galao* comes with a lot of milk.) For entertainment options — clubs, concerts, movies, everything but discoteques — pick up a copy of the weekly magazine *Sete*, which comes out on Wednesdays.

Restaurants

Numerous *almocos-jantares*, cheap restaurants catering to the working crowd, line the Baixa's narrower streets. Closer to the water, try the **Restaurante Central** for local atmosphere and a simple meal at only 200$00 to 500$00. But the **Rua das Portas de Santo Antao**, parallel to the wide Avenida da Liberdade, is the real "restaurant row" of Lisbon. **Escorial** and **Gambrinus** are the finest and most expensive (15,000$00 to sky high), serving the best shellfish and roast baby goat in town. Escorial features a superb stuffed *santola* (spider crab), while one of Gambrinus' highlights is deep-dish partridge pie. The best deal on the street is **Churrasco**, as the jammed tables show — 5,000$00 to 10,000$00 buys a great meal of fish or ribs, but shellfish will cost more. The **Cervejaria A Brilhante** is also reasonable, and serves a rich *sopa de mariscos* (shellfish soup) and a heaping platter of *porco a alentejana* (chunks of pork and baby clams in a mildly spicy sauce). **Bonjardim** is the place for *frango assado* (roast chicken) or *leitao* (roast suckling pig) in a more rustic setting — try to get a table upstairs.

Not surprisingly, seafood is the specialty in maritime Portugal. *Atum* (tuna), *peixe espada* (sword fish), and *lulas a sevilhana* (batter-fried rings of cuttlefish) are some of the standards. For dessert, pineapple from the Azores is plentiful — try it doused with Madeira wine (*ananas au Madeira*).

Dozens of good nightclubs are scattered throughout the city, but slightly effervescent *vinho verde* white if you don't stick to house wine.

For a light meal, drop in the **Cafe Gare**, across from the Rossio train station. This bustling tavern specializes in *freiduria* — dozens of the small fried goodies are piled in the window, next to huge cast-iron skillets of stewing meat. Ask for a *bifana* or a *prego* — pork or beef, respectively, on a soft Portuguese roll. Freiduria makes great travel food for daytrips — pick up a *rossol* (pastry with a fish paste filling), a *chamuca* (spicy beef in a pastry crust), or an *empanada* (pastry stuffed with meat and vegetables).

Nightlife

Although most bars, clubs, and discos open at 10:00 and some even earlier, the action usually doesn't pick up until near midnight. The big nights are Saturday and Sunday, but Friday is busy, too. Don't climb into a taxi and tell the driver to take you to a *"discoteca,"* or you'll wind up at a record store. In Lisbon, a place to dance is a *boite* (rhymes with "watt"). We'll cover the Libson nightspots here, but some equally exciting nightspots are at the nearby beach and are discussed in the "Escaping Lisbon" section below.

Dozens of good nightspots are scattered throughout the city, but some of the best are difficult or impossible for tourists to get into. To control their clientele — men more than women — some discos have a *cartao* system, giving or selling passes only to select people. Forget **Stones**, a favorite disco of the political establishment. A 4,000$00 cartao (if they would sell you one, which they won't) entitles you to enter, but you still have to pay another 800$00 a couple at the door. **Bananas**, probably the city's most popular disco, is a hangout for more radical politicos and other offbeat public figures. It also has a cartao system, but couples usually can get in without a pass for a 500$00 minimum. (Unaccompanied females often can enter Bananas without a cartao since the owner likes to have more women than men on the dance floor.) Several other discos also waive the cartao if men enter *"acompanhado,"* although single men still have problems.

Fortunately, two terrific discos keep their doors open to all. **Trumps** is where the fashionable youth go and one of the few places that cooks on weeknights. No other place in town emanates its spirit and atmosphere. They play international tunes, everything from straight to new wave, but the striking crowd is almost all Portuguese. There are quiet wood and marble booths on the ground floor for talkers, but the real action takes place on the jammed dance floor in the basement. Sometimes there's a 500$00 minimum for guys. **Whispers**, in the first basement level below the Sheraton Hotel, is a more conventional disco with black paint, mirrors, and flashing lights. They only turn people away at the door if the disco is *cheio* (full) — and Whispers reaches that point almost every night. For a 1,000$00 minimum, worth two drinks or four beers, you can wedge your way into the sea of singles and try your luck.

To get a feel for the more traditional side of Lisbon, spend an evening at the bullfights, followed by a night of *fado* singing. The Portuguese *tourada*, held from April to October, differs dramatically from the Spanish. The bull leaves the **Praca de Touros** alive after an amazing display of horsemanship, courage, and acrobatics. Sit in the cheap seats, where regulars give a running commentary. Tickets can cost under 200$00, and are available in advance at the green *quiosque* (kiosk) in the Praca dos Restauradores or at the Campo Pequeno bullring (take the Metro).

The emotional fado songs traditionally are sung by by women, accompanied by guitars and mandolins. Most fado taverns (*adegas típicas*) are in the Bairro Alto or the Alfama, and begin to get busy about midnight. The majority have a minimum but no cover. Let the night slip by, while you sip some wine or try the traditional ginja at **Lisboa a Noite** or **Senhor Vinho**, two of the best fado places.

Gays gather in two discos not far from Trumps in the Bairro Alto. Bustling **Bric-a-Bar** is the most popular meeting place and has the busiest dance floor. Two streets away, **Finalmente** has a reputation for the best *travesti* (drag) shows and has several shows most nights between 2:00 and 6:00 a.m.

If mellow be your mood, slip behind a table at shadowy **Pe Sujo** in the Alfama for soft and rhythmic Brasilian music. The same guitarist and percussionist sing every night and encourage the student audience to join in, using the soda-can shakers judiciously scattered throughout the tiny club. The air is hot and smokey, but you can cool off with a dozen different *cachaca* (Brasilian cane liquor) and rum drinks — try a *caipira* (lemon) or a *batida de limao* (lime). To get there, walk up to the Se and take the left fork — ring the bell to get in.

A warning: it's doubtful any Lisboan has ever been to **Maxime**, or it wouldn't be one of the first nightspots they suggest to tourists. Stay away. The club is seedy: tired hookers make up a quarter of the sparse crowd, the music is canned, and the 1,000$00 ticket price ought to buy both better drinks and more skin.

Prostitution is a major industry in Lisbon — the result of the poor economy, some say — and discos are some of their best markets. Young prostitutes perch in many bars and discos in the Bairro Alto, while more expensive callgirls roam discos near the wide Avenida da Liberdade and the Praca Marques de Pombal.

Escaping Lisbon

Lisbon's frequent trains put travelers within easy striking distance of both beaches and fairy-tale castles in the hills. But check which of Lisbon's four stations you want before starting off on a daytrip: Rossio for Sintra and west, Cais do Sodre for Estoril and Cascais, Santa Apolonia for northern, eastern, and international lines, or Barreiro (across the river by ferry) for the south.

The pink palace at **Queluz** mixes Portuguese and French style in its ornate halls and elaborate gardens. Be sure to see the Don Quixote Room and the festive scenes on the walls of the Tea Room. Sintra is a sort of "Palace Wonderland," with five in town or close by. The odd **Palacio da Vila** is easy to spot from a distance — two huge cones, actually the roof and chimneys of the kitchen, stick high up above the town. Its highlights include a room decorated with ceramic tiles of all the royal shields, and two rooms with birds painted on their ceilings, the *Por Bem* room with its magpies, and the hall with swans. The **Palacio da Pena** on the hill above is a storybook castle that would have made Walt Disney proud. Like the Palacio da Vila, the Palacio da Pena (ironically the "Palace of Regret") has great ceramic tiles. Be sure to look for the sea portal with its marine carvings. Walk back down — it takes awhile — and wander the ruins of the old 7th-Century Moorish castle that ramble over the hillsides.

The finest beach near Lisbon is the **Praia do Guincho**, a half-mile long and backed by white dunes and pine trees. The Guincho's rolling waves are popular with surfers, and its remote and uncrowded location make the beach the favorite of topless sunbathers. To get there, take the train to Cascais (the end of the line) and change to the bus to Guincho. The ride along the rocky coast lasts half an hour — get off when you see the **Restaurante Muchaxo**. The sunset over the Atlantic Ocean is beautiful, but be sure to catch the last bus back to Cascais, which leaves a little after 8:00 in summer.

Many small beaches punctuate the rocky coast from Lisbon to Cascais, but the Lisboans' favorite is **Estoril**, where the train drops you off only a few meters from the water. Although Estoril and its casino are no longer the darling of the jetset, they still draw plenty of beautiful people and brief bikinis. A bus from Lisbon's Praca de Espahna makes the half-hour trip under the huge aqueduct and across the river to the beach at the Costa de Caparica. The tawny sand stretches for miles and the crowd is strictly local — daytrippers from Lisbon or tourists from elsewhere in Portugal, staying somewhere in the pile of apartment buildings and beach houses at Caparica. This is the place to get a feel for the average Portuguese. Walk or take the mini-train south toward Fonte de Telha for more singles and a less crowded beach.

Beach Nightlife

Many Lisboans contend that the nightlife in Cascais is better than in the capital, perhaps because of the cozy atmosphere and the concentration of vacationers. But the best rock disco — some say the best disco period — is about six kilometers and a 200$00 taxi ride from Estoril on the highway to Sintra. The magnificent sound system of **2001** (*Dois Mil e Um*) blasts the latest British and American rock from 11:00 to 3:00 under the stands of the Estoril race track. International tourists, American soldiers from the nearby NATO base in Oeiras, and mostly Portuguese locals shell out a 400$00 minimum on weeknights and 500$00 on weekends to boogie in the flashing black-and-orange day-glo underworld of 2001. The setting's bizarre (you can tell you're under stadium seats), the dance floor's big, and the music's great. The hat-check girl can call you a cab at the end of the night, but watch the time if you're not staying nearby. The last train from Estoril to Lisbon leaves at 2:30, and a taxi all the way back to the capital costs over 1000$00.

Drop by the wharf on the Praia da Ribeira in Cascais around 6:00 and watch the fisherman unload their catch. The tiny **Rua das Flores**, right behind the market where the fish are auctioned off, has no flowers but six excellent seafood restaurants in a row (and a seventh around the corner). The **Beira Mar** is the prettiest; the **Sagres** is a little more informal. Checks can run anywhere from 700$00 to 2500$00. The shops and nightlife are much better in Cascais, so many people staying in Estoril make the short trip. The **Beefeater**, a British-owned bar near the Baia Hotel, is the best meeting place in town and host to a boisterous multi-lingual crowd, well-spiced with Americans, Brits, and Irishmen. The classy and intimate **Rolls Royce Club** lies buried in a basement on a small alley and is badly-marked — look for a sign that says "Bar and Boite" with a picture of a Rolls' front end. The doorman decides whether to charge the minimum and how much (usually 500$00 to 1000$00 — cheaper with a large group including some women, or a little Portuguese). For a romantic and tranquil finish to the evening, walk the massive seawall from Cascais to Estoril — except for a few fishermen, the mist and the sound of the waves will be all yours.

The **Casino Estoril** is straight up from the beach and train station. In addition to the gaming room and slot machines, the complex includes a movie theater, shops, and a restaurant and lounge, where international superstars like Julio Iglesias have performed. Tourists need a passport and 250$00 to enter the gambling rooms. A sign also states that a jacket is necessary after 8:00 — though this now is interpreted to include sweaters, windbreakers, and even denim jackets. (In the last couple of years, the casino has been looking for customers.)

Jeans are also acceptable. The one-armed bandits steal 5$00, 10$00, and 25$00 coins. The *Sala de Jogos* has roulette, blackjack, baccarat, French bank, and low "American-style" minimum bets — 200$00 for roulette and 100$00 for blackjack. Although the casino opens at 3:00, the gaming room doesn't fill until 11:00.

LISTINGS

Attractions

Mentioned in the text:
Mosteiro dos Jeronimos, Praca do Imperio, Belem.
Torre de Belem, Avenida Marginal, Pedroucos.
Se, Largo da Se.
Igreja de Sao Roque, Largo Trindade Coelho.
Castelo de Sao Jorge, Largo do Chao da Feira.
Praca de Touros, Campo Pequeno.

Not mentioned:
Museu da Fundacao Calouste Gulbenkian, Avenida da Berna, 45. Custom built for personal collection of Armenian oil tycoon. Little of everything: Rodin, Rubens, Rembrandt, Manet, Persian rugs, Italian tapestry, Lalique jewelry, Catherine the Great's tableware.
Museu Nacional de Arte Antiga, Rua das Janelas Verdes. Primitives, Bosch, Cranach, Durer, Holbein the Elder. Highlights: St. Vincent polyptch by Nuno Goncalves, gold monstrance of Belem wrought by poet Gil Vicente.
Museu Nacional dos Coches, Praca Afonso de Albuquerque, Belem. World's best collection, 16th-Century to Victorian coaches in former Royal Riding School.
Feira Popular, Avenida da Republica. Metro Entre Campos. Amusement park, open May through September. Games, rides, shops, two discos, many restaurants. Snacks: try *caracois* (snails) and beer, or *farturas*, the Portuguese' huge spiral version of doughnuts.
Tours of the **Tagus** (*Tejo*) River, Estacao Fluvial (near Praca do Comercio). Two-hour trip daily at 3:00 p.m. for 850$00. Great views of Lisbon's seven hills. Office of Turismo, Palacio Foz, Praca dos Restauradores, phone 36-25-31, also arranges three-hour tours at 3:00 p.m. every Sunday, June through September.

Restaurants and Cafes

Mentioned in the text:
Malmequer Bemmequer, Rua de S. Miguel, 23-25, phone 87-65-35.
Solar do Vinho do Porto, Rua Sao Pedro de Alcantara, 45, phone 32-33-07.
A Brasileira, Rua Garrett, 120-122.
Confeitaria Nacional, Praca da Figueira, 18B-C.
Pastelaria Suica, Rossio, 96, or Praca da Figueira, 3, phone 32-80-92.
Cafe Gelo, Rossio, 64-65, phone 32-62-88.
Restaurante Central, Rua da Madalena, 4, phone 87 06 23.
Escorial, Rua das Portas de Santo Antao, 47-49, phone 36-37-58.
Gambrinus, Rua das Portas de Santo Antao, 25, phone 32-14-66.
Churrasco, Rua das Portas de Santo Antao, 83, phone 32-30-59.
Cervejaria A Brilhante, Rua das Portas de Santo Antao, 105, phone 36-14-07.
Bonjardim, Travessa de Santo Antao, 10, phone 32-43-89.
Cafe Gare, Praca D. Joao da Camara, 5-6.
Restaurante Beira Mar, Rua das Flores, 6, Cascais, phone 28-01-52.
Restaurante Sagres, Rua das Flores, 10A, Cascais, phone 28-08-30.

Not mentioned:
Restaurante Baleal, Rua da Madalena, 277, phone 87-21-87. Portuguese favorites at low prices.
Michel, Largo de Santa Cruz do Castelo, 5, phone 86-43-38. Excellent and expensive French food near the castle.
Leao de Ouro, Rua Primeiro de Dezembro, 89-107, phone 32-61-95 and 36-94-95. Right door: folkloric tourist hall. Left door: bustling local crowd. Friendly waiters, large portions, about $5.
Jao do Grao, Rua dos Correeiros, 228, phone 32-47-57. Typical *almocos-jantares*, a Portuguese "Joe's Eats." In business since 1810 because it's cheap.

Shopping

Mentioned in the text:
O Mundo do Livro, Rua da Trindade, 12.
Fabrica de Sant'Anna, showroom, Rua do Alecrim, 91-97, phone 32-25-37. Factory, Calcada da Boa Hora, 96, phone 63 82 92.
Sarmento, Rua do Ouro, 251.
Ouriversaria Alianca, Rua Garrett, 50.
Phoebus, Rua do Ouro, 287.
Coco Loco, Rua de Sao Juliao, 78.
Por-fi-ri-os Contraste, Rua da Vitoria, 63.

Not mentioned:
Ouro Negro, Rua da Madalena, 189. Small tea and coffee shop with inexpensive blue ceramics from Alcobaca, north of Lisboa.

Portico, Rua da Misericordia, 27-31. Everything from wooden phones to ceramic dogs. Best collection of antique doorknobs we've seen.

Vista Alegre, Largo do Chiado, 18, phone 36-14-01. Portugal's most famous porcelain maker.

A Carioca, Rua da Misericordia, 9. Coffee shop with good selection of those unique Portuguese coffee makers that look more like chemistry sets.

Casa Quintao, Rua Ivens, 30, phone 36-58-37. Tapestries and rugs on second floor.

Nightlife

Mentioned in the text:

Stones, Rua do Olival, 1, 66-45-45.

Bananas. No street address, but near the Largo das Fontal in Alcantara. Any taxi driver knows.

Trumps, Rua da Imprensa Nacional, 104-B, phone 67-10-59.

Whispers, Centro Comercial Imaviz (beneath the Sheraton Hotel), Avenida Fontes Pereira de Melo, 35, phone 57-54-89.

Bric-a-bar, Rua Cecilio de Sousa, 84.

Finalmente, Rua da Palmeira, 38, phone 37-26-52.

Pe Sujo, Largo de S. Martinho, 6-7, phone 86-56-29.

Maxime, Praca da Alegria, 58, phone 36-53-66.

Lisboa a Noite, Rua das Gaveas, 69, phone 36-85-57.

Senhor Vinho, Rua do Meio a Lapa, 18, phone 67-26-81.

2001, Autodromo do Estoril, phone 269-05-50.

The Beefeater, Rua Visconde da Luz, 1A, Cascais.

Rolls Royce Club, Travessa Afonso Sanches, 6-B, Cascais, phone 286-61-29.

Casino Estoril, phone 268-45-21.

Not mentioned:

Farol, Estrada da Boca do Inferno, 7, Cascais, phone 286-01-73 and 286-47-32. Disco on the coastal road toward Guincho, in the basement of a hotel and restaurant. Young crowd, but not cheap.

Wellington, Rua Federico Arouca, 32, Cascais, phone 28-03-94. English pub, and a lot of English spoken.

Brown's, Rua Conde de Sabugosa, 21-A. Off the Avenida da Roma. Dark basement disco popular with university students and singles. A 300$00 minimum for guys, 500$00 on Friday and Saturday.

Beat Club, Rua Conde de Sabugosa, 11-D and 11-F, phone 89-58-68. Near Brown's, also popular with students. Couples only, 400$00 a person.

*London is most
uniquely British when
you sample its extremes*

London

In the afternoon, you sip tea in the Palm Court at the elegant Waldorf Hotel. Squadrons of black-jacketed waiters flurry about, serving the slightly stale upper-crust of British society. A few couples waltz sedately on the well-polished dance floor. The orchestra plays "In the Mood" as you try to catch the eye of the handsome man sitting at the next table. Feeling self-conscious when he finally returns your stare, you look down at the enormous scone in front of you and wonder how to eat it elegantly. The mood is broken when his wife and two children return. Well, there's always the scone, and the princes at tomorrow's polo match...

Late that evening, you're at the Bat Cave, with its black walls and slam dancing, talking to a punk singer named Scratch. From a distance, he looked scary, but you discover that he's a 20-year-old from Wales who's nervous about his new look: floppy black mohawk, earring, eye make-up, and tattoo. You assure him that his mohawk looks just fine, and he smiles at your friendly tone...

London is most uniquely British at its extremes. Maybe after a night at the Rock Garden, you're ready for some Shakespeare at the Barbican Centre. A lunch of pastrami and egg rolls at Cohen and Wong can be followed by dinner at an inexpensive restaurant Princess Di frequents. An afternoon jaunt to the countryside to see a polo match at a British manoral estate puts you in the mood for a drunken pub crawl.

Finding this British individuality can be a challenge for the American tourist. After you get used to the accent and learn to look right before crossing the street, you'll begin to notice a lot in London that is American or American-influenced. American restaurants and bars are so popular that you could spend your entire stay eating hamburgers and drinking rum and cokes. But you could do that back in Dayton couldn't you? And anything you could do in Dayton is not worth doing in London.

The customs and language in Britain so resemble our own that visitors often forget they're in a foreign country. There are differences, though. Remember, for example, that the British speak English, not American. Movies are "films," appetizers are "starters," and the letter "z" is pronounced "zed."

Britain's people need some explanation, too. Sloane Rangers and punks mark the extremes of Britain's populace. Sloane Rangers will remind you of preppies, except that they tend to be called Caroline and Henry rather than Buffy and Chip. *The Sloane Ranger Handbook* provides the complete Ranger profile. Sloanes live near Sloane Square, the old-money party of town. Henry works in the City (the financial district), if he isn't in the Horse Guards, and spends his evenings at pubs like the **Antelope**. Caroline either takes cooking lessons at Cordon Bleu or studies art in Florence. As for clothes, a Rangerette wears either a navy blue pleated skirt and a Cacherel blouse, or just goes totally Laura Ashley. Henry wears a double breasted pinstripe suit (like Dad's) to work and shows up at the Australian pub in baggy beige wide-wales and a thick sweater. The crucial difference between Sloanes and preps is that Sloanes never wear pink and green.

Punks do wear pink and green, but mostly in their hair. They congregrate near Oxford Streeet or on the King's Road. To a certain extent, punk has become *passe* in London. Fewer mohawks hang out on the King's Road than in years past. But punk culture persists, even if Americans and Sloanes tend to view them as a mutant race. For the punks, however, the uniform has become so standardized that it no longer expresses their anarchical ideology, and is becoming as much of a uniform as a three-piece suit. Watch a punk woman fixing the smudge in her outrageous eye make-up and suddenly you'll feel much less intimidated.

To blend in with the Sloanes, just be as subtly preppy as possible. For the punk scene, wear black pants and a black t-shirt. Men can wander anywhere in London in this outfit. Skip blue jeans — they're a dead give-away because the English wear theirs skin-tight. And no, Ralph Lauren shirts don't count.

Rain is about as constant in London as civility, so bring an umbrella. If for some reason you forgot one and you're too cheap to buy another, go to the **Lost Property Office** at the Baker Street Tube Station and tell them you left a black collapsible umbrella on the tube. They will smile and hand you one from their vast collection.

Four information sources will vastly ease your stay. Find a good map, like *London A-Z* (pronounced "zed," remember?), not the freebie that has pink rectangles where the museums are. London isn't organized like New York, so don't look for logic in the sprawl. Get a basic, fully indexed book form because 1) the British buy it, and 2) you won't look like an idiot unfolding a huge map on the street. *Time Out* magazine, published every Thursday, contains a weekly calendar of everything going on in London. The editors write unashamedly biased but always entertaining reviews. Not only does *Time Out* list theater, films and concerts, but also it includes night clubs, sports events, political action meetings, and literary activities. *What's On and Where to Go,* another weekly magazine, provides a second opinion.

The *London Theatre Guide* is given out free. There's usually a stack in every hotel lobby, but if not, try any theater or ticket agency. Published every two weeks, the guide lists all shows along with the phone numbers. It even has a little map on the back. Other than these items, the only thing you need to remember is to dial 353-4242 if you have questions. That's the **Daily Telegraph Information Service**, and they know everything.

Nightlife

At night, London loses its customary reserve. Punks strut their finery and feistiness at clubs like the Bat Cave. Sloanes cut loose, too, shedding their ties or removing their sweaters. And London theaters put on some of the most innovative and controversial productions in the world. Read on for details, but first, a word about a universal activity, drinking.

Drinking establishments come in three types in London: the pub, the wine bar, and the cocktail bar. Pubs, which have been around for centuries, serve mostly beer with cold and/or hot food. Londoners go to pubs for cheap lunches or a beer after work. Pubs can be found in all shapes and sizes, from the **George Inn** with its courtyard theater, to the artsy **Queen's Elm**, to the Sloane sophistication at the **Antelope**. The best pubs use hand pumps to draw their beer, eschewing the pressurized beer of America. Look for the long handles or ask for hand-pumped beer. Britons prefer to drink lager or bitter. Lager tastes like strong American beer, while bitter tastes, well, bitter. Men should order a pint, and women a half-pint, in order to avoid being considered, respectively, effeminate or uncouth. However, British chauvinism does not dictate how many half-pints a woman may drink.

Wine bars sprang up because few pubs serve decent wine. The wine bar's popularity is declining, except for a few that have attracted a loyal crowd or possess a great location. Many wine bars draw a middle-age crowd, but not all. For example, don't let the name of **Brahms and Liszt** fool you into thinking that it's for sedate classical music lovers. "Liszt" rhymes with "pissed," which means wasted in cockney slang — quite appropriate for this very loud and rowdy wine bar.

British cocktail bars resemble American bars, except they specialize in blender drinks. The atmosphere is generally raucous and loud, excluding bars at big hotels. **Downstairs at the Pheasantry** tops London's list of cocktail bars, with its friendly crowd, great drinks, but high prices. At Europe's longest bar (or so they say), they sell their drinks in large cups, sized like bras. A "B" cup will serve four, a "C" cup six, and so on. The cups come equipped with two-and-a-half foot straws, so you won't bump heads. The Pheasantry has happy hours between 5:30 and 7:00 each day.

A pub provides a good warmup for London's finest tradition, the theater. By American standards, the London theater is inexpensive and daring. Discount tickets, available either at **Leicester Square** or at individual theaters as student standby, run about 5.00 pounds (£). The half-price booth at Leicester Square opens at 2:30, with the queue starting at 1:00. Signs indicate which shows are available. *The London Theatre Guide* will tell you which theaters offer student standby tickets. The lines for these tickets start thirty to forty minutes before the show.

The National Theatre and the **Barbican Center** feature sparkling traditional performances. **The Royal Shakespeare Company** performs at the Barbican; tickets usually have to be purchasaed in advance. The National Theater, London's largest company, usually keeps at least six shows in repertoire. Find the National Theatre monthly schedule of performances in any ticket agency, or dial 928-8126 for recorded information. On the day of the performance, all remaining seats cost 4.50 £ (3.50 £ for students forty-five minutes before the performance). Tickets often remain available until the last moment.

The National will entertain you for an evening, even if you don't have tickets. Street musicians, souvenir hustlers, and three cafes make the south bank of the Thames come alive. There are free concerts (6:15 every evening and also 1:30 on Saturdays), not to mention rehearsed readings for 1.50 £ . The buffet and bar in the foyer serve reasonably priced sandwiches, pastries, and drinks. Don't miss the chocolate chip cookies at the **National Film Theatre Restaurant**. Cap off an evening on the town by viewing the skyline from the Charing Cross Bridge. The view of London at night, particularly of Saint Paul's, is spectacular.

When the plays let out and the pubs close, the night action moves to clubs. Most clubs are private, but there are a variety of ways to get in. The most famous, **Annabel's** and **Tokyo Joe's**, remain next to impossible, but if you look affluent (and actually are), it's worth a try. Londoners like formality, so this class of establishment expects dresses for the ladies, and as formal as black tie for the gentlemen. If the doorman refuses you, you can wait outside and try to convince someone to take you in with them. Most of the clientele is snootier than the club, so this may be tougher yet. A variation on this ploy is to join a crowd at a wine bar or a pub like Blushes or the Australian, and hope for an invitation to a club. If you're having problems, remember: the less glamorous the club, the easier the entrance. Hotels often have special deals with clubs, so check with the porter. *Time Out* also lists entrance information; some clubs have members-only nights once or twice a week.

For a punk/new wave night, go to the **Rock Garden** at Covent Garden rather than a chic club. Unless you're an ultra-purist punker, this converted vegetable warehouse packs enough leather and chains to satisfy any novice. It won't cost much, particularly if you have dinner at the restaurant. **Camden Palace** is of higher quality, and looks more like Studio 54. In fact, *Time Out* gave Camden Palace its Studio 54 Memorial Trophy for its sound and light shows, and noted its surprising lack of snobbery. Unfortunately, Camden Palace's out-of-the-way location means a cab or bus-ride after after the Underground closes.

The really adventurous should try to get into the **Bat Cave**, which holds court every Wednesday night at Fooberts, a club just off Carnaby Street. The walls are black, the tourist very rare, and the contact dancing very physical. Even if you hide two or three steps up the stairs, bodies will hurl into you. Around 2:00 a.m. the place explodes when the DJ plays the club's theme song, which is, of course, the theme from "Batman." To get in, arrive around 11:00, but expect to wait at least until midnight. The line is entertaining enough to make the effort worthwhile, but getting in to hear the live bands and watch the show is spectacular. Just remember your black pants, black shirt, and most degenerate look.

For those whom The Bat Cave turns away, or justifiably frightens away, **The Wag Club** serves as a good alternative. It won a prize from *Time Out* for "resisting the temptation to milk the hip hordes dry...and trying to cultivate a regular clientele." Then there's always **Le Beat Route**, which sells drinks for 25 pence after a 5.00 pound cover on Wednesday nights.

Restaurants

Most guidebooks seem to regard reviewing London restaurants as an unwanted chore, and they thus counsel readers to minimize their losses, apparently by starving. London merits its international reputation for bad food. The key is to search for great atmosphere, so you'll have a good time, if not a great meal. And surprisingly, you'll often find decent food in places with good atmosphere, even if it's just pizza or hamburgers.

The fine British institution of afternoon tea makes up for some of the inadequecy of the other meals. It will introduce you to scones, a true delicacy, and it will provide an opportunity to see how the other half percent of the population lives. There are two kinds of tea, "regular" and cream. "Regular" tea means just a cup of tea. Cream teas, on the other hand, feature clotted cream, a cross between the French *creme fraiche* and whipped cream, and a whole horde of delicacies. The first course consists of finger sandwiches, usually cucumber, tomato or butter. Next come the scones (except at the Waldorf where you get English muffins first). The sweet round biscuit known as a scone, when piled high with jam and clotted cream, is one of the finest edibles in Britain. If the tea offers more pastries after the scones, consider asking for another scone. Crumpets, if you should ever be served them, look a lot like English muffins — which, by the way, are an American invention.

The big hotels cater the stuffiest teas, so they are the best bets for true British atmosphere. The **Palm Court** at the Waldorf has the most elegant setting, and is less crowded and expensive than the **Ritz** (6.95 £ versus 5.95 £ — get to the Ritz by 3:30). **Harrods** offers the best value, an all-you-can-eat feast at tables piled high with goodies for only 3.95 £ . At **Fortnum and Mason**, the menu is a la carte, which lets you avoid the cucumber sandwiches and concentrate on scones.

The Waldorf and Ritz both sponsor tea dances, a typically declining British institution. Ladies are requested to wear hats, gentlemen should come in tie and jacket, and they should dance together with restraint to string quartets. The Waldorf's Friday afternoon tea dance costs just 6.95 £ .

Lunch is a necessary evil in London. But if you are famished, **Cranks**, a health food cafeteria near Oxford Circus, serves a mean *ratatouille*, decent quiche, delicious salads, and a great dessert. The best and probably cheapest quiche in London can be found at **Oodles**, a chain of country food cafeterias. Real men who don't eat quiche should try a Ploughman's lunch (bread, cheese, and chutney) at a pub. Pub grub is alway inexpensive and filling. Don't leave without trying steak and kidney pies, pork pies, or Cornish pasties (rhymes with "nasties").

Dinner, generally, has more potential than lunch. There are good Indian, Chinese, and Italian restaurants in London, and surprisingly enough, a few good English ones, too. At nicer restaurants, you must book ahead.

For a sophisticated atmosphere, visit **Avoirdupois**, the sister restaurant of **Menage a Trois**. Menage a Trois, though fairly expensive, recently became very popular because Princess Di lunched there. Menage a Trois serves only starters (appetizers) and desserts; their signs mention that there is "No Intercourse" on the premises; that's the British way of saying that there are no main courses. You can proceed directly from delicacy to delicacy. Avoirdupois, on the other hand, does have intercourse on the premises. At both restaurants, feel free to order as much or as little as you wish. Both serve excellent food, but Avoirdupois wins with its atmosphere. Solid black walls and framed posters of lips loom over your shoulder, and the menu arrives tucked in your napkin. Your copy of *Private Pie* — it's a spoof on the gossip magazine, *Private Eye* — lists exotic cocktails and standard English favorites, as well as more gourmet delights. Their "Menage a Trois" dish, which includes a boursin and spinach pastry, will make your stomach wonder if it's still in London.

At **Borscht 'n Tears**, the atmosphere is boisterous and Russian. Upstairs, there's live Russian folk music, while downstairs a guitarist croons sixties songs. The placemat dictates the few rules of decorum, noting that the lack of a licensed dance floor hasn't stopped people from dancing on the tables. On the placemat is a drawing of a credit card which says, "If you've got a stolen credit card, practice your signature here." The menu, while not particularly overwhelming, includes such specialties as the "Moscow Kremlin burger" ("a large, light, rich bundle of beef — just like our Dear Mr. Brezhnev"). Borscht'n Tears, and its sister restaurant, **Borscht 'n Cheers**, are best with a crowd.

Across the street from Avoirdupois, the **King's Road Jam** serves suprisingly good food in an equally unique atmosphere. At "The Jam," tables are stacked on two decks. Although complicated to describe, it works on the same principle as a bunk bed. The waiters dash up and down tiny steps, trying not to spill food on the patrons below. The food ranks a cut above burger fare, despite the diner-like atmosphere. A knob at each table controls the volume of the taped rock music, so you can drown out the rest of the world if you like.

Most of London closes down early, but late night snacks can be found at **Up All Night**, a late-night diner on the Fulham Road. They serve burgers, steaks, and snack food, all night long. For a ritzier late night snack, visit **Wichity's** on Kensington High Street. They serve a "Sloanish" breakfast or dinner until 7:00. They also have indoor and outdoor dancing areas for those who suddenly get a second wind.

Shopping

The Kings Road is the best street for clothes, especially shoes. Some shops are super punk, but most are just young and trendy. **The Brompton Road** and the **Burlington Arcade** on Piccadilly carry more expensive goods. Sloane Rangers frequent **South Molton Street**. Across from the British Museum, **Westaway & Westaway** stocks the cheapest wool and cashmere. **Fortnum and Mason**, across from the Burlington Arcade, sells food at outrageous prices, but the salesmen in tails make it worth the trip. Upstairs is a decent, if stodgy, department store. Their restaurant lets you sample the food first. The **General Trading Company**, around the corner from Sloane Square, houses the ultimate giftshop, while a great cafe downstairs serves all three meals plus afternoon tea. **Laura Ashley** sells its rejects on Lower Sloane Street, two blocks from Sloane Square.

London is famous for its markets. On Saturdays, follow the signs from Nottinghill Gate Tube to **Portobello Road**, if you're searching for antiques or amusing junk. Go there early, very early, for the best bargains. **The Petticoat Lane** is an enormous market open on Sundays where everything from clothes to furniture to animals is sold.

Petticoat Lane traders move their stalls to **Roman Road** at Bethnal Green during the week. With no tourists, Roman Road is less crowded and much cheaper.

Escaping London

A plethora of day trips surround London, ranging from the elegance of Bath to the studiousness of Oxford.

Perhaps the most typically British excursion is to view a polo match, conveniently located on a manoral estate. Low admission prices and lovely parks lure loads of London families to a sporting day in the country. There are three fields reachable from London. **Cirencester Park**, home of Earl Bathurst, contains 3,000 acres of woodlands and cultivated gardens, Roman ruins, 16th century homes, and a Norman church. Polo matches occur on Tuesday, Thursday, and Saturday, but the official matches are Sunday. Closer to London lies **Cowdray Park**, home of Viscount Cowdray. Prince Charles makes an occasional appearance; matches are Wednesday, Friday, Saturday, and Sunday. The Gold Cup Final highlights the season. For a fee, and if suitably dressed (blazers for men, dresses for women), one may enter the member's enclave and have tea. The most stylish is the **Smith's Law Windsor Great Park** at Windsor. Prince Charles' team, Guards Polo Club, plays there. During Royal Ascot Week, the Prince dashes from the races to the daily polo matches. The main event is the Imperial International Polo, Britain's only international tournament, which attracts over 15,000 spectators. The British regularly lose to their South American rivals, but it is quite the sporting event.

LISTINGS

A quick look at the listings will show that most of the restaurants and bars are found in a couple of neighborhoods. Covent Garden draws large crowds day and night. It's a good place to shop, eat, drink and watch free sidewalk shows. At night, there are rock clubs, jazz clubs and other various drinking establishments. If you want to go on a pub crawl (such a more accurate term than bar-hopping!), this is the place.

The other shopping and dining area centers around the King's Road and the Fulham Road. Chelsea is the area's artsy neighborhood, with exceptional shopping, not to mention the drinking and dining. Hotels near here (Cromwell Road, for example) charge reasonable prices.

Pubs

Antelope, 22 Eaton Terrace, SW1, phone 730-7781. The Sloane Ranger Handbook claims that "Toby practically lives" here, often arriving in his double-breasted suit. Should be seen.

Australian, 29 Milner Street, SW3, phone 589-3114. Incredibly Sloane.

Cartoonist, 76 Shoe Lane, EC4, phone 353-2828. Housed in the London International Press Centre, it's a haven for journalists. Also doubles as headquarters of the Cartoonist Club of Great Britain, with their artwork on the walls.

Dirty Dick's, 202-4, Bishopsgate EC2, phone 283-5888. The pub is dirty, and often filled with equally dirty old men. Dead cats hang on strings from the ceiling, and when you reach for your drink a carcass may fall in front of your face.

Finch's (King's Arms), 190 Fulham Rd., SW3, phone 352-7469. A pub for the artsy Chelsea crowd.

George Inn, 77 Borough High St. SE1, phone 407-2065. Touristy, but worth a visit. Shakespeare is performed in the courtyard.

Tavern, 49 Great Russell Street, WC1, phone 242-8987. Opposite the British Museum, but not touristy. Superb food, and don't miss the collection of umbrellas and bowlers.

Princess Louise, 209 High Holborn, WC1, phone 405-8816. A Victorian house with a vast selection of beer from the hand pump. Wine bar upstairs popular with Americans studying in the area.

Queen's Elm, 241 Fulham Rd., SW3, phone 352-9517. Queen Elizabeth took shelter from the rain under a nearby elm in 1567. The British remember things like that.

Sherlock Holmes, 10 Northumberland St., WC2, phone 930-2644. Replica of the 221b Baker Street study along with a large collection of Holmes memorabilia.

Two pubs are popular for their live music, the **Hope and Anchor**, 207 Upper Street, N1, phone 359-4510, and the **Stanhope**, 97 Gloucester Rd., SW7, phone 373-4192.

Wine Bars

Brahms & Liszt, 19 Russell Street, WC2, phone 240-3661.

Blushes, 52 King's Road, SW3, phone 589-6640. A trendy, European spot. The ground floor loosely imitates a French cafe, downstairs is a smoky lounge.

Dover Street, 819 Dover Street W1, phone 629-9813. Wine bar and restaurants with the trendier young execs. Live music on Tuesday, Thursday, and Friday.

Ivana's, 49 Hollywood Rd., SW10, phone 351-5852. Although they advertise as "London's first non-alcoholic art gallery," they serve drinks. What this means, we don't know.

Bars

Downstairs at the Pheasantry, 152 Kings Road SW3, phone 351-3084. Upstairs are two restaurants. Downstairs is the self-proclaimed "longest and friendliest cocktail bar in London."

Rumours, 33 Wellington Street, WC2, phone 836-3308. (Covent Garden.) A favorite with natives and tourists, housed in a converted flower market.

Hilton Hotel, 22 Park Lane W1, phone 493-8000. (Hyde Park Corner.) Worth it only for the great view of London from the rooftop bar. Drinks are expensive, so sip slowly.

Fridays, 24-26 Russell St., WC2, phone 240-0735. Some bars hide their U.S. origins better than this New York-style hangout.

Clubs

Fooberts (home of Bat Cave), 18 Fouberts Place, W1, phone 734-3630.

Annabel's, 44 Berkely Square, W1, phone 629-2350.

Tokyo Joe's, 85 Piccadilly W1, phone 409-1832.

The Wag Club, 35 Wardour St., W1, phone 437-5534.

Le Beat Route, 17 Greek Street, W1, phone 734-1470. Like Fooberts, it houses different clubs on different nights. Can be tough to get in.

Camden Palace, Camden High Street NW1, phone 387-0428. Dress well. Saturday night is "Dance Your Ass Off," but Thursday is the only night to go, according to those in the know.

Rock Garden, 6-7 The Piazza, Covent Garden, WC2, phone 240-3961. Try to look a little punky to distinguish yourself from the other Americans in their LaCostes.

Titanic, 1 Lansdowne Row, Berkeley Square W1, phone 499-1520. (Gren Park.) A membership club, but non-members get in easily. Worth the effort. Disco, cabaret, movies, bands and cheap food. Breakfast is served after 1:30 a.m.

Jazz

Canteen, 4 Great Queen Street, WC2, phone 405-6598. A little expensive, but if you're looking for good jazz, here it is.

Pizza Express, 10 Dean Street W1, phone 439-8722. The cover varies with the band, but it's cheaper and livelier than the Canteen. The pizza is fine at all the Pizza Express restaurants, but only at Dean Street is there live jazz.

Pizza on the Park, 11 Knightsbridge, SW 1, phone 437-9595. The banner out front asks you to help save Pizza on the Park, and it's probably a worthy cause.

Restaurants

Mentioned in text:

Cranks, 8 Marshall Street, W1, phone 437-9431.

Borscht 'n Tears, 45 Beauchamp Place, SW3, phone 589-5003.

Borscht 'n Cheers, 273 King's Rd., SW3, phone 352-5786.

Avoirdupois, 334 King's Road, SW3, phone 352-4071.

The King's Road Jam, 289a King's Road, SW3, phone 352-5390.

Up All Night, 325 Fulham Rd, SW10, phone 352-1996.

Wichity's, 253 Kensington High Street, W8, phone 937-2654.

Menage a Trois, 14/16 Beauchamp Pl., SW3, phone 589-4252.

Not mentioned:

Joe Allen, 13 Exeter Street, WC2, phone 836-0651. A converted warehouse, open-space with brick walls, and red-checked tableclothes. American food, but the crowd consists of British shoppers, artists, actors, and businessmen.

Tarts, 2a Kensington Park Road, W11, phone 229-6731. Burgers, salads, exotic cocktails, very eclectic crowd.

Leonardo, 397 Kings Road, SW10, phone 352-4146. Chelsea residents crowd into this neighborhood restaurant for good if unspectacular food. Friendly, noisy, and no tourists.

The Hungry Horse, 196 Fulham Road, SW10, phone 352-7757. For a really English meal, you can't beat this place, where you can have Yorkshire pudding in some form with all three courses.

19 Mossop St., 19 Mossop St., SW3, phone 589-4971. A Sloane bistro, with candles on the scrubbed wooden tables. Inexpensive Continental food.

Rules, 35 Maiden Lane, Strand WC 2, phone 836-5314. One of the most famous restaurants in London, Rules offers typical English fare from steak and kidney pies to roast beef.

L.S. Grant's Chicago Pizza Company, 12 Maiden Lane, WC2, phone 379-7722. Good deep dish pizza, huge mural of the Windy City on the wall.

Peppermint Park, 13-14 Upper St. Martin's Lane, WC2, phone 836-5234. Very pink, very green, very American, and very good hamburgers until 2:00 a.m.

Khyber, 56 Westbourne Grove, W2, phone 727-4385. Good Indian food in a clean, pleasant setting.

Cohen and Wong, 39 Panton St., SW1, phone 839-6876. A combination delicatessan and Chinese restaurant. The concept is better than the result, but still, worth the visit.

The Hard Rock Cafe, 150 Old Park Lane, W1, phone 629-0382. Perhaps the only place in London where Americana is entertaining. Long lines outside; hot fudge sundaes, burgers, and Elvis memorabilia inside. Beat the line by saying you just want drinks, then tell the maitre d' that you changed your mind. Closes at 12:30.

Wolfe's, 34 Park Lane W1, phone 499-6897. The best burgers in town, but Howard Johnson-ish interior.

Swiss Centre, 10 Wardour St., phone 734-1291. There are four restaurants in this huge complex; the basement restaurant serves wonderful cheese fondue or raclette.

The Good Earth, 91 Kings Road, SW3, phone 352-9231. Get some take out food, walk across the Albert Bridge to the south side of the Thames, and have a picnic in Battersea park.

Wong Kei, Rupert Court, Rupert St., W1, phone 437-3071. Rushed Chinese lunches, relaxed dinner. Excellent food until 2:00 a.m.

For fast food, stick with Wendy's or Burger King. They're better than the local variation, Wimpy's.

Tea

Harrods, Knightsbridge SW1, phone 730-1234.

Ritz, Picadilly W1, phone 493-8181.

Waldorf, Aldwych, WC2, phone 836-2400.

Shopping

Portobello Road, W11, Saturdays.

Petticoat Lane, Middlesex Street, Club Row and **Brick Lane**, E1, Sundays.

Roman Road, Bethnal Green, weekdays.

Laura Ashley Discount Outlet, 75 Lower Sloane Street, SW1, phone 730-5255.

Gay London

Complete listings can be found in Time Out, *or try the Gay Switchboard at 837-7324, or the Lesbian Line, 837-8602.*

Discos:

Heaven, Villiers St., WC2, phone 839-3852/3863. Europe's largest, and London's best, gay disco. On Tuesday, Heaven welcomes straights, but otherwise is exclusively male.

Heds, 5a Stratford Place, Oxford St., W1, phone 493-4454. Although Heds is predominantly for women, gay men are welcome. The crowd is well-dressed and friendly.

Pubs:

The London Apprentice, 33 Old Street, EC1, phone unlisted. Very popular but a little cruisy.

The Kings Arms, 23 Poland Street, W1, phone unlisted. Gay-run and friendly, one of the best central pubs.

The Cricketers, 317 Battersea Park Rd., SW11, phone 622-9060. Pub with drag shows every night and Sunday at noon. Drag pubs are popular in London, and this one seems to be the favorite.

*Some expect Madrid
to supplant Amsterdam as
the Continent's drug capitol*

Madrid

Madrid strides along at its own pace and style, waking grudgingly in the morning, taking a long lunch, and bursting into activity late at night when the sun finally sets. During the day, Madrilenos and tourists alike seek relief from the summer heat, fleeing to the long, cool corridors of museums or relaxing under the shade of a cafe's umbrellas. By late afternoon, the locals begin the daily ritual of *tapas*, cruising from bar to bar for the traditional appetizer (*pincho*) served free with the first drink.

Dinner starts late in the city, around 10:00 p.m., with the nightlife kicking off after midnight. The city has created a new use for the shopping mall, making bar-hopping easy for the lazy. **Orense**, a two-story complex popular with the young, houses a dozen different drinking and dancing establishments. Some are open-air, others are indoor, and all are enjoyable. For the hungry, another mall, **Aurrera**, is home to several dozen restaurants and bars, ranging from pizzerias to Brazilian samba bars to Irish coffee houses.

Despite their puritanical reputation, Madrilenos enjoy life, albeit with less wildness than their British or Parisian counterparts. Madrid had long been known for its oppressive summer heat and oppressive morals. But with the coming of democracy and a Socialist government, all this has changed. Madrilenos, who once expected their daughters back by sunset, are now glad to see them back by sunrise. Drug laws, formerly as strict as Turkey's, are now among the most liberal of all of Europe — some expect Madrid to supplant Amsterdam as the Continent's drug capital.

Because of both its geographical location and its status as the country's capital, Madrid draws from all the diverse cultures and peoples of Spain. Other cities may be more famous for a particular art form or cuisine, but Madrid contains a little bit of everything. The Spanish-language *Guia del Ocio* can help you plan your days: it lists the times and prices of all of Madrid's attractions, from museums to restaurants to night clubs.

Start your day by visiting the **Prado** museum and the **Palacio Real**, the Royal Palace. For a glimpse of old Madrid, walk south from Plaza Mayor to Lavapies, along the narrow roads that twist and wind between old homes and convents. Or wander near the **Puerta del Sol**

Promenading remains the favorite pastime of many Madrilenos. It's a show in which the spectators are the cast and the actors improvise. The best pageant is the Sunday afternoon *paseo*, a country tradition that still survives in the city. Between 4:00 and 6:00, Madrilenos stroll down the streets near the Plaza Callao and Plaza de Espana, showing off their families and Sunday finery. For a comfortable view of the parade, seat yourself at one of the streetside cafes.

Although you can go for tapas anywhere in Spain, the Madrilenos justly claim their city is tops in tapas. A tapa is a good-sized snack available for sale; a *pincho* is a small portion of that snack, provided free with the first drink. Pinchos range from seafood like sardines, squid, octopus, to olives or *patatas a la brava* (fried potatoes with a spicy sauce). Since restaurants don't start serving lunch until 1:00 or 2:00, and dinner until 9:30 or so, pinchos often sustain starving Americans. The bars that serve pinchos are known as *mesones* and *tabernas*. Going for pinchos means bar-hopping, because you should never have more than one drink in the same place. The procedure works as follows: enter the bar and order a small beer (beer is *cerveza*, but just ask for *una cana*, the smallest-size glass). If they serve olives, custom often dictates that you throw the pits on the floor. After downing your cana and munching your pincho, move on to the next bar. Repeat as necessary.

Tabernas line certain streets, so making the rounds involves short walks. The best-known streets center around the Plaza Mayor. Begin on a street called Cava de San Miguel with two classics: the **Meson de la Tortilla** and the **Meson del Champinon** (mushrooms). Continue down the Calle de Cuchilleros to the Calle de la Cava Baja. For a less-known, less-touristed region, wander between the Plaza del Sol and Plaza de Santa Ana. A third popular stretch for tapas lies between the Plaza Canalejas and the Plaza Jacinto Benavente. The best streets here are the Calle de la Cruz, Calle Nunez de Arce, Calle Victoria, Calle Barcelona, and Calle Cadiz.

Bullfighting still draws large crowds of Spaniards and tourists. Some love it for its pageantry, others detest it for the carnage. The **Plaza de Toros** of Madrid is located next to the metro stop Ventas. Buy tickets for seats in between the sun and shade (*sol y sombra*). The regulars gather there, providing an expert running commentary. Shortly after the show starts, shadows cover this section and cool it off.

Those who like a wild crowd but want to avoid watching bloodshed — or at least most of it — should see a soccer game, a much loved event in Spain. Even tourists who don't understand Spanish or the rules of the game have a great time. After an afternoon at the stadium, you'll at least learn how to insult the referee with a dozen words they don't teach in Spanish I. For safety's sake, be sure to root always for the home team. The city's best team, **Real Madrid**, plays at its stadium on Paseo de la Castellana, near the Station of Chamartin.

The more sedentary athletes can try their hand at chess, backgammon, and other games at **La Veneno**. An empty board is an invitation to play and to make a new Spanish friend. Games are free; besides the usual fare, the bar sells sandwiches and Irish coffee.

The more intellectual can attend a *tertulia*, a Spanish academic-social custom. At the turn of the century, Spanish avant-garde intellectuals gathered at cafes to discuss the latest in the arts and politics. These events soon became semi-formal, with scheduled appearances by speakers. The **Cafe Gijon** upholds the tradition every afternoon. Madrid's intellectuals still gather to discuss the latest in cultural and political happenings. This is not a standard tourist location, so keep a low profile if you are not proficient in Spanish and current in the day's topic. The **Cafe Comercial** still maintains the tertulia atmosphere but has lost the formal discussions.

Spain created and perpetuates two unique art forms, *flamenco* dancing and the *zarzuela*. Flamenco dancing has become an expensive but delightful treat, best seen at dinner night clubs such as the **Cafe de Chinitas** and the **Corral de la Moreira**. Avoid the touristy **Arco de Cuchilleros**. The zarzuela is a short, showy opera, akin to Gilbert and Sullivan. Some zarzuelas are well-known plays, set to music. The **Teatro Nacional de Zarzuela** and the theaters at the Plaza de Colon both put on performances.

Finally, the Spanish impressionistic artist Sorolla, generally neglected abroad, deserves a word. The **Museo Sorolla** houses an excellent collection of his work.

Restaurants

In Spain, you can eat lots while spending little. The *Menu del Dia* (meal of the day) offers two or three dishes, bread, wine, and dessert for much less than the items cost separately. A typical Menu del Dia features a mixed salad, thick lentil bean stew, a main course of veal and potatoes with red Spanish wine, all for about 400 pesetas (pts.). The menu limits your choice of dishes, but you're bound to find something you like.

In restaurants, customers usually order a first and second course. The first course consists of vegetables, pasta, shellfish, soup or tortillas. (Spanish tortillas don't resemble Mexican ones; the Spanish are egg omelettes combined with potatoes and cooked in olive oil, often mixed with cold cuts or vegetables.) The second dish usually is meat. Some Madrid specialties that deserve a try include *cocido madrileno* (Madrid's hotpot — a winter dish of chick peas with meat and vegetables), *callos a la madrilena* (stomach lining — delicious), with *tarta helada* (ice cream pie), *tarta al whiskey* (whisky-soaked pastry) or *tarta de manzana* (custard and apple pie) for dessert. For a distinctive breakfast, try *chocolate con churros*, Spanish hot chocolate with strips of fried dough. Spanish hot chocolate is thick enough to stand a spoon in, and can also be ordered in the late afternoon (i.e. 7:00 p.m.). Spain's best wine comes from the Rioja region; less expensive but good varieties include Valdepenas and Jumilla. For a non-alcoholic drink, try a *limon granizado* (like a lemon slurpee) or an *horchata*, available at bars and horchata stands.

The bill usually includes the service, but a 25 to 50 pts. additional tip on 500- to 700-peseta bill is a nice courtesy. In cafes, leave a couple of 5 peseta pieces or the change. Of course, if the service is bad and you're really angry, ask for the official *Libro de Reclamaciones* (Book of Complaints) that every bar and hotel must have. The government will examine complaints noted here, so just mentioning the book often solves problems.

Avoid self-service restaurants at all costs. They save you little money and the food stinks. Spain, of all European countries, should be the one place where you can eat well while staying within a budget. Restaurants aren't the only place to get good food: some of Madrid's bars, like British pubs, dish up wholesome meals in an entertaining atmosphere.

The **Casa Gallega**, across from Mercado de San Miguel, specializes in the spicy cuisine of Galicia (northern Spain). Start with the region's wine, *vino gallego*, along with *pulpo a la gallega* (octopus in hot paprika sauce) as an appetizer. Try their *tortilla gallega* as a first dish and *cochinillo* (roasted pig) as a second, *tarta helada* for dessert, and then plan for a long siesta for digestion and recuperation. This splurge will run about 1,000 pts. per person.

The **Restaurante Amadis** serves inexpensive working-class dinners for under 500 pts. This blue-collar locale definitely does not cater to tourists. **Restaurante Valencia** does cater to tourists with its English menu, but retains a good atmosphere and good-sized portions. Its Menu del Dia makes it a good bargain. Roast lamb or suckling pig lends credence to **Botin's** rustic atmosphere, but dinners cost 1,000 to 1,500 pts.

The **Restaurante Valdes** houses both a tavern and a dining room. Both serve the same food, so choose according to your mood. You can eat very well for 1,000 pts., but their *merluza a la romana* (cod) for 1,000 pts. is worth the splurge. For a touch of international flair, visit **La Argentina**, with its Spanish and international cuisine. Their specialties include pastas and *asados de ternera* (veal). Dinner will run about 700 pts.

Many Madrileno bars will feed you cheaply and entertain you as well. **Casa Mingo** serves Spanish cider, which unlike the American, packs an alcoholic kick. Order it by the glass (it's on tap) or by the bottle. Young folk flock to Casa Mingo, but tables can be found. The place serves *empanadas* (meat turnovers) as snacks, and great roast chicken. Or try a northern specialty, *chorizo a la sidra* (sausage in cider). Hot dogs (*perritos calientes*) are 50 pts.

Cerveza means beer in Spanish, so *cervecerias* are places that serve beer. **Hartzenbusch,** a local institution, stays open from 11:00 a.m. to 11:00 p.m. Though the beer is imported, the crowd is local and ready to mix. The kitchen turns out Franco-German cuisine, with good crepes. The Menu del Dia costs just 385 pts. The **Cerveceria Santa Barbara**, another popular choice, serves shellfish and beer.

Those lusting for a big juicy hamburger should visit **Hollywood** at one of its three locations. These hamburger joints stay open from 1:00 p.m. to 1:00 a.m. (1:30 on Saturday). Besides surprisingly tasty burgers, they make good *costillas de cerdo a la barbacoa* (barbecued spare ribs). Hollywood will stuff your stomach for less than 500 pts. During the school year, students hang out at **Bocaito**, known for its sandwich specials. Bocaito's long hours and short prices draw the crowd.

The indecisive shouldn't forget the Aurrera mall, mentioned earlier. Its twenty varied bars and restaurants, located near the university quarter, make browsing simple. The student bars and pizzerias clustered around Aurrera make for even more choices.

Nightlife

The nightlife starts late and ends after daybreak. In Madrid, it's hard to go wrong. You can dance to sultry samba music, swing to the newest jazz, or bop to the latest rock. The prices won't empty your wallet, and Madrilenos welcome a new face. Those who go early in the evening may well find the dance hall filled with teenagers, but the youngsters get booted out at 10:00 p.m. or so.

The hottest clubs for rock 'n roll and new wave are located under the same roof and run by the same people. **Rock-Ola** and **Marquee** play the latest tunes and attract the fastest crowd. Marquee caters to hard rockers, while Rock-ola (ola means wave) is for *nuevaoleros* (new wavers). Though few discos still play disco music, many of them still look like John Travolta hangouts, with Marquee and Rock-ola being welcome exceptions. When there's a band, which is almost always, it's 500 pts. at the door. Drinks cost about 350 pts. Prepare for a swinging night.

Joy-Eslava rivals Rock-ola for crowds, but draws a different set: more conventional, more affluent. People here dance in the elaborate remains of the old theater Eslava, complete with a stage and various levels. The sound system, complemented by the constant play of lights, outclasses anything in Madrid. Subterranean couches function as spots for those desiring to know one another better. But don't go there thirsty: drinks in the afternoon are 400 to 500 pts., and the prices double at night.

Madrid's most popular bowling alley, situated inside a discoteque, gives new meaning to the term "rock 'n *roll*." **Stella Disco Bowling** boasts bowling and dancing every afternoon, and on Fridays and eves of holidays until midnight. The clatter of pins intrudes into the disco, and bowlers roll to the latest Clash tune. Here, you can strike out at the lanes as well as on the dance floor.

Speed, another hot club, plays new imported tunes that attract a jumping local crowd. The special Speed cocktail will get you whizzing. For Madrid's first *pista electronica* (electronic dance floor), not to mention a good time, visit **Mississippi** in the student quarter. It opens at 6:00, goes all night, and even serves dinner until 5:00 a.m., along with German beer on tap and fine Irish Coffee. To dance to a different beat, samba at **Oba-Oba**. Live Brazilian music sets the stage for dancing every night until 5:00. For jazz, visit the **Arenal Jazz Club**, which earns its reputation for Madrid's best jazz. Politicians and *literati* hang out at the disco **Boccaccio**, a trendy but friendly establishment.

To check out the most night spots in the least time, head for **Orense**, the two-story mall filled with clubs. Browse there for the clientele and tunes of your choice. (Note: there is a nearby red-light zone, so single women shouldn't stray too far away.) Three of the best are **Dallas Club Jazz**, **Ravel**, and **Select**. Most clubs here stay open until 5:00 a.m., and few demand a cover charge.

To retreat back to the mellow 1960's, wander the Calle Santa Maria and Calle Huertas. Bars like **Miel**, **El Raton**, and **Kasbah** have as few as a dozen seats, so people hang out on the streets. The zone of Malasana (Metros Bilbao and San Bernado near Plaza 2 de Mayo) was a lot more popular a few years ago, but it still draws a crowd of unconventional university students and low-lifes. The crowd and drugs make this area a bit unsafe, by Madrileno standards. Two places that haven't lost their appeal are **Manuela**, with live jazz, and **Cafe de Ruiz**, which has newspapers, good coffee drinks in the mornings, and samba music at night. **Cafe Estar** is a quiet establishment for those seeking tranquility.

The **Cuevas de Sesamo** is Madrid's literary hangout, even giving out its own literary awards and recording its favorite quotations on

the wall. It mixes honky-tonk piano, great Sangria, a smokey atmosphere, and Andalucian decor. Film buffs should visit **La Filmo**,
a cafe bar that serves drinks like "The African Queen." Movies with
the accompanying soundtrack are played on the wall.

Escaping Madrid

It's hard to escape Madrid's summer heat. Reaching the best refuge,
the ocean, involves an overnight trip. The choices on afternoons usually
boil down either to your bath tub or a municipal pool. The biggest
and best pool, **Casa de Campo**, can be reached on the *suburbano* from
Plaza de Espana to El Lago. It stays open until 8:00. The **Parque
de Retiro**, although it doesn't permit swimming in its lake, rents
rowboats and paddleboats.

The sun in Spain doesn't set until after 10:00 during the summer,
and the hill of **Cuartel de la Montana** is *the* place to celebrate the
sunset. Find a seat near the fountain: the city is to the left and the
sun sets to the right over rolling hills. It's a great place for falling in
love and forgetting all about dinner.

Shopping

The best all-round shopping area centers around the Gran Via and
the streets extending from the Puerta del Sol: Calle del Arenal, Calle
de Preciados, Calle del Carmen, Carrera de San Jeronimo, and Calle
de Carretas. The two big department store chains, **el Corte Ingles**
and the **Galerias Preciados**, both have locations on the Calle de
Preciados. They are open from 10:00 to 8:00 and are air-conditioned
and stocked with just about anything you could need. For boutique
clothes in this area, visit **Femina** and **Cortefiel** on the Gran Via, next
to the movie house Coliseo. **Sesena** has Spanish capes. **Va Com Va**,
has shoes to match any mood: classical, elegant, or punk, from 750
to 2,050 pts. For native handicrafts, go to the **Rastro flea market**,
which runs from the Plaza de Cascorro to the Ronda de Toledo. Vendors sell everything from blouses to hardware. Or else visit the **Mercado San Miguel** in the Plaza de San Miguel.

LISTINGS

Restaurants

Mentioned in the text:
Casa Gallega, Bordardores, 11, phone 241-90-55.
Restaurante Valdes, Calle Libertad, 3, phone 232-20-52.
La Argentina, Valgame Dios 8, phone 221-37-63.
Hollywood, Magallanes 1, phone 448-91-65; or Calle Apolonio
  Morales 3, phone 457-79-11, or Calle Tamayo y Baus,1, phone
  231-51-15.
Bocaito, Libertad, 6, phone 232-12-19.
Casa Mingo Sidreria, Paseo de Florida, 2, phone 247-79-18.
Hartzenbusch, Calle Harzenbusch 8.
Restaurante Amadis
Restaurante Valencia, Jose Antonio 44.
Botin, Cuchilleros, 17, phone 266-42-17.
Cerberia Santa Barbara, Fernando VI, 3, phone 419-10-48.

Not mentioned:
El Restaurante Vegetariano, Marques de Santa Ana, 34. Vegetarian
  only, lunch only. Open Tuesday to Sunday. Menu 475 pts.
El Salmon, Calle Larra, 23, phone 221-57-44. Tops in tapas in university area. Their specialty is *ahumados* (smoked fish). Also try their
  chopitos (small squid) for 350 pts. The backroom restaurant charges
  twice the price of the barroom.

Nightlife

Mentioned in text:
Rock-Ola and **Marquee**, Padre Xifre, 5, phone 413-78-39.
Joy-Eslava, Arenal, 11, phone 266-54-40.
Speed, Luna, 4, phone 232-71-89.
Mississippi, Princesa, 45, phone 247-54-32.
Dallas Club Jazz, Orense, 34, 456-36-25.
Ravel, Orense, 28.
Select, Orense, 22, phone 456-61-26.
Oba-Oba, Jacometro, 4, phone 221-97-59.
Cuevas de Sesamo, Principe, 7, phone 232-91-19.
La Filmo, Plaza de Matute, 4, phone 228-76-39.
Manuela, Calle San Vicente Ferrer, 29, phone 231-70-37.
Cafe de Ruiz, Calle de Ruiz, 14.
Arenal Jazz Club, Arenal 15. Phone 247-91-89.

Boccaccio, Marques de la Ensenada, 16, phone 419-10-08.
Stella Disco Bowling, Arlaban, 7.
Cafe Estar, San Vicente Ferrer, 20, phone 448-60-87.
La Veneno, Juan de Herrera, 6, phone 247-19-34.
Cafe Commercial, Calle Genova and Plaza Bilbao.
Cafe Gijon, Calle La Castellana.
Cafe de Chinitas, Torija 7, phone 248-51-35.
Corral de la Moreira, Moreira, 17, phone 265-84-46.

Not mentioned:
Caviarisimo, Calle Serrano, 53, phone 431-33-55. Serrano is one of the most expensive streets in Madrid, and the prices in this tiny bar are no exception. But if your tast buds are tingling for something exquisite, then go all out with their fresh caviar from Russia and Iran, and their smoked salmon and eel.
Griots, Barco, 32, phone 30-06-68. A bar with African music, drinks and cuisine from 9:00 until 2:30.
Al-Mounia, Recoletos, 5, phone 225-06-42. Arabian teas, pastries and dried fruits until midnight.
Suzie-Q, Noviciado, 12, specializes in rock 'n roll from the '60's, with decor and atmosphere to match. German beer on tap, hamburgers and Irish coffee from 6:00 p.m. to 2:00 a.m.
Gizeh, San Mateo, 28, phone 419-21-60.A disco-pub, not a discoteque, plays reggae and new wave. Dancing is only in the aisles or on the tables. Sandwiches, salads or complete dinners from 8:00 p.m. to 2:00 a.m.
Pacha, Barcelo, 11, phone 446-01-37, Madrid's version of Studio 54, housed in the old theater Barcelo. Drinks 700 to 1000 pts. Friday, Saturday and Sunday afternoons from 7:00 to 10:00, nights from midnight to 4:00.

Shopping

Corte Ingles, Calle de Preciados and Paza Callao.
Galerias Preciados, corner of Calle de Preciados and Plaza Callao.
Femina, Calle de Preciados, 12.
Cortefiel, Gran Via 74.
Sesena, Calle Cruz, 23.
Va Com Va, Calle Atocha.

Attractions

Teatro Nacional de Zarzuela, Jovellamos, 2, phone 221-43-41.
Museo Sorolla, Calle General Martinez Campos, 37.

*Naples is dirty,
chaotic, and treacherous,
and you should go there*

Naples

Naples is dirty, chaotic, and treacherous, and you should go there. The city has never generated ambivalence: it will either enchant you or remain in your mind as a warren of thugs and criminals. The city is at once Sunny Naples, port of music and poets, and Naples of the Thieves. It has long been Italy's hard-luck city, overrun by invaders from the Visigoths to World War II G.I.'s, convulsed by earthquakes, strangled by the mafia.

Nevertheless, perhaps because they have seen so much come and go (or because they never have had enough free time or space to stay away from their neighbors), most Neapolitans remain the most generous and sociable of people. Every Neapolitan, thief or artist, is a salesman — clever, quick-tongued, and amiable. The entire city functions like an open market, where everything could be for sale — just ask. Yet there are those who take advantage of the chaos and treat the tourists and others as their prey. The city works with words; silent and aloof visitors will be treated as simple prey, but anyone who talks and jokes with the Neapolitans will be treated well.

Begin at the train station, **Piazza Garibaldi**, which at any hour of day or night seems a hellish chaos. Anything is sold, any price is asked, every language is spoken, everything is stolen. It serves as an aptly inhospitable welcome to Naples. On the near right hand corner of the piazza, just across from the baggage deposit room, is the **Pizzeria Birreria**. There you can sit, enjoy an inexpensive meal and begin getting accustomed to Neapolitan atmosphere.

Naples boasts the most and the finest *banche di acqua* (lemonade stands) to be found in Italy. Installed permanently along the streets, lemons and oranges piled high on marble and colored stone, they of-

117

fer juice or soft drinks. To the right of the station (with your back to it) is the street Corso Novara: follow it three streets to Via Venezia. On the left you will find one Banca di Acqua, run by a most courteous and wild Signora and whichever of her two dozen relatives show up that day. Early in the morning, the ice man still cometh with his wagon to deliver the block of ice for the Signora. Nearby, at the corner of Via Firenza and Via Bologna, is **Da Caterina**, a good, cheap restaurant with outdoor tables where customers relax in the sun over a three-hour meal.

In the evening, during the ceremonial *passeggiata* (promenade), people fill the streets again. Strollers move arm-in-arm along Via Caracciolo, following the road between the Castel Dell'ovo and Mergellina along the Bay of Naples. From sunset until past midnight, all of Naples turns out for this procession of vamps, lady-killers, chic debutantes, and huge families, who gossip and flirt, joke and laugh. Vendors set up shop, selling beer, *spicche* (pronounced ''spee-kay,'' it's roasted corn on the cob), *taralli* (a Neapolitan specialty: dry, round biscuits with almonds and various seeds), and the usual fare of peanuts, chestnuts, and Coke. At one end of the road looms the black hump of Vesuvius; at the other sparkle the lights of the glamorous Mergellina quarter.

Between Piazza Vittoria and Piazza Repubblica, at the beginning of Via Caracciolo, the parks of the Villa Communale face the sea, luring the visitor with their fountains and placid, tree-lined vistas. Though at night this area fills with prostitutes, you can sit safely here until 1:00 a.m. at two open-air cafes, hidden among the trees, where waiters will serve you with silver trays. The breeze blows gently from the sea, and you will not want to leave.

At the end of the walk lies a quarter called **Mergellina**, crowded with restaurants and bars. The best are in the Piazza (on Sannazzaro, just off Via Caracciolo), where you begin to get a view of the docks and a small harbor. On the far side of the Piazza, at the beginning of Via Giordano Bruno, hide two good pizzerias. **O Giardiniello**, at the corner, stays open late and serves especially fine pizza in a genial setting. **O Pigniatello**, next door, a bit more elegant and expensive, hosts a mixture of young thinkers and transient vendors. Nearby, at the ocean, a fine strip of bars with outside tables lines the water.

Close by, near the gardens (midway between P. Vittoria and P. Repubblica) on Via Ischitella, is **Il Pulcinella**. Its dark, carnivalesque atmosphere often attracts the flamboyant scions of the great fallen families who live in this area. The restaurant, named after a Commedia dell'Arte character, serves moderate fare at equally moderate prices.

If you walk about ten minutes or take the bus on past Mergellina, toward the gorgeous villas and cliff gardens of Via Posillipo, you will find **Vini, Olio, Cucina**, a small, humble, and very good restaurant at #268 Via Posillipo. New and managed by young people, it has one of the most beautiful views in Naples — for those lucky enough to get an outside table.

The most beautiful and most famous restaurants of Naples are found on the little island of the **Borgo Marinaio**, at the edge of the quarter of Santa Lucia. Halfway between Mergellina and Vesuvius, the isle offers a stunning view of both. People flock here for the sunrise and sunset. The enormous Castel dell' Ovo, a castle which seems as big as Vesuvius itself, takes up half the island. The restaurants, built right at the edge of the sea, all face a small harbor between the island and Naples. You could dip your toes in the harbor with little effort.

At **Ciro's Pizzeria**, you'll find white tablecloths and waiters with bow ties. An ancient gray-haired waiter, if you get him talking, will tell you of the fifty years he spent roaming the world. He speaks broken English, so you'll have to bribe the maitre d' to translate. Next to Ciro's is a birrreria, a humbler place serving antipasti and light foods, all good and moderatetly priced. **Starita**, a full-fledged *ristorante*, boasts a little porch built out over the water. This restaurant, with its sense of elegance, outshines its neighbors. Starita dishes out superb seafood at moderate prices.

At the end of the row stands **Vongolaio**, a simple but excellent family-run place that serves only clam and mussels in broth. The tables wobble, the lights flicker on and off, but the good food and fun-loving proprietors make it an enjoyable evening.

During the day, the heart of Naples throbs between Via De'Tribunali and Via Di S. Biagio Dei Librai. Ancient, fallen, repaired, and fallen again, the area is the playground of the city. The streets are at their best in early morning or late afternoon. As the bells ring for Mass, the merchants open or close their stores, and the smells of either new bread or dinner hover in the air.

Hidden in the gloom of the *portici* (covered sidewalks) that begin where Via de'Tribunali meets Vicolo dei Cinque Santi, there's a little-known spectacle. Perhaps you've never paid much attention to butcher shops, but look at these. You wouldn't expect hamburger to be made here, but rather sacrifices, martyrdoms, or executions. The floors and doorways are of inlaid stone; the meat lies on huge slabs of pink marble that slant back like a little stage. These three shops are their eeriest at night. A large altar looms in the back of each, the Virgin Mary and the *Bambino Gesu* hovering in orbs of blue neon. In the day these shops are less haunting, but the butchers provide enough entertainment to draw a crowd. They speak only the local dialect, yet whatever you say to them they'll jabber back with gusto. Neapolitan, Italy's "jive" talk, will entertain you, even if you don't understand a word.

In this area, look for Santa Maria della *"Pace-e-Bene,"* the resident saint. She's an ancient, bent, and wizened woman, dressed always in black wool and pulling behind her a miniature caravan of black bags — her belongings and her "hotel." She decided years ago to live homeless for Christ, but rather than be a   sanctimonious reformer, she became a loose-tongued wild-woman, calling out *"Pace e bene"* (peace and well-being) to all who pass. She says she'll live forever, and we believe her. Look for her at S. Lorenzo Maggiore at closing time.

To eat in this area (and the rest of Naples) you'll have the most fun in an *osteria* or *cucina casalinga*, both informal places run by families, where you sit down wherever there's space and eat whatever they cook that day. You eat well and pay little. Across from the butcher shops is one — **Cucina Casalinga**; and one block down on the same side of the street is another, between Via Nilo and Via di S. Gregorio Armeno. Another good cucina, **La Cantina**, is found on a narrow roller-coaster street that will remind you of San Francisco. These places open only for lunch.

An unusual sort of religious decor surrounds Via De' Tribunali — a flirtatious, ostentatious, nearly grotesque tribute to religion that Fellini would endorse. Wandering around here at night, you'll notice that the streets glow irregularly with the colored lights from the shrines to the Madonna. This is not the lovely, chaste virgin of northern Italy, nor the "Fifth Avenue baroque" lady of Rome, but a painted, hot-eyed vamp posing within her Broadway-style cloister of neon, gold, and fur. The Neapolitans love the Madonna and can't bear to deprive her of the pleasures of life. Via Di S. Maria in Purgatorio houses a fine "strip" of these shrines.

If you want a Madonna of your very own, go to Via Di S. Gregorio Armeno at Christmas time when it is transformed into a crecherie. Rows and rows of stores sell animals and saints for the manger, tropical mangers, art deco mangers, mangers of all sizes and styles, from pastoral to penthouse deluxe. The more unusual styles you can find sometimes in a back room on an upper shelf; they are not part of the regular display but show up now and again.

There are some similarly high-spirited churches in this area — spectacular like a circus, dramatic, taunting. Enter, for example, **S. Gregorio Armeno** at dusk, when Naples slides back to medieval times. You walk up the steps and cross the wide porch of black stone. Here the sisters of S. Gregorio (a convent) loiter and chatter, seeing which of the sinners show up to confess. Inside all is light: the ceiling floats up, bedecked with gold and fresco, dazzling like a mirage. The side chapels, little black estuaries of passion, house the stories of the saints and martyrs, depicted with detail and violence rarely found in churches. Everything here glistens; no area bigger than a fingernail was left unworked. If you walk in before mass when the church lies empty, when candles provide the only light, you can feel all the reverie and terror of a past era's religous fervor.

Up the street is **S. Lorenzo Maggiore**, where Via di S. Gregorio meets Via de' Tribunali. The interior of the enormous cathedral opens like a chasm in the city. In contrast with S. Gregorio, this cathedral is vast and bare, the wide floor open and luminous. The chapels, harmed by floods and only partly restored, remain little Baroque jewels. Finally, visit the **Cloister of Santa Chiara**, open from 9:00 a.m. to noon, and from 4:30 to 7:30. It's a rococo orchard, covered with vines, overgrown with trees and bushes. Painted tiles cover all the columns. The Cloister is a beautiful spot, quieter and cooler than the outside world, and the monks won't object if you take a nap here.

You should go in the early morning to see the **Palazzo Reale**. Pretend that you are neglected royalty, returning to a minor holding. (Despite your lineage, you still have to pay 1000 L, and it's closed Monday). The palazzo will be almost empty, and you will have miles and miles of exquisite rooms opening into gardens by the sea. Fortunately, it has not yet been glassed off and labeled by overzealous curators, and you can sit down in the chairs or stretch out on a bed. Take a long stroll and invent your own history for the rooms, the people you have entertained here, the parties you've thrown.

The **Museo Nazionale Di Napoli** (at Piazza Cavour) combines Naple's squalor and distress with its extravagance and spectacle. The atmosphere is overpowering, the acoustics deafening. Dozens of self-proclaimed guides will conduct tours in any language, but they earn their pay only in the entertainment they provide. Upstairs you will find perhaps the finest collection of Pompeiian frescoes and mosaics in Naples, while downstairs an enormous terracotta model of Pompeii sits, so covered with dirt and so poorly kept that it will soon resemble post-Vesuvius Pompeii. The ground floor is awash with second-rate Roman copies of Greek statues. In contrast, the restored wing, which houses the Egyptian collection, is spacious, well-designed, and beautiful. Large black and white photographs of the re-discovery of ancient Egypt fill one room; another contains a number of mummies, surrounded by their opulent belongings and jewelry in silver and glass cases. The whole arrangement eerily resembles an ancient fashion show.

Shopping

Naples is one of the cheapest and finest places to shop in Italy. The street merchants, especially at the far side of Piazza Garibaldi near the station, often sell very decent shoes and nice clothes for reasonable prices. They also sell a lot of junk, but what is good there is very good. Best bets for store shopping center around Corso Umberto (from P. Garibaldi) and Via Toledo (from P. Plebiscito). Here are the most inventive and gorgeous styles of shoes in Italy. The August sales are the best, with everything at about half price.

Near the Palazzo Reale is **Galleria Umberto**, a bit of grand old Naples. This is what a shopping mall should be. It was built in the form of a Greek cross, with huge marble floors as smooth and wide and lustrous as a skating rink. The walls rise three stories to an arched, stained-glass ceiling. A number of swank clothing stores hold court here. Each morning at the famous **Bar Brasilero**, the old men sit at the tables and talk about the good old days when Naples had a king.

Nightlife

There are two ritzy discotheques in Naples, but they have little to recommend them. You can lose your money much faster on the streets with less effort and perhaps more pleasure. Along Via Nazarion Sauro, **Anthony Club**, a large spacious spot, has good music, but a cover charge of 10,000L. The drinks are stiff, too, at 7,000L.

Nearby is the **Shaker Club** which often has good live music, though it is all Neapolitan (akin to early Frank Sinatra). Admission runs from 7,000L when there is a DJ, to 20,000L when there is a good band.

Red Light Naples

Because it is poor, a port, and near American naval and military bases, Naples has an extensive and remarkably squalid red light district. The action centers almost entirely around Piazza Municipio. Whatever your interests in the area, you will find something. It's at least entertaining and always well-trafficked. Start with Via Agostinio Depretis at P. Municipio. On your immediate left (moving away from the piazza) is **Boston Blackies**, a masterpiece of a sleaze pit. Beginning in the late afternoon, prostitutes, faces painted in garish colors, gaze out from their stools near the doorway. Further along, off a tiny street to the left called Via Orazio Massa, lurks the **Red Lantern Dancing Bar**. There are better places to go dancing. Here again there is the wild display of "hostesses" lined up at the bar. You wander in through the red fog from the "mood lights" to a tiny dance floor surrounded by couches and, further back, private booths. Drinks American-style cost 4,500L.

None of these bars caters exclusively to prostitution, but some are more wholesome than others. The Red Lantern is fun for dancing, if you go with friends. Otherwise, the prostitution gets oppressive. **El Marocco**, a downstairs lounge, is the wild spot, with its large dancing floor and flashing lights. It has the best dancing, and you can go alone without the fear of being viewed as a "client." Here too you'll find the private booths in the back, sunken into a sort of mirror-paradise behind the dance floor. A DJ starts the music at 9:30.

The cheapest and most destitute of these bars is the **Saddakan** at #34 Piazza Francia (go to where P. Municipio meets Via Cristofero Colombo and turn left, and the third door will be this bar). The same creatures sit chatting on stools in yet another downstairs pleasure grotto. The music here is good, and sometimes you'll find good dancers.

Follow Via C. Colombo around to the right, along the port, past a huge castle on the right, and you'll find the most lurid and picturesque night vendors of all sexes and sexualities. This truck route and sailor hang-out provides a year round spectacle.

*Paris fashion separates
the beautiful from the ugly,
the rich from the poor, and
the Europeans from the Americans*

Paris

If you're in Paris and bored one day, ask a Parisian what in his city is *not* the best. Does any other city do something better? Tell him, for example, that you've heard that London's nightlife is more exciting. He may think that this question is impudent, that it forces him to brag about his city. But when pressed, he'll admit that Parisian women are the world's most beautiful, and the men the most suave; the food is the tastiest, the shopping the most glamorous. And, of course, Paris sets the world's standard for fashion and chic nightlife... Eventually, he may concede something — like the Metro, though it's the world's most pleasant subway, really needs more express stops, or the city's theater hasn't produced much since Ionesco and Beckett.

Though his homage should be taken with some skepticism, your Parisian has a point: Paris is a spectacular city, often justifiably boasting of the "best" of this or that. And of course, living among all these "bests," the residents of Paris consider themselves the world's most discerning judges of class and culture. To put it bluntly, many French are snobs, and the Parisians are the worst. Unabashedly, unashamedly, they will judge you on your looks, evaluating your wealth and sophistication with a highly-trained eye. And many Americans, with their baggy blue jeans, oversized backpacks, and overloaded wallets, just don't pass the test.

Fashion in Paris distinguishes the beautiful from the ugly, the rich from the poor, and the Europeans from the Americans. The French use an English word for it, the "look," but they give it more importance than the haughtiest American. It's more than just money: after all, the French gave us the phrase *nouveau riche*, and more importantly, *savoir faire*. It's knowing how to do everything with individuality and flair that the French respect. That's part of what makes Paris so much fun: if you can get into a French private club, or engage a Parisian in conversation, you know you've accomplished something.

Parisians in general treat strangers formally, but nothing works like a strong dollar and a strong personality to improve foreign relations. You can use the innocent (but double-edged) pick up line "*Tu as du feu?*" which means "Do you have a light?" and is pronounced "ta doo feuh?" This line usually works anywhere and anytime — even if you don't smoke.

Paris herself remains very much what she was fifty, or even one hundred years ago, with three exceptions: the Eiffel Tower, the Champs Elysees, and the month of August, which have become tourist property. The rest of Paris belongs to the Parisians, and they, too, have changed very little. Long-legged, Dior-clad beauties still sip coffee in the Place de la Madeleine, while long-haired jeans-wearing students drink wine from the bottle in the Place St. Michel. Let both parts of the city entertain you: eat a hearty dinner in a student bistro and follow it by a night at one of Paris's jet-set night clubs. Complete a picnic lunch of home-made *Breton pate* on French bread with an ice cream from elegant Berthillon's. Paris caters to gourmets; become one. Permit no luxury to pass you by, and remember that the finer things of life are better and cheaper here than anywhere else.

Nightlife

Paris is the city of light and of lights. White — and red — lights gleam all over the city at night, marking the places where nightlife is the only way of life. "Nightlife" in Paris can mean anything from walking along lamplit avenues to dancing to the rhythm of flashing lasers. But despite the fact that France has one of the highest alcoholism rates in the world, the French don't go out to drink. A mixed drink will cost you 40 francs and up almost anywhere. The typical French youth returns sober from his evening on the town.

The French regard the concept of a plain bar as boring. Drinking only makes other things more pleasurable. Music, for instance. Discos still dominate the most chic element of Parisian nightlife. Trying to get into elite clubs is still a favorite pastime, with success a sign of social distinction. The "in" places change faster than French fashions, but you're sure to meet a star if you make it past the doors of the Elysees Matignon, Castel, or Le Privilege. To do so, you should look very rich, very beautiful, or very arrogant. You needn't look all three, and the last usually will suffice. If you don't fit into any of these categories you can at least amuse yourself at the door by watching the people who do fit — you may recognize some celebrities.

Le Privilege is just that, a privilege for those who prefer soft lights, soft music, and plush seats to the hard-core festivites which occur upstairs in Le Palace. What used to be the roller rink for Le Palace was turned into this tiny club and reserved for the select few. Don't despair if you aren't one of them, because it's worth the trip even if you end up upstairs at Le Palace.

Anyone and everyone gets into **Le Palace**, a huge disco that fills up with 2,000 people every night. People work hard to make themselves stand out in the crowd; success comes in the form of exotic costumes, multi-colored punk hairdos, some very provocative dancing, and ambiguous sexuality. Waiters and bouncers, clad in satin jump-suits with quilted silver wings, patrol the floor, looking like space-age angels. An excellent sound system blasts music, while videos light up a screen that covers a full wall of this converted theater.

If possible, **Les Bains Douches** surpasses Le Palace in character. Converted from an old Turkish bath, Les Bains Douches became the center for punk, hard-rock, and ska fashion at the end of the 1970's. At that time only the truly bizarre got past the stone statues at the door. But with changing times and a few cocaine raids, Les Bains Douches has become a more accessible, if not less desirable, place to pass the hours between midnight and dawn, listening and dancing to new-wave music. Or swimming — it has a small stone-lined pool, one of the many remnants from its days as a bath house.

In the summer of 1984, **120 Nights**, perhaps the trendiest club ever, became a smashing success. The club epitomized chic, you see, because after being open for just 120 nights, it closed for good. The idea was such a hit, though, that many people have talked about opening a similar place next summer, but whether they will remains to be seen.

At the **Elysees Matignon**, you're likely to run into older movie stars, young social climbers, and prepubescent models trying to make a name for themselves. This makes for easy pick-ups, provided you are well-dressed and behave yourself. Tell the bouncer you are from California and he'll probably forgive you anything. Elysees Matignon is on the same block as Keur Samba, "78," Regine's, and L'Apocalypse, four of the other most elite discos. If you strike out once. you're only minutes from your next opportunity. **Keur Samba** has the distinction of closing the latest — 9:00 a.m. Just rememer, though, that drinks cost 90 francs at all these spots.

Castel-Princesse opens its doors to a more heterogeneous crowd. Considering the diverse crowd of hippies, dandies, men in three-piece suits, and women in much less than that, you may conclude you have a chance of getting in. You can try, but the key here is fame: if you are an unknown, or if Corinne (the woman at the door) decides you won't ever be known, you will stay on the sidewalk.

Les Halles, the section surrounding the former market, has been the trendiest section of Paris for the past couple years, full of the *branche* ("in") people, but the area surrounding La Bastille is rapidly supplanting it. A club called **La Mousson** typifies the newly renovated

125

region. For just plain dancing, an spot called **Opera Night** draws a large crowd of young folk; spontaneous exhibitions of dancing some nights are the highlight. The **Rock'n'Roll Circus** and the **Depot-Vente** (in Neuilly) are two of the trendiest clubs for the young. Other good rock and roll establishments include the **Bus Palladium** for endless dancing and **Gibus** for the truly bizarre.

Jazz clubs typically offer a less elitist, more relaxing evening than the discos. The young and the swinging love to gather at jazz bars to enjoy an evening over a cool drink and some pretty hot music. Paris and much of Europe was for years a haven for black jazz musicians fleeing the racism of the States. Don't be surprised if the Europeans are better informed on this American art form than you.

Le Caveau de la Huchette, a traditional jazz establishment, these days puts more emphasis on rowdiness than rhythm. There is almost always something happening at this student hang-out, but it isn't usually the dancing. The wildest patrons here usually aren't French; nor, for a change, are they Americans. The cheap cover charge and low drink prices draw students from just about everywhere. Le Caveau is an institution, for better or worse.

Le Furstemberg is a little more intimate, and a lot more French. A few steps down from a St. Germain side street, this old wine cellar has been remodeled with soft leather booths and a brown lacquered ceiling. The regulars are as well-dressed (especially the men) as the place is decorated, and the drinks are as smooth as the jazz. Although Le Furstemberg appears to be fairly quiet, things do start to hop around 11:00, as quiet talk turns into lively discussion and sometimes even off-tune singing.

Le Petit Opportun surpasses Le Furstemberg in intimacy, if you can call brushing buttocks with your neighbor intimate. This tiny bar makes up for its size with its music, which many call the best jazz in Paris. Smoke surrounds the friendly, out-going crowd.

Old newspapers mix with modern video screens at **Le Petit Journal**. This club manages to balance old music with a young, hip audience. Forty-year-old newspapers cover the walls, but the current day's paper is given out free.

London Tavern hosts some decent jazz on Saturday nights and always serves good beer. If you simply crave beer, go to **L'Academie de la Biere**, which serves over a hundred varieties of beer from across the globe. And the people are usually more friendly than the average Parisian sipping a Pernod in a sidewalk cafe.

Most bars and night clubs don't get going until 10:00 or 11:00, so the cafe-theater was invented to fill the gap between dinner and drink or dance. Songs and acts are performed in front of (and sometimes on top of) tiny tables where drinks and light meals are served. Acts vary from full-fledged plays to songs and stand-up routines. The material varies as well, changing from week to week. All the same, each cafe/cabaret maintains a certain reputation.

Le Cafe d'Edgar puts on three different shows a night, but since they all center on the same theme, sex, they're fairly easy to understand. **Le Club des Poetes**, by contrast, caters to a more intellectual crowd, featuring poetry readings of anything and everything by anyone and everyone. Feel free to let them have it with a few verses of your own. The reactions are usually as amusing as the poems and poets themselves. Americans in search of the quintessentially French go to **Chez Georges**. Despite being quintessential, the place is fun; if you don't understand the songs that are the standard here, someone will be glad to explain them to you.

While you can get hard liquor in many cafes, the best places for cocktails are advertised as *Bars Americains*. Tropical and exotic drinks are just that in Paris — the drink being tropical and the price exotic. Exotic drinks and American bars can still be found: the former at **Le Montgolfier** and the latter at either Harry's or Mother Earth's. **Harry's New York Bar** is true to its name, differing from its New York counterpart only in that the New Yorkers sipping whiskies here are transferred businessmen who read the *International Herald Tribune* instead of the *Wall Street Journal*. **Mother Earth's** caters to a younger and funkier set of ex-patriates, especially college students, struggling artists, and Grand Tourists sick of wine and cheese. If you have really despaired of meeting a sociable Parisian, try here, for the occasional Parisian frequenting these places is obviously looking to meet Americans.

An older but equally international crowd can be found at **Le Montgolfier**. This bar, located atop of the Meridien Hotel, offers excellent drinks, good jazz, a great view of Paris, and the atmosphere of an airport — international and impersonal. Another chic bar/restaurant sits on top of Tour Montparnasse, Paris's sole skyscraper. Although the building mars the city's architectural integrity and the drinks are mediocre, the view makes the trip worthwhile. After a hard day of museums, enjoy a drink for an hour or two atop the building, soothed by gentle piano music.

Paris has long been known for its Moulin Rouge, Folies Bergere, Lido and other great cabarets. Like many other famous attractions, they charge high prices and draw large number of tourists. However, in all fairness, the cabarets put on a great show: it's like the Rockettes in Radio City Music Hall — the crowds are huge, natives rare, and the shows perhaps dated but well-done.

Paris's red-light district is known as **Pigalle**. As one American said, "It's like New York's Times Square, but safe." Tour buses deposit large numbers of Italians, Germans, Americans, and Swiss who stop at the Moulin Rouge before taking a peek at some of the peep shows. A tour bus driver observed that the Italians prefer watching many women with one man, the Germans like lesbian sex, and the Americans like everything. We leave the sociological implications of all this to others. Prostitution lurks nearby, especially on Rue Frochot where every bar has a lady with keys in hand. Those with a great deal of daring and a valid insurance policy can visit the **Bois de Boulogne** after the sun sets, when the area attracts muggers rapists, pimps, prostitutes, and transvestites. People cruise through in their Mercedes, looking for a bisexual male to complete their foursome, or the like. But until they're sure of their find, they keep their doors locked.

Restaurants

Eating in Paris should be entertaining, inexpensive, and delicious. For pure fun, visit **Chez les Fondus**, near Sacre Coeur. If you wander down Rue des Trois Freres, halfway down the street you will encounter the waiting line for this illustrious establishment, where wine comes in baby bottles and the owner weilds a plastic hammer, allegedly to preserve order. Chaos reigns; you can hear shouts, laughter, and slurred singing well down the block. The restaurant only serves fondue — both cheese and meat — and the obligatory wine. Eating fondue becomes even more fun if you observe the tradition of kissing the person to your left when you drop your bread. With the tight tables, this could be just about anyone, so use your imagination. If you want to be sure to get a table, call ahead to reserve. Just be prepared to shout over the racket.

To meet students or to avoid French stuffiness, visit **Zero de Conduite** or **Bistrot de la Sorbonne**. In French schools, *Zero de Conduite* means "F" for behavior. Waiters earn this mark as they tease and gossip with their clients. Zero de Conduite serves surprisingly good food for a place that charges only 40 francs for an all-inclusive meal. Don't be frightened by its black exterior.

Bistrot de la Sorbonne resembles a cafe, but forget about quiet dining here. The people at the table next to you will have their high-brow discussion on anything from Plato to "the-quality-of-the-girl-at-the-first-table-over-there's-legs" in high decibels. If your French is good enough, join in. In any case the food is inexpensive and good, so if you strike out the first time don't feel bad.

Typical home-style French cooking is at its best in family-run places like **Au Gourmet de l'Ile** or **Polidor**. Typical home-style means chicken, meats, and fish, in different sauces and broths with a green vegetable and some form of potatoes. Family-run means that the father or the grandfather will sit at a small bar, making sure that his wife or daughter finds you a place among the myriad tiny tables, and that the wine is satisfactory. Parisians go to Au Gourmet de l'Ile for its food, while tourists go there for its location on the Ile St. Louis. In either case, it is almost always full, so it's best to reserve a table. In the past, Polidor has served such luminaries as Joyce and Hemingway. Today, it retains much its turn-of-the century atmosphere. Students, locals, and others who appreciate the low prices — between 20 and 50 francs for an entree and appetizer, frequent the place.

Chartier rivals Polidor both in prices and atmosphere. At Chartier, waiters run between the narrow tables, writing patrons' orders down on the place mats. A dinner of salad, chicken, french fries, red wine, and coffee will cost you less than 30 francs.

If you want to sample the lighter *nouvelle cuisine*, or if you want to eat outside away from tourists and traffic, try **La Cour St. Germain**, with its red checkered table cloths. For the price, the food is excellent, making the restaurant successful enough to open several branches throughout the city. At La Cour St. Germain an appetizer and entree will run 48ff. The desserts are extra-money and extra-rich.

For really good steak and french fries — *steak frites* in French — try **L'Entrecote**. There is no menu; your only choices are your wine, how thoroughly the steak is cooked, and whether to have dessert (which is large and delicious, but an added expense to the rest of the 48ff tab). Parisians and tourists flock to L'Entrecote, and since the restaurant takes no reservations, you can expect a line. Most find that it's worth the wait.

A formal French lunch lasts two hours and probably is best enjoyed at a restaurant with outdoor tables. If you want a quick meal, order a cafe's *plat du jour* or a steak frites. Or for less money than you would pay for a "ham-beurre-ger," you can get a quiche or a small pizza at a *boulangerie* (bakery). *Charcuteries* also provide quick meals, but have more exotic dishes, some served hot, as well as a wide assortments of pates and cold meats.

Not only are French restaurants superb, but the markets and boulangeries make for excellent eating for those on a lower budget. A diet of bread (French) and water (Perrier) isn't that bad, after all. Following Marie Antoinette's advice ("Let them eat cake ") won't lead you too far astray, either. Shopping at an open-air market solves the low-budget woes with spectacular fresh vegetables and fish, homemade *pate* and cheese. *Paris par Arrondissement*, the most popular city map, lists these markets. Some of the better ones are in the fifth arrondissement (Place Monge; Wed.,Fri.,Sat.,) and the sixteenth (Ave. President Wilson; Wed.,Sat). Less expensive ones are in the Les Halles area and in the twelfth arrondissement. Even if you only buy an apple, you're bound to learn some new words, as vendors hawk their wares to pushy housewives.

If you want Paris's best picnic, stop by **Androuet** for cheese, **Lenotre** for pastries, and **Berthillon** for ice cream and sherbets. Or practice one-stop shopping at **Fauchon**, the gourmet's supermarket. It stocks everything from Argentine biscuits to American clam chowder. These shops all specialize in making addictive little foods with large prices.

(Consider that your wallet will lose the weight that your hips are gaining, so the scales won't note the difference.)

Shopping

Spend some time wandering around the side streets of the left bank's St. Germain to see what's new in the fashion world. The boutiques are trendier and more eclectic than those on the right bank. The traditional establishments, like **Christian Dior**, **Louis Vuitton**, and **Hermes** still dwell in the Eighth on or near Rue St. Honore and the Champs Elysees. When you have an idea of what you are looking for, walk over to Blvd. St. Michel, across the river to the Forum des Halles, or to one of the big shopping stores (**Au Printemps** or **Galeries Lafayette**) on Blvd. Haussman. There you'll find what you can afford. Parisian department stores such as Au Printemps offer a wide range of prices and much more sophistication than their American counterparts. The bargain section of town is in the sixth arrondissement, on Rue St. Placide. Many outlets sell clothes marked *degriffe*, meaning they bear no labels. Two other bargain basements are **Bab's** in the first arrondissement, and **Mendes** in the second. Both sell last year's designer items at half price. Bear in mind that last year's Yves St. Laurent still is not cheap.

If you have time to spare and want to find some very inexpensive or unusual clothes, take the Metro out to the Porte de Clignancourt for the **Marche aux Puces**. This flea market covers several long blocks and sells nearly anything you could imagine and includes an exotic furniture store with live baby alligators in the window.

Paris also is home to three classier "flea markets," modeled after London's Portobello Road. These markets offer "antiques" and *objets d'art* from the 18th-century to Art Deco. Sometimes their offerings seem to range from the useless to the truly useless, but both the shopkeepers and the merchandise can be entertaining. If you're planning to buy something expensive, you'll do better here than the Marche aux Puces. The biggest and ritziest is **Le Louvre des Antiquaires**, housed in a part of the Louvre, then the **Village Suisse** near the Champs-de-Mar, and the **Village St. Paul**, not far from Notre Dame, in a bramble of homes and courtyards. Wandering around the courtyards of Village St. Paul is a treat in itself.

The latest section of Paris to be revitalized is **Les Halles**, with its Le Forum des Halles. Le Forum resembles an American shopping mall, but with specialized stores and a touch of Parisian sophistication. This combination has gained mixed reviews. Near Les Halles on roads such as Rue des Lombards, a set of funky stores have sprung up. They display the latest fashions, which are often old American fashions: one store had fifties-look sweaters next to fly-fishing vests.

Wandering

For those with too little interest or money to go shopping, the **Bois de Boulogne** during the day will beat window-browsing. With its model boat pond and real boat pond where you can rent row boats, the Bois de Boulogne is more or less to Paris what Central Park is to New York. It doesn't have a zoo (the zoo is in the Bois de Vincennes) but it does have La Bagatelle, an extensive rose and flower garden, and le Jardin d'Acclimatation, a small amusement park. The race course there attracts a classy crowd on Sundays.

Luxembourg Garden, a park in the city, is the home of the Guignol marionettes. The productions, with their sly sense of humor, amuse both children and adults. There's also always a show at **Le Centre Pompidou/Beaubourg**, the city's latest major museum. This structure, which resembles an above-ground model of a subway station, would look more in place at Disney's Epcot Center. But it does have some decent exhibits, an accessible library, and street shows (usually flame-swallowers, for some reason) out front. Across the way at the *horloge automatique* (automatic clock), three mechanical figures fight on the hour, every hour, with the wildest melees occuring at noon and 6:00. The figures symbolize earth, air, and water, and supposedly, the one which "wins" that hour's fight is selected at random by computer.

For a more traditional vision of beauty and art, visit the **Musee Rodin**. This house and garden is home to much of the sculptor's finest work. The enclosed statue garden, especially when its myriad roses are in bloom, is perhaps the most lovely and tranquil picnic spot in Paris.

Nothing is more traditionally Parisian than to sit at a cafe, sip a coffee, and watch the world go by. Since the best seats are outdoors and the fare always simple, pick your cafe by its location. Several cafes, however, have developed reputations and attract a loyal following. **Les Deux Magots**, despite its touristy atmosphere and an unbelievably snobby menu, still packs them in with its view of the chic Boulevard St. Germain. **La Coupole** draws a mixed crowd of long-haired intellectuals, down-and-out movie stars, and out-of-town models. On the right bank, the **Drugstore des Champs-Elysees**, which sells everything from tennis rackets to suitcases, has a very popular counter-restaurant.

Les Gobelins has been the royal tapestry-making center in France for centuries. It is *not* a museum, though these days its biggest customers are museums doing restoration work, such as Versailles. When you enter, you feel as if you have stepped back several centuries, as you watch the weavers work with such painstaking care.

Pere Lachaise has been *the* cemetery for proper French families for years, though it's hard to see why. Lachaise is a shantytown of a cemetery, with garish tombs covering every square foot. There's a long list of famous people buried here, topped by Moliere, Oscar Wilde, and Jim Morrison. The gatekeepers will sell you a map of this eerie establishment.

If it is really hot or if you aren't going to make it to the Riviera — "I'm afraid not this year, darling" — you might want to visit the local substitute, **La Piscine Deligny**. The pool retains one of the Riviera's finest traits: topless and often nearly bottomless women. You can get a pretty close look, too, since towel space is limited and there is quite a bit of overlapping.

LISTINGS

Nightlife

Le Palace, 8 Faubourg Montmartre, phone 246-10-87.
Les Bains-Douches, 7 rue Bourg l'Abbe, phone 887-34-40.
Castel-Princesse, 15 rue Princesse, phone 326-90-22.
Elysees Matignon, 2 ave. Matignon, phone 225-73-13.
Le Privilege, 1 ter cite Bergere, phone 246-10-87.
Bus Palladium, 6 rue Fontaine, phone 874-54-99.
Gibus, 18 rue du Faubourg-du-Temple, phone 700-78-88.
Rock'n'Roll Circus, 6 rue Caumartin, phone 268-05-20.
120 Nights, 10 blvd. de Strasbourg, phone 240-57-61.
La Mousson, 9 rue de la Bastille, phone 271-85-20.
Le Depot Vente, 17 blvd. Vital-Bouhot, Neuilly, phone 637-33-99.
Opera Night, 30 rue Gramont, phone 296-62-23.
Caveau de La Huchette, 5 rue de la Huchette, phone 326-65-05.
Le Furstemberg, 25 rue de Bac, phone 354-79-51.
Le Petit Opportun, 15 rue des Lavandieres-Ste-Opportune, phone 236-01-36.
Le Petit Journal, 71 blvd. St. Michel, phone 326-28-59.
L'Acadamie de la Biere 88 bis. blvd. Port Royal, phone 354-66-65.
London Tavern, 3 rue du Sabot, phone 548-42-39.
Cafe d'Edgar, 58 blvd. Edgar-Quinet, phone 320-85-11.
Chez Georges, rue des Canettes, phone 326-79-15.
Club des Poetes, 4 impasse Marie-Blanche, phone 606-49-46.
Harry's, 5 rue Danou.
Le Montgolfier, 8 rue Louis-Armand, phone 554-95-00.
Mother Earth's, 60 rue des Lombards, phone 236-35-57.

Restaurants

Mentioned in the text:
Bistrot de la Sorbonne, 4 rue des Carnes, 5th, phone 329-42-93.
Chez les Fondus, 17 rue des Trois Freres, 18th, phone 255-22-65.
La Cour St. Germain, 156 blvd. St. Germain, 6th, phone 326-85-49;
  263 blvd. Pereire, 17th, phone 572-06-66; 19 rue Marboeuf, 8th,
  phone 723-84-25.
l'Entrecote (le Relais de Venise), 271 bvd. Pereire, 17th,
  phone 574-27-47.
Au Gourmet de l'Ile, 42 rue St. Louis en l'Ile, 4th, phone 326-79-27.
Polidor, 41 rue Monsieur le Prince, 5th, phone 326-45-34.
Zero de Conduite, 64 rue Monsieur le Prince, 5th, phone 354-50-79.
Chartier, 7 rue du Faubourg Montmartre, phone 770-86-29.

Not mentioned:
Chez Toutounne, 5 rue de Pontoise, 5th, phone 326-56-81. Good food
  for 85 ff.
A Nos Ancetres Les Gaulois, 39 rue St. Louis en l'Ile, 4th,
  phone 633-66-07. A quality restaurant with 109 ff price tag.
l'Amanguier, 160 rue de Richelieu, 2nd, phone 296-37-78; 43 ave.
  des Ternes, 17th, phone 380-19-28; 15 rue de Theatre, 15th, phone
  577-19-28. Good but not cheap at 95 francs.

Food Shops

Cheese: **Androuet**, 41 rue d'Amsterdam, phone 874-26-93.
Ice cream: **Berthillon**, 41 rue St. Louis en l'Ile, phone 354-31-61.
Everything: **Fauchon**, 26 place de la Madeleine, phone 742-60-11.
Pastries: **Le Notre**, 44 rue d'Auteuil, phone 524-52-52.

Shops

Mendes, 65 rue Montmartre, phone 263-83-32.
Babs, 34 rue du Marche-Saint-Horne, phone 260-07-87.
Galeries Lafayette, 40 blvd. Haussmann, phone 282-34-56
  (other branch in 15th arrondissement).
Au Printemps, 64 blvd. Haussmann, phone 285-22-22 (other
  branches in 12th and 13th arrondissements).
Village Suisse, corner of ave. de la Motte-Picquet and l'avenue de
  Suffren.
Le Louvre des Antiquaires, the Louvre.
Village St. Paul, rue St. Paul.

*Your hotel may have
been Virgil's poolhall
Constantine's bath, Caesar's
stables, and Giovanni's bird shop*

Rome

You may never leave.

Rome is irresistable, spectacular, gorgeous — the most seductive of all cities. It's not that you actually decide to stay; rather, you just postpone leaving. Another day, another week, another year; another government, another husband. And there is little reason to leave. You could spend two lives wandering around in ecstasy, muttering to yourself how beautiful it is. Every Emperor and every Pope tried to make it the most lovely of all cities, and it goes on and on like the interior of a jewel. Rome is a moody city, kaleidoscopic, exhaling history in mirages. As the light changes from day to dusk to night, the past ages of the city seem to take control of the streets and draw you in. You'll see it written on the subway trains: ROMA Is Magic.

Rome is not a museum city, like Florence, nor a museum, like the center of Venice. Little has been glassed-in and made untouchable. Instead, the city is being used and re-used as the Romans need. Much of Rome was built through this kind of constructive anarchy: new Rome was built over older Rome, which was built over an even older Rome, and so on. You can find pockets of an isolated style in very few places; there is no Gothic quarter, no Byzantine ghetto. Nothing has been left untouched, and everything is recycled. Your hotel may have been Caesar's stables, Virgil's poolhall, Constantine's bath, and Giovanni's bird shop.

Rome is a modern ancient city. This is both a charm and a curse. You will have to adapt yourself here to two ancient and unchanging systems: Rome-time and Roman-reason. Rome-time moves more slowly than standard time. It has nothing to do with either clocks or

134

deadlines, but rather with rates of digestion and contemplation. Roman-reason is a way of thinking, not far from contradiction. Ask directions from two people, or follow the developments of the government, and you will find it. These are ancient Roman modes, sometimes amusing, but equally infuriating. They have not helped Rome rush ahead in this century, and you will find here a city split between a desire to modernize and a refusal to disrupt tradition. Watch the cars race around the Colosseum and figure out which looks out of place.

Rome is big, and most of it is worth seeing. It is a city to walk in, but also a city to take the bus in, as the bus service is cheap and very good, and half the local spectacles (gossip, romance, feuds, flirtation) happen on buses. You can buy a bus pass (*una tessera*) good for all buses for a month, for 12,000 lira (L) (ask for *la Tessera Intera Rete*) or for a week, for 7,000L (*la Tessera Turistica*). They should be for sale in the Tabbacchi the first week of each month.

Morning starts slowly in Rome. A good place to take your coffee is **Caffe Colonna**, on Via Del Corso, across from the Parliament. The cafe spreads its tables on the pearly floors under the vast marble arcade of Galleria Colonna. At the edge of the Galleria, on the corner of Via del Tritone and Via del Corso, vagrant chalk artists recreate Renaissance masterpieces. As often as not, faces of various members of parliament replace saints and sinners, and movie stars like Marilyn Monroe make an appearance as Venus or Delilah.

For a panoramic early morning view of Rome, stroll to the cafes of **Villa Borghese**. Walk up the Spanish steps and follow Via Trinita dei Monti up to the left, higher and higher, until you can see all seven hills. Here is a spectacular garden, lush and tropical, overlooking the splendid city. At the top of the road stands a small white villa that has become a cafe. Tables sit beneath grape arbors, beckoning you to rest your feet and emjoy the view.

Further on, in the middle of the park, lies the peaceful tranquility of **Viale dell'Aranciers**. The leaves blot out the sky; all you hear is the gurgling of fountains and the creaking of trees. At the edge of the lake stands **La Casina Del Lago** (The Little House of the Lake), straight from Hansel and Gretel. Little clusters of broken marble gods and satyrs surround the lake. At a tiny marina with its tiny dock you can rent green and red rowboats.

After the coffee, it's time to begin your day by wandering amidst the churches and ruins. The Vatican and the like have been described too often to need much more attention. But a trip to one church will reward the visitor with a view of both faces of the Catholic church. **Santissima Giovanni e Paolo** stands on the hill Celio, near the Colosseum. Follow the tiny road Salita di S. Gregorio from Piazza di Porta Capena. Pass the church and convent of S. Gregorio. The road changes its name to Clivo di Sauro. The exterior of the church is starkly medieval; its interior resembles the lobby of the Hilton. But at the back of the nave, an entrance leads to a stairway descending into the labyrinth of ancient Roman homes that the church was built over. In the traditional Roman style, new buildings were simply built over the older (usually they waited for an earthquake or emperor to demolish the old ones; this time they didn't). Down below, everything is brick, and the temperature drops. House is stacked over house, with patches of mosaic lining the walls. It is dark, so be careful of getting lost. John and Paul, the namesakes of the churches, were two Christians who hid here from the Romans, and a cult grew up around them.

There is an equally unusual church on Via Veneto 27, **La Chiesa Del' L'Immacolata Concezione**. The church itself is a murky Baroque cavern, inhabited by the Capuchin friars that run it. Next to it, though, is the **Monumental Cemetery**, a series of six tiny vaulted chapels decorated with human bones. At the door a friar shakes a plate to ensure that you donate something for the spectacle. This chapel testifies to the zealousness of the Catholic church: sacred earth was imported from Jerusalem by Pope Urban VIII, and the bones of almost 4,000 monks were brought here. There are walls of skulls, arabesques of vertabrae, floral patterns of ankle bones. The pamphlet reads, "These skeletons which adorn the walls and the ceiling invite us to meditation and prayer."

On Sunday morning, before mass, everyone goes to **Porta Portese**, the market. There's a price for everything, and anything for a price. The market begins at dawn when the vendors, who usually move from town to town with their little caravan of goods, wake up in the front seats of their trucks and set up. You can find anything that has been made in the last three hundred years. You will also find offers of things even older — pieces of the Cross, unknown paintings by Raphael, "ancient" coins, etc. The market is a training ground for con artists and shysters. Never even consider paying the asking price. Offer at most one-third of what is asked and hold it out toward the vendor. At Porta Portese, money shouts.

Afternoons

Rome sleeps from about 1:00 to 4:00 every afternoon. When the city revives, many people head for *gelaterias* (ice cream stores).

Behind the Pantheon hides the *gelato* district of Rome, where three Meccas of the gelato world can be found. All three are excellent and serve their own concoctions, which you don't find often — flavors like mango, ricotta, avocado, kiwi, amaretto, and so on. The first is **Gelateria della Palma** on Via della Maddalena 23: slick, chic, full of tile and mirror, the young and beautiful dwell here. Across the street is a smaller and untitled gelateria, with lower prices, better service, and nicer people. The most famous is **Giolitti**: follow Via della Maddalena up one block where it ends and turn right. Giolitti may not have better gelato, but it is classy and elegant. There are tables outside, and in the inner "salon" you will be served on silver platters by waiters in black tie. There are groups of people who come here daily to stage their intrigues and love feuds, whose dramas you can follow word for word, because they often conduct them at the top of their lungs. However, since Giolitti is ice cream for aristocrats, most of what goes on here is genteel.

On your right when leaving Giolitti is **Via Del Corso** and the fashion jungle of Rome. Every evening the area between the Spanish Steps and Via Del Corso is mobbed with the daily fur-and-diamond parade. This is where the clothes are the most bizarre, the most beautiful, and the most expensive. All the professional dressers turn out here. Have you ever seen fur pants or peacock feather blouses? After hanging out on Via del Corso for a while, you will never feel so bland and traditional.

Those seeking natural beauty should visit the **Campo de' Fiori**, where every morning half the piazza becomes a greenhouse populated by flower vendors, and the other half is Rome's finest fresh produce and fish market. One block away is the **Bottega Artigiana Neria**, a lace shop, selling blouses and shirts often made by Neria herself, a grandmother with a family of 300. The prices are reasonable, and with a little encouragement, Neria will show you how to make lace. Just up the street is **Fornaio**, a high-fashion baker, specializing in exotic breads that will make your sandwich blush.

Next to Campo de Fiori is **Piazza Farnese**, with its single sculpted bench, that seems a quarter mile long and doubles as Rome's modern-day Forum. From time to time, a circus sets up in the piazza, and the restaurants move their tables outside. You can eat a meal while above your head a fat lady rides her unicycle on a tight rope.

The next piazza over is **Piazza del Ferrocavallo/Piazza della Quercia**. As you cross the couryard of the Museo di Palazzo Spada, you'll see a long, ornate *galleria* (corridor) leading far back to a small garden. If you wonder how such a long galleria and garden can fit into this small palazzo, you'll soon find out: the walls and floor are slanted slightly inward, deceiving your perception of the true length (actually less than 10 yards).

Babington's and **Cafe El Greco** are two of the most famous and ancient cafes in Rome. Babington's is an authentic old English tea house, stuffy and high brow, where people sit and chat all day. El Greco is like a series of dark caverns, wooden and smokey, where all the famous foreigners sit and carve their initials in the tables as they let the day flow by.

Restaurants

Back in the good old days when the Empire was still intact, the Romans ate and built and conquered. These days, it seems, they eat and loiter and talk. As Mussolini allegedly said, "It is not stone but spaghetti that makes an empire strong." Surprisingly, Rome is not famous for her own cuisine — the best restauranteurs in Rome come from other regions in Italy. But despite this, Rome seems to have as many restaurants as churches, and Romans love to stay at their favorite spot from 6:00 p.m. until midnight.

For a dinner set in typical Roman chaos, go to the **Viale Trastevere**. This region is Rome's Greenwich Village, a section of town untouched by time and inhabited by artists and ex-patriates. Beneath the trees at numbers 57 and 73 are two big *pizzerias-birrerias*, where wild and hungry young Romans come to eat until past midnight. The food is good yet cheap, but you'll almost have to shoot your waiter to get his attention. Since the atmosphere resembles a circus, half of the action consists of the acrobatics people perform trying to catch a waiter's eye.

Romantic Rome lurks by a little garden by the river at **Il Porto**. Statues of Venus and Bacchus, amid the grape vines, overlook the tables for two. The maitre d' here is licensed to marry, like the captain of a ship. And the food — heaps of antipasto — is piled on silver platters by the wall.

Between the Piazza Venezia and Teatro Marcello, at the Piazza Campitelli, the **Vecchia Roma** holds court, its tables spread across the piazza. The waiters, dressed in elegant black and white, run the restaurant like stately servants of a king. Many diplomats and wealthy recluses live in this area, and they all come here to dinner. The excellent meal will cost 30,000L a person.

The most elegant restaurant in town sits atop the **Hassler**, Rome's hotel of hotels at the Spanish Steps. You may have to mortgage your house to eat here, but when you watch the Roman sunset as you eat, you won't regret it. The whole city takes fire and fades like a mirage, and when evening follows, Rome looks like a fleet of gold domes drifting in the sea. The Hassler is the Sistine Chapel of eating establishments, built of silver, linen, and a jealousy of heaven. The splendid dinner starts at 50,000L.

A new and very good restaurant just opened up off Via della Lungara, at Vicolo della Renella 94, called **Associazione Culturale L'Ultima Isola**. It was organized as an association to save taxes, and they may issue you a membership card after a meal. The card entitles you to nothing at all, but this system lets the restaurant operate at lower costs. It is run by young people, and mostly young people go there.

Nightlife

Rome is at her best at night, when the ghosts come out. The city flickers in the street light like scenes from dreams, and the Romans come outside and walk among them. People wander arm-in-arm from piazza to piazza, stopping at cafes, watching the street shows. Rome has no sense of hurry at night — the city is a large party with no host and no rules. There are three big rooms at this party — Piazza Navona, Piazza del Pantheon, and Piazza S. Maria in Trastevere — connected by ancient labyrinths. Each piazza has its own crowd and costumes.

Piazza Navona is the most beautiful and bizarre. It stretches on between three fountains, with Bernini's Seven Rivers at the center. Up the piazza are vendors, crouching on the ground with piles of jewelry and Indian clothes. By the sides little men tend coal fires, selling warm chestnuts. Down the piazza art dealers, slouching in director's chairs, sell their hideous paintings Gypsies slink through, with their babies and their fast hands.

Piazza del Pantheon attracts the young and fashionable. Its two cafes are streamlined, filled till late evening with thousands of "beautiful people." It is the piazza of the motorbike, the leather skirt, and the diamond earring. Around the corner is the cafe at **Piazza di S. Eustacchio**, which sells the best coffee in Rome, and perhaps all of Italy. On the walls plastic bins hold hundreds of types of coffee from around the world. As you walk outside, look up to the top of the church on your right, S. Eustacchio. Attached to the cross are the antlers of a deer, a symbol of cuckoldry. No one has been able to figure out this little Roman mystery, but, not surprisingly, it is not a popular church for marriages.

The third night piazza is **Piazza di Santa Maria in Trastevere**, Rome's version of Greenwich Village. People play guitars and bongos on the steps of the central fountain, fifties greasers mix with sixties hippies, and drug dealers do a lively business with all. Piazza Santa Maria, the liveliest piazza, stays buzzing later than the others. Piazza S. Callisto, right nearby, is home to the **Bar S. Callisto.** This cafe, the informal headquarters of the punk-mod crowd, has a more raucous atmosphere than the ones on Santa Maria. All languages are spoken here, all drugs taken, all laws broken, and ice cream and drinks are served until 2:00 a.m.

During the summer, the government sponsors the **Estate Romana**, the Roman Summer, that brings a series of outdoor concerts and events to the city. The film festival of **Massenzio** goes on all night every night in the Circus Maximus in August, showing old films, cowboy movies, horror and romance movies — each night has a new theme. Entrance is 4,000L for as many as you can sit through. A series of classical music concerts takes place at the **Campidoglio**, Michelangelo's piazza, every night from the beginning of the summer until August. Entrance is 3,000L and 6,000L. The music is good, the location stunning. Finally, there are frequent concerts on Tiber Island down on the bank during the summer. The music is classical or jazz, and the tickets start at 3,000L, depending on who is playing. The schedule for Estate Romana is always posted on the walls of the city. The best daily listing of everything going on is in *Repubblica*, a daily newspaper famous for its culture section.

Between July 15 and August 15, a party definitely *not* sponsored by the government takes place at the Villa Ada: a month-long dance called **In Cerca del Ballo Perduto** ("In Search of the Lost Dance"). The sponsors create a huge dance floor, and upon entering, each guest must give his name, astrological sign, birthday, size, etc., to a computer. At midnight, the dance is interrupted, and the night's computer-matched couples are announced. The music is incredibly loud.

Organized night life in Rome is not easy to come by. Rome is an outdoor city, and indoor entertainment is not its specialty. The most raucous late-hours drinking establishment in Rome, **Fiddler's Elbow**, is a pub run and frequented by the British. This place is loud and has casual concerts put on by whoever brings guitars.

The closest to a straight dance-club in Rome is the **Piper 80**, which always has either a DJ or a decent local band. A big club, popular with foreigners, the Piper is wild when full.

Currently, the most "in" club is **Bella Blu**. Less raucous than the Piper, the Bella draws a chic, swanky crowd into its interior of mirrors and black light. Bella Blu (7,000L cover) sits in Parioli, one of the richest and most fashionable areas of Rome — which is reflected in its occasionally cliquish atmosphere.

In Trastevere, the **Scarabocchio** houses a small dance floor and many plush booths. This small disco charges 8,000L at the door, which includes one drink. **Jackie O**, a very beautiful, very swank establishment, is frequented by the over-30 crowd, but when it fills, it catches fire and becomes fast and lurid. 10,000L at the door.

Nearby, **George's Piano Bar** resembles an American bar, with its long, elegant brass-and-leather lounge. The front door has a sign saying "Gentleman are required to wear a jacket," which gives an indication of the clientele's character. In the back section, a gorgeous white wooden porch opens onto a Renaissance courtyard with a restaurant, home of the **Scuola di Arte Culinaria Cordon Bleu.** Dinners start at 50,000L.

Across from the Chiesa Nuova off Corso Vittorio Emanuelle stands a punk cafe, a rendezvous point for the small but spicy Roman punk crowd. Just near Piazza Navona on Via della Pace is **Bar Pace**, a mixture of intimate brass and wood, French windows, and a little Art Deco. They play good music and attract interesting people.

LISTINGS

Restaurants and Bars

Gelateria della Palma, Via della Maddalena 23.
Il Porto, Vicolo del Canale 26.
Vecchia Roma, 18 via Tribuna Compitelli, phone 656-46-04.
Associazione Culturale L'Ultima Isola, Vicolo della Renella 94.
Caffe S. Eustacchio, Piazza S. Eustacchio 82, phone 656-13-09.
Caffe Greco, Via dei Condotti 86, phone 678-25-54.
Bottega Artigiana Neria, Via de Baullari 145.
Fornaio, Corso Vittorio Emanuelle and Via de Baullari.
Babington's, Spanish Steps.
Fiddler's Elbow, Via Dell'Olmata 43.
Piper Club, Via Tagliamento 9, phone 85-44-59.
Bella Blu, Via Luciani 21, phone 360-88-40.
Scarabocchio, Piazza Ponziani 8, phone 580-09-95.
Jacky O, Via Buoncompagni.
George's Piano Bar, Via Marche 7, phone 48-45-75.

*The routes to the
major points are marked, but
you should try to get lost, anyway*

Venice

A picturesque maze of tiny alleys and canals, exquisite hand-blown glass, friendly natives, and, of course, the gondolas: this is the Venice that hordes of summer tourists expect to find. This is also why Venice can be the quintessential tourist trap. Like so many major stops in Europe, you can have a great time in Venice if you just stay away from any place that looks like it can accomodate a few dozen tour buses.

If they have the money, native Venetians flee their city in the summer. Those who do stay take their vacations in the fall, after a summer of catering to the sightseeing crowds. No matter how crafty you are, you'll probably see lots of Joe Texas and his family, their cameras clicking away atop the Rialto. But with just a little perseverance, you'll have no problem finding some off-beat adventure on a murky evening in a mysterious alley, some relatively unspoiled beauty, and maybe even some relatively unspoiled beauties.

Daytime

The heart of Venice lies in the **Piazza San Marco**. By day the square swelters and swarms with tourists, but you should see it anyway so you can fully appreciate the contrast of its evening appearance. When the sun sets, the Piazza glows with its renowned old-world charm. **Cafe Quadii** and **Cafe Florian**, perhaps the most famous cafes in Italy, fill up as their orchestras begin to play. (Their prices go up at night and get even higher during the orchestra sets, so order and pay before or after the music starts.) Couples dance in the Piazza, and everyone's out for an evening of people-watching.

And while in Italy, do as the Italians do: sample a bitter Campari. Although this drink hasn't become popular in the United States, it's the Italians' favorite. It is really bitter, so you may want to temper it with soda or orange juice. Likewise, vermouth is perfect before dinner. But Italians order *espresso*, not *cappuccino*, after dinner, since cappuccino is strictly a breakfast drink in Italy and considered crass to drink at night.

Next to San Marco, Venetians' favorite gathering place is the **Rialto** bridge. Early in the mornings, the fish and fruit markets there flourish, and an early-rising tourist can catch the natives in operation. Vendors and customers play tug-of-war, pinching fruit and cruising the stalls to find the best deals. Close to the Rialto, carts filled with sweaters, t-shirts, and souvenirs line the streets, spilling onto the bridge. Avoid them. If you must have something, sweaters are fairly good bargains, as are the coral necklaces that became a rage last summer but remain uncommon in the U.S.

From the Rialto, you'll also get one of your best views of the **Grand Canal**. Some visitors find the dirty color and bad odor of the canals distasteful, but don't close your eyes or hold your nose — this is an integral part of Venice's historical charm. Crowds of boats, from the *motoscafi* (motor boats) to the gondolas, make canal traffic as snarled as rush-hour in Manhattan. Though the quaint gondolas still drift by, they are no match for the larger and noisier charter boats on which families will often take a floating meal. (To hire your own, call **Piazzale Roma**, 71-69-22, 71-62-86, or 71-61-24, or **Piazza Marco Polo**, 3-83-41, and ask for *motoscafi per escurzione*.) Keeping order in the canals is nearly impossible, and the *vigili*, the waterlogged traffic police, attempt it mainly by shouts, gestures, and sheer stubbornness. A further tribute to the modernization of the canal system, and as incongruous as the water cops, is the fire station, a garage with a canal for a floor. You can catch a glimpse of it on the right when riding the Diretto from San Marco to Piazzale Roma on the Rio Foscari.

Venice's labyrinthine alleys have inspired visitors' imaginations at least as much as its canals, and they reflect a little less our modern times. You may consider it fortunate that routes to the major points — the Ferrovia, Piazza San Marco, Rialto, etc. — are clearly marked with signs, but you really should try to get lost, anyway. It's easy and delightful to spend an hour traversing the distance between the Academia and San Marco, which could be only a five-minute walk.

By day the streets are crammed with tourists. If you tire of the mobs, try strolling into the **Jewish Ghetto** and the streets to its northeast. The ghetto lies across the first canal which traverses the Lista di Spagna. Or walk in the area behind the **Public Gardens** (not the Gardens themselves — they're dirty and full of bums). Both are primarily residential, where the denizens hang out of windows talking to friends and gathering in the squares. To round off this daytime view of the city, cross to the island of **San Giorgio**, opposite San Marco, and climb its tower for an unpublicized but ideal panorama. Venice looks like the maze it is from the tower, and your guide will be a monk. Ours was unhampered by the language barrier and full of stories about Jimmy Carter's visit to Venice.

Finally, when the city shuts down for the night, prowl through the deserted streets and squares. What was by day rather tacky, at night becomes almost sinister — an aura that has inspired writers to choose Venice as the scene for tales of isolation, creeping evil, and murder. You can safely wander for hours through damp passageways and beneath shuttered buildings without meeting a soul, as the canals lap furtively at the foundations, slowly but surely eroding the city.

Escaping Venice

Venice offers plenty of daytime diversions beyond its physical boundaries. The islands of the lagoon are well worth a stop and can yield unexpected fun. On one trip, we got off the *vaporetto* at the wrong island, **San Senvolo**. Stuck there for three hours, we decided to take a look around. Most of the island was deserted, but at its farthest end was the site of an old psychiatric hospital and a spooky abandoned laboratory. Through a broken window we saw rows of skulls and preserved brains lining the shelves. After we terrified ourselves with an unauthorized tour of the dissecting room and the incinerator, we scurried back to the vaporetto stop. This is not necessarily a recommended excursion, since you'll be stranded for half a day, but it does prove the value of expansive adventuring.

Other islands of note include **San Lazzaro degli Armeniani**, a welcome respite from crowds and "sights." The Fathers here will guide you in French and Italian around their fantastic collection of Armenian art and artifacts. These treasures have been here since the Republic of Venice gave them refuge early in the 18th century, after the Armenian diaspora. From San Lazzaro, the vaporetto will take you to the **Lido**, Venice's most famous beach. Though most of the best waterfront is private, you can rent a cabana or try to sneak onto the beach. Riding lessons are available at the **Scuola d'Equitazione** — difficult but not impossible if you don't speak Italian (11,000 lira per hour for excellent facilities and fine horses). The best time to swim at the Lido, however, is during the Nuadalonga and Nuadacorta in July. These are races open to everyone and are basically non-competitive. Or, in August, there's the Byron Cup, which also offers a swim-along.

But the Lido holds the most fun for the traveler at night. Take a walk along the southeastern segment of the beach, opposite the Malamocco; it's deserted after dark and perfect for a skinny-dip or a romantic stroll. Back in the populated parts there's a disco, **Club 22**, near the Hotel des Bains, and the a casino for those with money to lose. A boat from the Ferrovia provides direct service to the casino for a stiff price, but it might be necessary — when you're all dressed up for an evening of baccarat, the vaporetto is out of the question. Unfortunately, the casino, large and impressive as it is, attracts mostly middle-aged tourists. It's not quite polyester city, but you won't find many Giorgio Armani suits at the tables, either. The Lido's best event is the annual film festival, partly held in the theater of the casino at the beginning of September. This festival rivals Cannes's and attracts an even more artsy bunch, though not as many stars. The festival seems to blend successfully a party atmosphere with serious artistic intent.

In the lagoon, the **Murano**, the birthplace of all the art glass in Venetian shops, is overrun with tourists, but it does have some of the better glass boutiques. If you must buy some glass, check out **Mazzaga**. Their prices, like those in other good boutiques, run from 20,000L and up — way up.

Murano glass is the only indigenous product of Venice, but your shopping need not end after you've bought a piece. Clothing and leather are abundant but slightly more expensive than in other cities. Nevertheless, try the tiny shops for some ritzy stuff, always cheaper than the prices back home. The shopping district begins around the Rialto and extends to San Marco along a street called Mercerie. It is, however, absolutely forbidden to buy a straw gondolier's hat or one of their striped shirts. They only look good on a real gondolier, and absolutely ridiculous on anyone else. Trust us.

Around the Mercerie, **Le Nostri Occasioni** sells good leather in the 100,000 to 200,000L range, and **Elysee** and **La Cupola** has high-priced, high-quality clothes for men and women (if you've been looking all over for that sequined bikini, La Cupola's got it). When you're tired of traditional fare, stop at **Kaleidos**, which offers hand-painted t-shirts in wild designs, also around 100,000L. The annual carnival in Venice has created a supply of off-the-wall gifts. Many shops carry elaborate carnival masks (40,000 and up), and the best are the boutiques on Calle del Scaleto 2199, near Campo San Polo, selling "*originali di Gampi*," and 2600a Rio Tera, near the Rialto. Feel like dressing up for your own private carnival? The **Fiorella Shop** is a bizarre place, filled with outlandish costumes festooning the bus that's parked inside.

Another potential gift, or just a fun pastime, is a caricature. Don't sneer — it may be touristy, but it's amusing. We found a good artist near the Ferrovia, and for 5,000L we had a great time attracting a crowd and discovering what we *really* look like. Most of the other sidewalk artists are not worth a second look; buy a poster instead.

Restaurants

After walking all around Venice you'll be looking forward to a delicious, prolonged meal of Venetian specialties. Alas, you'll be disappointed. The one, huge problem with this city is that it has bland, poor food, perhaps the worst in Italy. Thus, there are few real bargains. Most menus run from 7,000L for a cheap *menu touristico* to 10,000 or 15,000L for a la carte. It really makes little difference where you eat, with the following exceptions:

The trattoria at **Locanda Montin** gets the best ratings for quality, cost, and atmosphere. For 50,000L, two people can eat a three-course meal with wine and coffee in a pleasant garden. Though it's not a Venetian dish, they make a fine *spaghetti ala carbonara* and good *spaghetti alle vongole* (clams). Their *tartuffa* and *tirami su'* are fantastic for dessert. Keep a lookout for the newspaper clippings on the wall to the right as you enter, describing Locanda Montin's claim to fame: Jimmy Carter ate here. The clientele is unselfconsciously varied. Typical middle-aged Venetians eat next to a table of young punk-rockers, and neither group seems to notice the other.

Other good trattoria include **Trattoria Sempione**, known less for its food as for its two window seats which overlook a canal and the passing gondolas. **Trattoria Angelo Raffaele**, **Trattoria ala Bruno**, and, on the Lido, **Ristorante La Pagoda**, with a lovely view of the sea from its terrace, are also good, mainly in the 15,000-20,000L range.

Nightlife

After dinner, indulge in some cafe-hopping. Paris has its cafe society, and so does Venice in its own fashion. Nearly every little Campo or Piazza has one or two cafes that set out tables in the square. They are at their best in the evening and provide a great opportunity to meet people. Just play the same game everyone else is playing: catch someone's eye and smile. Unattached females may get a little more than they bargained for in this game, however — even a wicked scowl is no obstacle to the amorous Italian males. Watch the older crowd drink and talk at night; they're colorful, and always friendly. The **Campo Santa Margherita** comes highly recommended by a native Venetian, but other piazzas in Borsuduro are equally good.

With the plethora of cafes to choose from, there's no trouble finding a few pleasant ones, but keep in mind the **Cherubin Bar**, near Campo San Luco, as a special place. This bar is new and very different. Most importantly in this town which shuts down early, Cherubin opens at 11:00 p.m. and closes in the wee hours of the morning. This may not sound unusual to Americans, but when you find yourself heading home at 10:30 because every bar is shut, the place is a godsend. Though Venetian cafes generally look alike and attract the same types of crowds, Cherubin gets a very young, chic, clean-cut group — more preppies, Italian and foreign, here than anywhere else. And if you're lucky enough to be in the city in the fall or winter, the wealthy upper-crust will also be hanging out at the Cherubin. The decor should give you a clue: the bar looks like a self-conscious parody of Art Deco, with black and white tiles, mirrors, and yes, cherubim in pink, blue, yellow, and green holding up the lights. Above all, Cherubin's young crowd is relaxed, which makes it infinitely easier to make spur-of-the-moment introductions and find dates.

Otherwise, decent nightspots are fairly hard to find. There's one at the Ferrovia called **New Life**, but it looks like a porno theater from the outside, and it's really not too hot. **Disco El Souk** is a smaller, nicer club, and **Ristorante La Pagoda** on the Lido has dancing, but it's more for an over-30 crowd.

Etc.

For all-night liveliness, the only time to be in Venice is during one of the festivals. The streets stream with revelers, yachts jam the canals (stick out your thumb — you never know, you might get picked up) and the cafes never close. The three-day **Festival del Redentore** in July kicks off its celebration with a solid hour of fireworks over the Giudecca, followed by endless drinking and general pandemonium. On the second day there are boat and gondola races on the Grand Canal.

Finally, what is a trip to Venice without a ride in a gondola? Unfortunately, you can't pole your own, but it's the gondolier that makes the ride worthwhile anyway. Take the time to find one who's charming and will show you the sights, and whatever you do, take your ride *at night*. It's far more romantic and prettier. Ask your hotel or gondolier to find you a musician, bring a bottle or three of wine (a glass for the gondolier is only polite), and sit back and pretend it's 1884. By the way, when Casanova escaped from prison, he made it to *all* his rendezvous via gondola. The going rate is 40,000L per hour. Occasionally, women can get a free ride, but we take no responsibility for the consequences. Generally, you can haggle gently about the price with the smaller outfits, but the big agencies along the major canals stick to their official rates. Groups should make reservations for both the boat and the musical accompaniment (the latter may be schmaltzy, but definitely appropriate).

LISTINGS

Nightlife

Cherubin, 4118 Calle San Antonio, (no phone listed).
Disco New Life, 124 Lista di Spagna, phone 71-66-43.
Disco Club El Souk, 1056a Academia, phone 70-03-71.
Cafe Florian, San Marco, phone 8-53-38. Red velvet chairs, white-jacketed waiters, many tourists, but pleasant.
Cafe Quadri, San Marco, phone 2-21-05. A close cousin to Cafe Florian.

On the Lido:
Club 22, Lungomare Marconi 22, phone 76-04-66. Pretty ordinary, rarely lively.
Euro Club Discoteca, 9 Via Usodimare, phone 76-87-97. Stick with Club 22.
Casino Municipale Venezia, Lungomare Marconi 4, phone 76-06-26. A nightclub, casino, and restaurant.

Theaters:
Teatro Goldoni, San Marco 4650b, phone 70-75-83, and **Venice Theater**, San Marco 1965, phone 2-39-54. Plays in Italian, and, very rarely, in English.

Restaurants

Sempione, 578 San Marco, phone 2-60-22.
Locanda Montin, 1147 Dorsoduro, phone 27-15-1. This locanda, Da Bruno, and Angelo Raffaele (below) are nice, family-run places in a slightly less touristy area.
Da Bruno, 2754 Dorsoduro, phone 70-69-78.
Angelo Raffaele, 22 Dorsoduro, phone 3-74-56.
Antico Pignolo, 451 Calle Specchieri, phone 28-12-3. Offers typical Venetian cuisine, with a garden.
Feschiettereia Toscane, 5719 Cannaregio, phone 85-28-1. Very cheap.

On the Lido:
Ristorante La Pagoda, Lungomare Marconi.
Ristorante Artigliere, and **Ristorante Albergo Il Fontane** are on either side of the canal behind the Casino. Both have outdoor seating, average prices, and not too many foreigners.
Ristorante Da Valentino, 81 Via S. Gallo. Not bad.

Shopping

Kaleidos, Calle della Cortesia.
La Nostre Occasioni, Calle de Lovo.
La Coupole, San Marco Frezzeria 1674/Calle Larga XXII Marzo
    2366.
Fiorella, S. Marco 3661.
Elysec, San Marco Calle Goldoni 4485a.
Mazzaga, Fondamento Da Muia 147.
Fiorella Shop, Calle de la Verona 3661.

Other Diversions

Sports and Boats:
Riding at **Venice Riding Club**, Ca' Bianco, phone 76-51-62. 11,000
    lira per hour.
Golf: **Alberoni Golf Club**, on the Lido.
Motoscafi Rentals: rates are 50,000 lira per hour and up.
    Piazzale Roma, phone 71-69-22, 71-62-86, 71-61-24.
    Coop San Marco, phone 85-93-0, 35-77-5.
    Marco Polo, Castello 1011, phone 38-34-1.
Gondole: available at all major points on Grand Canal, and inter-
    mittently on other canals. Rates: up to five people for one hour,
    40,000 lira; evenings, 42,000 lira and up.

Festivals
Carnival: usually the second week in February. Contact Tourist Info
    for exact dates.
Festa del Redentore: the third week in July.
Venice International Film Festival: late August or early September.
Festa della Salute: first Sunday in September.

Also, in 1984, Venice hosts the Maritime Regatta during the sum-
    mer. Contact Tourist Info for specifics.

*After you've sampled
the tortes and pastries,
move on to the hot desserts*

Vienna

A city that produced Brahms, Beethoven, Mozart, and Mahler shouldn't be expected to produce much more, and Vienna doesn't. Nor should it. Vienna should be savored slowly, just like the strong coffee served in its famous coffeehouses.

No other city can claim such a combination of rich musical heritage and current musical quality. The city's 1.5 million residents support four major symphony orchestras, two opera houses, and a host of theaters, in addition to the legendary *Sangerknaben* (Boys Choir) and countless smaller music groups. Century after century, Vienna has remained the world's proving ground for classical musicians. All Viennese are very proud of this continuing virtuosity, and their cultural events are not reserved for the upper crust of society — every audience is made up of people from all walks of life and of all ages.

But, of course, not everyone is obliged to be an opera fan or to live for the Philharmonic's next concert, and there is a second culture, as lively if not as famous as the first, flourishing on the banks of the not-so-beautiful, definitely-not-blue Danube. Popular culture, much of it imported from America, has as much a place in Viennese life today as classical culture. This dual nature translates into a welcome variety of entertainment options. You can go to the opera and hit a couple of discos later, or go to a *Heuriger* (wine garden) and listen to jazz instead of the traditional Schrammel-music.

Nightlife

Since descriptions of Vienna's classical music scene are legion, we won't dwell on the subject. But because the wealth of musical experience can overwhelm the visitor, here are a few pointers. You can't lose with a concert by the **Vienna Philharmonic**, but the problem is getting in. Every concert sells out long before the season starts, but a sympthetic usher at the Musikverein, persuaded by a coin or two, may be able to find one more place in the standing room space. Even if the better music makes little difference to your untrained ear, the pageantry and tradition of the hall make the effort worthwhile.

Don't despair if you can't get in; concerts by the **Vienna Symphony** are usually first-rate, and even the **ORF Symphony Orchestra** (the Austrian broadcasting system's own team) turns in several outstanding performances each season.

As for chamber music and recitals, if you don't recognize the artists' names, the hall they're playing serves as good indicator. No rank amateur would dare book the large hall at the Musikverein or Konzerthaus, so for the listener, performances in the smaller halls are riskier propositions.

The large opera house, the **Staatsoper**, has performances virtually every night from September through June. Casts change frequently because of the superstars' scheduling, but you can guage the quality on any given night by the length of the standing-room line outside. It's worth the three- to four-hour wait as long as you get a place either in the *Parterre* (orchestra section) or *Galerie* (top balcony). Where else can you listen to Placido Domingo (or learn why others want to listen to him) for less than a dollar? Don't overlook the other operas, either — the **Volksoper** can be just as good as the Staatsoper, but has a lighter repertoire.

There are dozens of other musical events every week. Suffice to say that if you're in Vienna during the musical season (October through June), you may have a hard time choosing among performances at the state theaters (which offer straight drama as well as opera and operetta), and concerts at the Musikverein, Konzerthaus, and several old palaces in the first district. May and June are especially good months for music because the Vienna Festival, which alternates between the two big concert halls, brings in an even greater number of star performers per week than usual. Finally, since we can't include everything, get your hands on a bi-weekly newspaper called *Falter*. For just 15 Austrian shillings (AS), you'll get all the listings of concerts, theater, and other happenings in Vienna, as well as some spicy personals if you happen to read colloquial German.

The pop scene hasn't been catalogued as extensively as its classical counterpart, largely because it's still in a state of flux. Many of the discos that were Vienna's pride five years ago have fallen upon hard times, and the same fate threatens those that are popular today. Although the decor may be lavish, the prices are still out of line with the quality of life, and you have to wonder how all those teenagers can afford to hang out in them. Clubs like **U4**, so named because it's downstairs from an elevated subway stop on the U4 line, survive because they have live shows and a slightly older, more sophisticated clientele. The **Metropol** is another survivor. Check out the posters showing their schedule, or you may wind up there on "amateur night." (Then again, that may be your idea of a great time. In any case, check.) The hot spot this year is a club with an impossible name, **Boonoonoonoos** (just wait to hear it pronounced with a Viennese accent). Its reggae and salsa pack them in every night.

Outnumbering by far the clubs where you can dance are those just for listening to jazz, blues, and latino music. Usually small and smokey, the atmosphere is genuinely funky enough to be convincing — despite the Viennese dialect you'll hear all around — and the performers are often fairly big names. The standard for jazz clubs is **Jazzland**. The cover varies with the fame of the band, but it's usually worth it. Latin American music has caught on in a big way in the past few years. Two of the most popular clubs reflect very different approaches: **America Latina** packs them into a cafe/bar upstairs to hear the bands down below. **Andino** takes a counter-culture stance (the room used for concerts doubles as a meeting room for political discussions and film showings), but the restaurant/bar is strictly free enterprise, if a little cheaper than most. In addition to Latin American music, they have reggae, blues, and folk music.

Of course, the quintessential Viennese institution is not the disco, but the coffee house. The Viennese say the hotel may be your bedroom, the restaurant your dining room, but the coffee-house is your living room, where the most important activities take place — talking, reflecting, and reading. The Viennese brew their coffee strong and then lighten it with condensed milk (for what they call a *brauner*) or top it with unsweetened whipped cream in a tall glass (an *einspanner*), or mix it capuccino-style with steamed milk (a *melange*). Whatever your preference, the experience can be transcendental for caffeine aficionados. A good coffee-house never rushes a customer; one cup can last for hours. The better ones supply newspapers and magazines, both Austrian and foreign, all hung on wooden rods on a rack. Many cafes in Vienna have become French-style espresso counters, where you drink standing up. Only a few traditional places have survived, sometimes thanks to government subsidies.

The **Cafe Central**, located in a posh, miniature shopping mall, has frescoes, marble columns, and fountains in an enclosed courtyard. This turn-of-the-century intellectual hangout serves the best *topfenstrudel* in Vienna (infinitely better than any cheese danish ever was) for AS 24. Behind the Hofburg, the **Braunerhof**, with its Art Deco fixtures and weekend concerts, retains the best of the coffee-house atmosphere and attracts an intellectual crowd. Across from the State Opera, the **Cafe Sirk** juxtaposes modern decor with classic coffee house decorum. The **Cafe Sperl** draws a devoted set of billiards players. On the Ringstrasse, the cafe **Schwarzenberg** is a traditional place, now operated by the city. At all costs, avoid the **Aida** chain (the Viennese cafe equivalent of White Tower) — their coffee is unnecessarily bitter. Also, the **Alte Schmiede**, though more than a cafe, provides a good atmosphere. It's a catch-all consisting of cafe, restaurant, gallery, and museum, all tucked away on one of those untouched-by-time streets in the first district.

Unlike cafes in other parts of Europe, Vienna's coffee houses close early. But evenings are probably better spent in the wine gardens surrounding the city anyway. **Grinzing** is the best-known area: every night during the summer, busloads of tourists head out there for an alcoholic adventure. But not only is the touristy atmosphere a little suspect, the wine isn't as good as it is just a thousand yards away in other parts of the Wiener Wald. Hunting for the ultimate Heuriger may become your favorite pastime in Vienna, and it's easy to find candidates if you go to Heiligenstadt, Sievering, Potzleinsdorf, or Neustift am Walde, all in the same general region northwest of downtown Vienna. Once you find a place that looks inviting, order a carafe of white wine and some mineral water (so you can "spritz" your wine, thus making it — and you — last longer), fetch some cold cuts and pickeled mushrooms from the buffet, and enjoy. Start your oenophilic odyssey at **Zimmerman**. The address won't do you a lot of good: once you've found the street, it's the second Heuriger up the driveway. Or try **Nierscher**, with a garden shaded by huge old trees, and rooms inside that are quite acceptable if the weather's bad.

Restaurants

As their girth will indicate, most Viennese eat well and often. Vienna seduces the palate with the variety and sweetness of its dishes. Austrian cuisine is an amalgam of the best from all of the countries that were at one time its empire, which means there's a lot of variety. Don't limit yourself to *wiener schnitzel* and *bratwurst*; as good as they are, they represent just one of many cooking styles. The Hungarians have donated *goulash* and paprika chicken, the Czechs are the source of *fritattensuppe* and a multitude of sinful sweets including *kolatschen* (danish-like pastries), and the Serbs are responsible for the *bohnensuppe* that makes bean and bacon look like a poor relation. In addition, the presence of foreigners from dozens of other countries means that there will be lots of ethnic restaurants — everything from Chinese to Chilean.

Two notable restaurants, **Brezel Gwolb** and **Vincent**, will entertain as well as feed you. Brezel Gwolb is almost too charming to be true, while remaining one of Vienna's best-kept secrets, largely because you won't find it without a concerted effort. (Hint: try near Am Hof.) The *krautsuppe* is beyond compare, the cheese plate and salads appetizing, and the wine list covers all the bases. They play classical music in the background, providing a way to tell your mother without lying that you heard an opera while you were in Vienna. **Vincent** combines a dinner restaurant with a trendy gallery. The food alone makes the journey worthwhile. The fried Camembert with cranberries is an award-winner; stuffed vegetables (with ham and cheese) are also good. A broad selection of beer and teas back up the menu.

Zu den 3 Hacken has been dishing up the goulash the same way since the Kaiser's days. Tavern-like inside, it places tables under the arbor out front during the summer. Try the *zwiebel-* or *vanille-rostbraten* (somehow "pot roast" doesn't do it justice). The desserts can be meals in themselves; complete dinners run AS 75.

Vienna is the place to indulge your innermost dessert fantasies. The city is famous for its *sacher torte*, of course, but that's just one (and according to many, a lesser one) of the delicacies beckoning from the display window of every konditorei. After you've sampled the tortes and pastries (filled with fruit, filberts, pistachios, marzipan, cream cheese, or — God forbid! — all of the above), move on to the hot desserts. There are two main divisions: the *palatschinken* (crepes) filled with fruit, nuts, and/or chocolate, and the *knodel* (dumplings) with various fruit fillings. (*Germknodel* are a special breed: made with a much heavier dough, filled with prune jam, and topped with melted butter and poppy seeds, they are usually as big as Whoppers and twice as filling.) And then there's *kaiserschmarren* — a fluffy pancake scrambled with raisins, dusted with powdered sugar, and served with plum compote instead of syrup.

As a final touch, there's even a reason for tourists to be glad they came to a city that's largely on vacation all summer: ice cream. Vienna's ice cream parlors are open only from April to October, but the profits from those six months allow the owners to relax on the Aegean all winter. The best one is at Schwedenplatz, right by the subway station. Try their fruit flavors (all kinds of berries, kiwi, melon, and banana), hazelnut, coffee, and/or After Eight (chocolate with mint, like the candy). You can order as many flavors at once as you dare, no matter what size of cup you get.

Shopping

There are few bargains to be found in Austria because of the 18% value-added tax on everything and the 30% tax on such "luxuries" as clothes, books, and records (as well as jewelry, furs, and appliances). For foreigners to get the tax rebated is a time-consuming, complicated process.

In keeping with the Austrians' overwhelming interest in edibles, open air markets flourish all over Vienna. The biggest and best is the **Naschmarkt**, located along the Wienzeile between the fifth and sixth districts. Empty out your biggest tote bag first, then wander the aisles picking the best of the produce, wurst, and cheese for a picnic in the park or in your hotel room. There's a natural food store, vendors selling nothing but pickles or sauerkraut, and stands with six kinds of marinated olives. Saturday mornings are not the time for this adventure, because all the *hausfraus* in Vienna will be scurrying madly to stock up before the market closes down at noon for the weekend.

Saturday morning is the time for the flea market at the far end of the Naschmarkt. Amidst all that junk is an occasional treasure, and the people (both buying and selling) are great subjects for people-watchers.

Other Diversions

Although Vienna is a city traditionally connected with things musical, there's more to life than meets the ear. Austrians are great sun-worshippers, and some of those gorgeous tans you'll see flaunted on the Karntnerstrasse are acquired not in Greece but at public swimming pools less than a half-hour's tram ride away. These aren't just expanses of chlorinated water, either: most swimming holes have playgrounds and Ping-Pong, and many have miniature golf courses and tennis courts as well. (If you don't want to go all the way to the suburbs to play miniature golf, there's a course in the middle of town, right behind the Votivkirche on Rooseveltplatz. Just be careful not to swing too hard or you may break a Gothic stained-glass window.) The prettiest women are reputed to hang out at the **Krapfenwaldbad**, which is only one of several pools where you can go topless. The **Schafbergad** is high up in the Wiener Wald where you get a great view of the city.

If your tastes in parks run to conventional, you can stroll through the **Stadtpark**, but beware the little old ladies who will give you an incredibly hard time if you walk on the grass. The Stadtpark does have two great attractions: the peacocks that think they own the place and the little orchestra that plays during the afternoons and evenings all summer. If you sit at the tables in front of the gazebo, the hovering waiters will force you to buy an outrageously priced cup of coffee or ice cream sundae, but you can hear the waltzes just as well from the sides or behind the stage. A couple of times during each set the concert master invites the audience to get up and dance. Don't be intimidated by the professional waltz troupe's exhibition — if this is the moment you've always waited for, seize it.

The biggest official amusement area in Vienna is the **Prater**, the site of the giant Ferris wheel immortalized in "The Third Man." (You may want to skip the *Riesenrad* unless you enjoy being cooped-up in a slow-moving box for ten minutes with nothing to do but look at Vienna through the summer haze.) The Prater has a lot to offer, from traditional rides (including the Cortina, a first-class roller-coaster), bumper cars, and a merry-go-round, to a video arcade and a bowling alley. It was originally a huge park, and there's still a lot of green space left, so it's also a good place to go walking or cycling. (You can rent bicycles by the hour at the Praterstern, the tram and subway stop.) And when you've worn yourself out reliving your childhood, you can stop in at a beer garden and refuel (see **Wieselburger Bierinsel** under "Restaurants" in the Listings below.)

If you're up to a slightly more demanding excursion, a day-trip out to **Baden** makes for a nice change from the city. It's a sleepy little resort town with lots of old people "taking the waters," but there's also a casino, a local version of the Stadtpark complete with orchestra, operattas in the evening, and a racetrack where the trotters run twice a week during the summer. You can hike in the hills around the town, catch a little civilized amusement in Baden itself, and retire to the Heuriger in nearby Soss or Gumpoldskirchen to mellow-out before returning to Vienna. (You can get to Baden via train from the Sudbanhof or on the S-Bahn's commuter train system, or you can take a bus from the stop across the street from the Opera.)

LISTINGS

Nightlife

Note: the Roman numeral indicates the district number.

Mentioned in text:
U4, XII, Schonbrunnerstrasse, phone 85-83-18.
Metropol, XVII, Hernalser Hauptstrasse 55, phone 43-35-43.
Jazzland, I, Franz-Josefs-Kai 29, phone 63-25-75.
American Latina, VI, Mollardgasse 17, phone 57-61-25.
Andino, VI, Munzwardeingasse 2, phone 57-61-25.
Boonoonoonoos, V, Margaretenstrasse 7, phone 57-12-29.

Not mentioned:
Even an early evening in town can be well-spent: check out the **Spittelberg**, a short street (closed to traffic) in the 7th district behind the Messepalast. There are a couple of Heurigen, an artsy cafe, and a pizzeria. Service at the outside tables stops at 10 p.m. because it's a residential area, but you can continue your revelry inside until at least midnight.
Miles Smiles, VIII, Langegasse 51, phone 42-84-814. A smokey little jazz club. It has live music only about once a week, but then it really fills up. Friendly folks.
Sowieso, I, Grashofgasse 1, phone 52-63-88. A restaurant/cafe/disco in the new Viennese tradition. The dance floor is miniscule, but the music is usually good.

Willi's Rumpelkammer, XVI, Lerchenfeldergurtel 17 (corner of Koppstrasse), phone 92-12-36. Jazz. Good atmosphere, a good record collection, and occasionally a really good group.

Restaurants

Mentioned in chapter:
Alte Schmiede, I, Schlonlaterngasse 9, phone 52-43-95.
Vincent, II, Grosse Pfarrgasse 7, phone 33-23-39.
Brezel Gwolb, I, Ledererhof 9, phone 63-88-11.
Zu den 3 Hacken, I, Singerstrasse 28, phone 52-58-95.

Not mentioned:
Wieselburger Bierinsel, II, Prater 11, phone 24-94-60. More than just a place to go when you're done at the Prater: this is a real family restaurant. A full meal with a large Wieselburger beer will run about AS 125.
Pizzeria de Francesco, I, Annagasse 4, phone 52-63-85. This place started out with one room and has expanded to take up the entire old building. Pastas about AS 54, lasagne or canneloni AS 64, pizzas AS 49-84.
Pizzeria Casa Bella, I, Johannesgasse 23, phone 52-16-24. Three minutes from da Francesco, this place is giving it a run for a money. Try the garlic soup (AS 22).
Orpheus, I, Spiegelgasse 10, phone 52-38-53. Generous portions of good Greek food, but a little dingy. Lots of intriguing hot and cold appetizers, moussaka (AS 50), lamb on a skewer (AS 125), baklava with an extra dose of cinnamon.
Tilt, IV, Pressgasse 30. Trendy, too, but not as well done as Vincent. The main attraction here is the late hours they keep in a city that closes down early. Still, there are some interesting salads ("psycho-chicken," "Hell's angels") for AS 45-50 and lots of fancy drinks
Motto, V, Rudigergasse 1/Schonbrunnerstrasse 30, phone 57-06-72. Very close to Tilt geographically, but this place is on a different spiritual plane. Posh decor not reflected in the prices, which are reasonable. Popular with gays and people who enjoy being called libertines.
Kardos, I, Dominikanerbastei 8, phone 52-69-49. Balkan restaurant with slightly overdone folk-art decor. Beef stroganoff (AS 110), Balkan grill for two (AS 210), shish kebab (AS 92).
Bukarest, I, Braunerstrasse 7, phone 52-37-63. Less pretentious than Kardos, slightly less expensive. Gypsy music in the evening. Balkan specialties for AS 59-82.
Shalimar, VI, Schmalzhofgasse 11, phone 56-43-17. Indian restaurant. The menu is large and varied, the portions big, the service good. Main course run about AS 80-100.

Alte Backstube, VIII, Langegasse 34, phone 43-11-01. This 17th century house really used to be a bakery, and they've made one room into a museum to prove it. The menu includes goulash and Fleischknodel (meat dumplings) for AS 58, a cheese plate for AS 60, venison (in season) for AS 120.

Cafes

Mentioned in text:
Cafe Braunerhof, Stallburggasse 1, phone 52-38-93.
Cafe Sirk, Karntnerstrasse 53, phone 52-73-79.
Cafe Sperl, Gumpendorgerstrasse 11, phone 56-41-58.
Cafe Schwarzenberg, Karntner Ring 17, phone 52-73-93.
Cafe Central, I, Herrengasse 14, phone 66-41-76.
Zimmerman, Mitterwurzergasse 20, Neustift am Walde.

Not mentioned:
Heiner, two locations: Karntnerstrasse 21-23 and Wollzeile 9 (both in the first district). Lots of proper Viennese ladies having tea here, but there's lots of space upstairs at the Karntnerstrasse location for you to relax while you wait for that sinfully rich torte to digest. A melange and a torte will run about AS 40-45.
Wolfbauer, I, Johannesgasse 23, phone 52-21-78. Nothing fancy about this place but the pastries. They vary daily and are, without exception, delicious. Tortes and pastries AS 8-25, palatschinken AS 26-44, soups and light meals AS 14-40.

Swimming Pools

Krapfenwaldbad, XIX, Krapfenwaldgasse 73, phone 32-15-01.
Schafbergbad, XVII, Josef-Redl-Gasse 2, phone 47-15-93.

Shopping

Bienenkorb, VI, Mariahilferstrasse 1a, phone 56-52-62. Baskets and other things made of wicker, rattan, almost anything that can be woven, all at very low prices.
Osterreichische Werkstutte, I, Karntnerstrasse 6. Don't expect to find any bargains here (it is the Karntnerstrasse, after all), but if you want a fine piece of Austrian enamelwork, this is the place.
Schonbichler, I, Wollzeile 4, phone 52-18-16. A delicious little shop filled with thousands of teas and other gourmet delicacies. Choose among dozens of *darjeelings* or go for the spicy (cinnamon, anise, pistachio) or fruity (sweet orange, pear, wild cherry) teas.

Tivoli Gardens
is the most romantic
amusement park in the world

Copenhagen

Danny Kaye, the king of schmaltz and the current patron saint of Copenhagen, hit the nail on the head: the city is "wonderful." It is not rowdy, lovely, wild, romantic, sleazy, sedate, bawdy, or any other adjective you can think of. Rather, it is a combination of all of the above, a mixture that, no matter how you serve it, always comes out "wonderful."

Copenhagen neither boasts nor bores. It seems to evoke a lovely kind of merriment that makes past visitors just sort of smile and chuckle. Perhaps the best way to describe the Danish capital is by analogy: if the city were a body, then its heart would be Tivoli Gardens, the best-natured, most romantic amusement park in the world, around which the city seems to have been built. All the main roads, like arteries and veins, lead to Tivoli, and Tivoli pump out its "wonderfulness" to the farthest reaches of the city.

Alas, there is one thing that makes Copenhagen a bit anemic: the debilitating 22% tax that the "progressive" Danish government imposes on everything from an ice cream cone to a mink coat. Though the government will refund the tax on your major purchases, it is a constant irritation when paying for meals, hotel rooms, and so on.

Before we get started on the fun, there's a big myth about Copenhagen that should exploded first. The city, for some reason, is renowned as especially "sexy." Although pornography and prostitution are entirely legal, the dirty bookstores are very standard, rather scurvy, and boring. Istedgade, the street directly behind the train station, is the main drag for the porn trade, and there are a half dozen magazine stores and a couple of "sex clubs" that feature high membership fees, adult movies, a topless waitress or two, and overpriced drinks. The two most famous striptease clubs, **Valencia** and the **Waterloo Disco**, are pathetic rip-off joints; it's absurd that they even stay in business. There's also a small "red-light" district off Istedgade where about five women display themselves in the windows, but the scene is definitely amateurish compared with Amsterdam's Zeedjik.

As with most other forms of Copenhagen fun, the real sensual action in town occurs behind closed doors. The city abounds with sauna clubs, escort services, and "drop-in" massage parlors. Both men and women can find any type of lover they want with these services, and though they aren't cheap, they are relatively safe. The customer is protected by law, and you can be reasonably sure that "escorts" who keep their jobs do not have VD. The top clubs and services include the **VIP Club**, **Rendezvous**, **Venus**, and **Exclusive Escort**, but the best way to shop for your intimacy is through the very thorough *Night and Day Tourist Guide*, available at all the porn shops for 60 Dkr. This book lists scores of escort services and masseuses and masseurs and also describes their specialties. Nothing is left to the imagination except their prices, so all you have to do is call around and compare the fees.

Daytime

In daytime Copenhagen you can go quickly from the noisy grind of big-city traffic to the peace of an 18th-century back alley. The major thoroughfare for both foreign and local shoppers is known as the **Stroget**, a mile-long, pedestrians-only "shopping street." You'll be able to pick up any form of souvenir for the home-folks here, from furs to sweaters to tacky t-shirts. The city's major department stores, **Illum** and **Magasin**, are within a few steps of the Stroget. Especially recommended browsing points are **Birger Christensen** for furs, the **Sweater Market** for Icelandic sweaters, **Nygade Ure** and other watch stores (especially for the gorgeous Bijoux Inex watches), and the various hand-made pipe stores.

But don't confine your browsing to this Main Street of materialism. The side streets like Studiestrade, Brolaegger, and Kompagnistrade harbor a collection of less flashy but perhaps more satisfying bookstores, clothing boutiques, and antique shops in which the serious browser could spend hours. And if you need a store comparable to K-Mart, **Daells Varehus** on Norregade should suffice.

After the long and potentially expensive walk down the Stroget, you'll no doubt want something refreshing and cheap. Obvious conclusion: a brewery tour. Copenhagen's two breweries, **Tuborg** and **Carlsberg**, both offer free tours and free beer—an unbeatable deal!

Carlsberg is the bigger brewery and offers the better tour: its architecture is more interesting, its tour guides are funnier, and its beer is better. (A warning: on the Carlsberg tour, do not ask if the swastikas on the elephants have anything to do with Nazis. They don't, and the guides can be very touchy about that.)

Nightlife

You've walked and you've quaffed—now you've really worked up an appetite. However, the restaurant scene in Copenhagen is really nothing to rave about.. The Danish specialty, called *smorrebrod* and found everywhere, consists of a slice of buttered bread piled with layers of fish or meat, cheese, and sundry vegetables. It's filling but not thrilling. Of course, Chinese, Indian, Italian, and seafood restaurants abound, but the most popular eating establishment remains the Burger King at one end of the Stroget.

However, those of you unable to visit Munich should not miss **Vin and Olgood**, Copenhagen's version of the Hofbrauhaus. This place is a total blast. A live oom-pah band belts international favorites in a cavernous room that somehow manages to retain an intimate atmosphere. (If you don't know any international favorites, there are songbooks on the tables.) Harried—but, yes, busty—maidens serve large steins of beer to their customers, who are often standing on the benches, singing loudly, toasting each other, and waving flags. And you'll notice a surprising absence of a generation gap—drunk retirees will lock arms and sing with sloshed newlyweds. But be sure to arrive by 8:30, or you'll be watching the action from the windows outside.

If you're a fan of the dinner-movie-drinking routine, especially the movie part, then you'll really think Copenhagen is wonderful. In the Tivoli area there are at least forty movie screens, and most of the flicks are in English with Danish subtitles. You'll see recent American hits as well as slightly old classics: last summer, for example, "Gremlins" was running with "Papillon," "The Godfather," and "The Shining." You're bound to find something to see at **The Palads** on the Axeltorv—it has twenty screens.

By the time the movie lets out, the city's nightlife has started to pick up. Though certainly no Amsterdam or Berlin, Copenhagen offers a decent range of bars and nightclubs, with the emphasis on a somewhat intimate, slightly mellow atmosphere. **De Tre Musketerer** provides delightfully peppy Dixieland and swing tunes, and **La Fontaine** has the small, smoky aura of a New York jazz club. Both clubs cater to an over-25, "aging hippie" crowd, but anyone will feel welcome, and both are great places to unwind after a long night.

For the younger set, **Daddy's** and **Exalon** vie every weekend for the title of #1. Daddy's supplies taped disco and new wave music in a very chic setting: the faces of Marilyn Monroe and Elvis Presley line the streamlined interior. Perhaps Daddy's most enticing feature is the fact that it's open until 7:00 a.m. and it serves breakfast from 5:00 a.m. Exalon combines a very popular bar in the front with loud, fun, live disco music in the back. Americans might chuckle at a singer who belts "Shake Your Booty" with a thick Danish accent, but no one else notices and everyone's booty does indeed shake. **Trocadero** is also a popular hang-out and tends to attract a more earthy, casual crowd than the two trend-setters above. Punks, quite the minority in Copenhagen, head for **Bonaparte** and face a demanding staircase to reach the dance floor. The crowd at Bonaparte is a little scary, and if you decide that green hair is not really an improvement, the **English Pub**, right next door, is a straight-forward, young professionals' pub with darts and Guinness on tap.

But everyone, from the aging hippies to the students to the punks, mixes and mingles at **Montmarte**, Copenhagen's largest nightclub. It attracts some of the top bands in Europe, as well as the occasional American act on tour. But Montmarte is not just another dance hall. In fact, even if Prince were playing you'd have trouble dancing because there's just no room. This club is for listening, and though some couples manage to carve out a little space between the tables to bop, most people are content to sit and drink and listen. Montmarte patrons take their music seriously, and you shouldn't miss it. But arrive early, because there are some really awful seats inside.

If you're unable to wedge into Montmarte, check out **The Purple Door**, which could be described as a "mom and pop" nightclub. Ruth Jourdan and Jo Banks, an affable couple serious about giving new talent a chance to perform, have run the place since the early seventies. The club probably can't hold more than fifty people, and it gets so hot that you'll sweat just ordering a beer, but the music (both rock and jazz) is engagingly fresh and raw.

Finally, if they'll let you in, you'll see the most chic crowd this side of Paris' Le Palace at **Annabel's**. Gorgeous women bop to pop with equally gorgeous men, and to cool off they wander onto a gorgeous patio just off the dance floor. Annabel's is officially a private club, but if you're gorgeous enough, you'll get in.

But back to the heart of the city, **Tivoli**, where you can rock 'n roll, gamble, quaff brew, and just mellow-out beside a lake lined with trees that twinkle with lights. Tivoli invites the teeny-boppers and their grandparents, the fans of the roller-coaster and the ballet. It would be futile to attempt to describe the joyful aura of the place, so we'll just recommend that you set aside a full evening to wander, explore, and marvel. The restaurants, though expensive, offer great views, and the rides are generally good—especially *Det Flyvende Taeppe* (The Flying Carpet) and the bumper cars. Simply put, Tivoli is wonderful.

Finally, there are two areas of Copenhagen that are often praised in guidebooks, but we found nothing great about them at all. **Nyhavn** the "sailors' district" and the old neighborhood of Hans Christian Andersen, is picturesque, schizophrenic, and fairly boring. Expensive seafood restaurants, scurvy bars, and tattoo parlors line one side of the canal, while drunks and deadbeats stagger along the road. The bars are billed in some books as rowdy and wild, but we found them (on a Friday night, no less) deserted, depressing, and disgusting. **Nyhavn 17** is the most famous bar and probably the safest, but that's not saying much. **The Hong Kong** and **Oresund** bars are side-by-side and neck-and-neck in the sleaze race. Nyhavn is a pretty place for dinner, but after dinner, forget it.

You might also read stories that extol the virtues of the huge commune of squatters at the corner of Prinsessegade and Badsmandsstrade, a settlement called **Christiania**. Actually, the area, which resembles a combination of Harlem and rural Mississippi, is a depressing statement of the realities of communal living. Every twenty yards someone will try to sell you hash, and as you walk through the rubble you'll be shocked that anyone could choose to live in such squalor. Naked children play with mangy dogs, broken bicycles rust in the weeds, and graffiti like "Fuck the law" and posters that claim "You Can Be a Witch!" adorn every building. Christiana is not fun, it is gross, and it certainly is memorable.

In many ways, Copenhagen will strike the visitor as a more real, more regular city than others in Europe. It does not overwhelm with either history or modernity, and it does not conceal its problems behind a facade of exuberance. You'll find that Copenhagen's charm lies ultimately in its normality, from the abundant Stroget to the seamy Istedgade to the good-natured grab-bag of Tivoli. Danny Kaye was right.

LISTINGS

Restaurants and Nightspots

Annabel's, Lille Kongensgade 16, phone 11-20-20.
Bonaparte, Gothersgade 15, phone 12-61-76.
Daddy's, Axeltorv 5, phone 11-46-79.
De Tre Musketerer, Nikolaj Plads, phone 11-25-07.
The English Pub, Gothersgade 13, phone 15-66-61.
Exalon, Frederiksberggade 38, phone 11-55-14.

The Hong Kong, Nyhavn 7, phone 12-92-72.
La Fontaine, Kompagnistraede 11, phone 11-60-98.
Montmarte, Norregade 41, phone 12-78-36.
Nyhavn 17, Nyhavn 17, phone 13-12-33.
The Palads (movie theater), Axeltorv, phone 13-14-00.
The Purple Door, Fiolstraede 28, phone 13-66-28.
Trocadero, Jernbanegade 6, phone 11-00-10.
Valencia, Vesterbrogade 32, phone 24-24-28.
Vin and Olgood, Skindergade 45, phone 13-25-26.
Waterloo Disco, Gammel Kongevej 7, phone 22-39-46.

Daytime Activities

Shopping:
Birger Christensen, Ostergade 30, phone 11-55-55.
Daells Varehus, Norregade 12, phone 12-78-25.
Illum, Ostergade 52, phone 14-40-02.
Magasin, Kongens Nytorv 13, phone 11-44-33.
Nygade Ure, Nygade 6, phone 13-98-08.
The Sweater Market, Frederiksberggade 15, phone 15-27-73.

Breweries:
Carlsberg, Ny Carlsbergvej 140, phone 21-12-21.
Tuborg, Strandvejen 54, phone 29-33-11.

Sex Clubs and Escort Services

Exclusive Escort, phone 86-00-32.
Rendezvous, phone 37-05-65.
Venus, phone 39-98-93 or 85-92-41.
VIP Club, Nygade 3, phone 11-46-01 or 13-70-74.

*Nightlife
in Munich means
drinking beer, lots of beer*

Munich

Munich is like a stereotypical Bavarian beer wench—big, busty, and over-flowing with laughter and generosity. When you're in Munich, you're in Bavaria first and Germany second, and despite the typical Bavarian weather (cold, drab, and drizzling) which Munich usually experiences, the sunny, lusty disposition of the Bavarians can make every day seem delightful.

On the other hand, Munich is expensive—cheap hotels and cheap meals with any flair are not easy to find. And since most American tourists visit Munich in the summer, they miss the two carnivals in town that make New Orleans' Mardi Gras look like a church social— the Oktoberfest in September and Fasching in January and February. But if you've got some bucks, Munich can make you very happy, and if you can plan to be in town during one of the carnivals, Munich can make you positively joyous.

Nightlife

Since many experts maintain the best beer in the world is brewed in Germany and sold in Munich, it's probably logical that nightlife in Munich means drinking beer, lots of beer. And undoubtedly the best place to drink lots of beer is one of the twelve historic *bierkellers* around the city. All of the beer halls are cavernous, friendly places that serve Bavarian dishes like *wurst*, chicken, and veal and huge steins of beer, and though they're great places to visit during the day, they really get rowdy at night.

165

To join the fun in a beer hall, just walk in and don't wait to be seated. Grab the nearest empty chair and sit down before someone else does. The next step is to holler *"A bier!"*—which is unnecessary to translate. Your timing must be just right for this exercise, though, as the hefty waitress with ten overflowing steins wrapped around her knuckles must be within earshot—that is, from zero to three feet from your seat—to react at all, since the noise from the oom-pah band and the patrons singing along makes simple shouting ineffective. And don't complain if you get more foam than beer in your stein—that's customary in Munich, and the liquid underneath the head is plenty enough to make you groggy.

To prolong the fun, order fried chicken (pronounced "hoon") or try pork sausages (*schweinswurstl*) and sauerkraut (it's the same in German) from the greasy menu lying around the wooden tables. Don't worry—if your stomach can take the beer, it can hold the food.

The most famous of Munich's beer halls is the **Hofbrauhaus**. You should check it out just because it is so famous, but it's patronized mostly by tourists, and the rowdiness can seem a bit forced. If you want a little more entertainment than the typical oom-pah band, the **Platzl**, across the street from the Hofbrauhaus, offers a floor show of Bavarian skits, yodelers, and so forth. The **Mathaser Bierstadt** (*stadt* means "city") is enormous and worth a full day's exploration. It features a number of different sections, each with its own atmosphere, restaurants, etc., and, of course, a cavernous beer hall with a large and loud band. Fewer tourists and more locals drink at the Mathaser, and if you're looking for the quintessential Bavarian beer hall experience, you'll probably find it there. **Donisl**, the oldest of Munich's beer halls (established 1715), is the place to hit during Fasching, when it stays open until 4:00 a.m. In the summer, the **Chinesischer Turm** and the **Aumeister**, both outdoor beer halls in the English Gardens, or the **Osterwald Garden** in Schwabing, are lovely spots for hoisting a stein or three. Most beer gardens have two sections, one with tablecloths and waitress service, the other with plain tables and self-service. Usually, the self-serve section is much cozier. People bring their own *knackwurst*, radishes, Limburg cheese, and other Bavarian specialties, or they buy a snack at the cottages. All the proprietor asks is that you buy your drinks at the Garden. For a refreshing change of pace, try a *radler*, a cyclist's mixture of lemonade and beer.

Remember, if you know just a little German, and if the people sitting next to you know just a little English, it should be easy to strike up a friendship in a beer hall. Unlike American restaurants, beer gardens are considered huge meeting places, and though many people come in groups and stick together, you should have little problem making new acquaintences.

For more traditional nightlife, head for **Schwabing**, the student district in Munich. Like Boston, Munich is known for having tens of thousands of students, and Schwabing is where most of them live and cavort. Though many guidebooks will call the area "Munich's answer to Greenwich Village," Schwabing is much earthier and less trendy than the Village, and it's also cheaper.

There are a good 200 restaurants and cafes, and dozens of small nightclubs, bars, and discos in this area. To find the spots that are really "in," check the area bulletin boards and ask the locals. There's a good chance that the spots we recommend now will be *passe* by the time you hit Munich, and they might even have changed their names, so your best bet is to ask around and check the area out for yourself. Discos like the **Ba-Ba-Lu, California**, and **Capt'n Cook** are currently very hot, and the **Galerie Tangente**—a hang-out for sophisticated models, fashion designers, and Schwabing's high society—boosts its drink prices by displaying real art throughout the club.

While in Schwabing, you should also admire the sidewalk artists who peddle their goods on Boulevard Leopold, where "working" frauleins parade late into the night, and where many visitors search in vain for some kind of nightlife. The action is on the sidestreets, especially Occamstrasse—try the **Haimhauser** (a good beer bar), **Puff** (very crowded, popular spot), **Nachteule** (dark, popular disco), the **Gaslight Club** (a dance club for the under-25 crowd), and **Domicile** or **Musicland** for jazz (**J.A.M.**, in downtown Munich, is also a top-notch jazz club). And if you still need more beer, the **Haus der 111 Biere** offers—you guessed it—111 brands to choose from.

Munich's authentic nightclubs are expensive and rather tame compared to the offerings in other European cities—mostly striptease at high prices. The leading nightclub is **Cabaret Eve**, which boasts about such patrons as Robert F. Kennedy and Anthony Quinn. The funniest Bavarian-style show takes place in the **Blauer Engel** ("Blue Angel," named for Marlene Dietrich's 1920's movie). There, waitresses climb the stage between servings and take off their Dirndl dresses to a serenade of brass music and yodelers. It's really quite silly, but people seem to get a kick out of it.

There are several gay bars in Munich, too, such as the **Chez Otto II-Spinne** or **Fred's Pub**. Lesbians congregate at the **Boccaccio**, the **Mylord Club**, or the **Pom Pon Rouge**. Finally, most bars in Munch close at 1:00 a.m., but the **Big Fifteen** piano bar stays open until 4:00.

The Oktoberfest and Fasching

Munich is world-famous for two periods of spectacular revelry, the **Oktoberfest** (usually the last week or so in September) and **Fasching** (the month preceeding Ash Wednesday). The carnival atmosphere during these celebrations infects the whole city and makes the normally jolly Bavarians simply ecstatic. While the Oktoberfest resembles a huge world's fair where beer has been substituted for all the boring exhibits,

Fasching is a bit more sensual and private, since most of the action takes place at wild, private costume balls around the city. Either festival, though, makes the Spring Breakers in Fort Lauderdale look like rank amateurs.

Beer lovers worldwide flock to Munich for the Oktoberfest, so a hotel room is impossible to find during the carnival. You'd better have reservations or friends in the city, or your only alternative will be to get plastered in a beer tent and wait for the police to take you to the shed on the fairgrounds reserved for stupified drunks.

Though the Oktoberfest is the world's biggest beer bust (over one million gallons of brew is served during the celebration), you can enjoy the fair even if you don't like beer. There are dozens of carnival rides and sideshows—the roller coasters are quite good, the bumper cars are fun, and the ferris wheel offers a stunning view of the raucousness below. Be sure to check out "The Devil's Wheel," a peculiar and hilarious form of Bavarian sadism that you'll have to see to believe (and don't be shy—jump on!). Of course, be sure to hit the rides first and the beer tents second, or you'll leave quite a mess.

The true fun lies in the beer tents, where thousands of guzzlers meet to drink, sing, dance, flirt, and make general fools of themselves. The image of an Oktoberfest beer bust that you have in your mind is 100% true: busty women carry armloads of huge steins overflowing with foam to tables filled with singing, red-nosed drinkers, while an oom-pah band plays German favorites loudly. The only way to do it right is to dive right in, and by the time you've finished your second beer, you'll no longer feel silly doing the "chicken dance" with total strangers, we guarantee you.

The beer tents don't serve food, so get a roasted chicken from a vendor before going inside and eat it with your beer. Most beer tents serve the last beer around 11:00 p.m., and the fairgrounds are usually cleared by midnight. The Hippodrome, however, stays open until 2:00 a.m. If you desire further refreshment at closing time, just follow the crowd up the slopes of the fairgrounds to the next beer hall, the **Pschorrkeller** or the **Hackerkeller**. These spots are the hang-outs for an international set of late-night beer-drinkers during the festival.

The Oktoberfest is not exactly cheap, since the big rides cost 5 marks and the smaller ones 2.50 to 3.50. The beer in the tents is 6 marks per liter, but two of them will put you away, so those on a budget should just confine themselves to the beer tents. (It's tough being on a budget, eh?) Also, don't try to sneak a stein out of a beer tent under your jacket. You'll most likely get caught, and you'll be charged a hefty fine. Anyway, the steins are for sale at souvenir stands.

Fasching is an indoor variation of the Oktoberfest. It takes place from mid-January through February, and always ends on Ash Wednesday, the official beginning of Lent.

To enjoy Fasching, you'll need a contact in Munich to help you get invited to one of the hilarious ballroom affairs like the "Suburban Wedding" or "The Poor Knights' Dance." Everybody wears costumes (often quite flimsy), and the dances usually last until the wee hours of the morning. Most Fasching fools come in pairs, but at most dances there are also lots of singles. The bands play everything from waltzes to rock, and German Fasching songs dominate. Anyway, the dance floors are usually so crowded that it doesn't matter if you don't know the proper steps.

Daytime

If "Bavarian sunshine," as American GI's sometimes refer to the steady drizzle, is not dripping from the skies, you might clear your head with a bicycle tour through the **English Gardens**, the giant park that virtually cuts the city in half and stretches along the Isar River. Ask your innkeeper where you can rent a bike, or try the Veterinarstrasse entrance to the Gardens.

Incidentally, on a warm day's stroll through the English Gardens, you will probably encounter a number of nude sunbathers. Tanning in the buff in the middle of the city has become quite the rage in Munich recently, and the naked and the red are more plentiful in the park these days than rabbits. The police, who once had to register all nude sunbathers, now pretend they just don't see them. If you get lucky, you might get to watch a hilarious tableau: white-robed Arab sheiks, a fairly common sight in Munich, followed by their veiled harem, strolling amongst the sunbathers and inspecting the naked offerings of western society.

With a good map, you should have no problem finding the countless cycling roads in and around Munich, all off the main highways, and many leading through forests and alongside small lakes. And if you're a seasoned cyclist, you'll enjoy the ride to the **Andechs Monastery** in the south of Munich. The Bavarians say that this monastery is "where the Bible has handles," since the Benedictine monks there have a thriving beer business.

At Lake Starnberg, Lake Ammer, and some of the smaller lakes as well, (all of which can be reached by the suburban train system called the "S-Bahn"), you can rent sailboats and surfboards at reasonable prices.

On a clear day, it pays to take a train to **Garmisch-Partenkirchen** (about an hour's ride) or to **Berchtesgaden** and take a cable car to the peak of the Zugspitze, the Hausberg, or any other mountain in the Bavarian Alps. The sights are truly overwhelming. If you're in good shape, you can climb to the top and ride down, but riding up and climbing down is not recommended, since it's really hard on the knees. Another fascinating day-trip from Munich is a ride to the **Partnachklamm gorge** near Garmisch or the **Hollentalklamm** ("Hell's Gorge") on the way up the Zugspitze. They're a must for photographers.

Also in Garmisch is the popular but rather small **Garmisch Casino**. If you're sight-seeing for the day in the area, you might want to stay and gamble in the evening. Or, you can take a special bus from the Munich train station directly to the casino. The bus leaves at 5:15 p.m., costs 10 marks for the round trip, and takes a really lovely route through the German countryside. Before you enter the casino, take a half-mile walk up Alpspitzstrasse to the railroad tracks. At dusk, with the open fields all around, the goat bells tinkling, and the Alps in the distance, the stroll is unforgettable. Unfortunately, the casino is no great shakes, and the bus ride back (you return to Munich around midnight) can be awfully long if you've lost at the tables.

If you can get a group together, try to arrange a trip on a wooden raft down the Isar River from Wolfratshausen to Munich. The voyage takes about five hours and is probably the best the city has to offer to friends of brass music and beer. The rafts, used in the olden days to transport logs from the mountains to the city, now only haul people intent on having fun. Two pilots guide the rafts safely past rocks and down several slides, while the band plays "When the Saints Come Marching In" or some such oldies and the passengers get drunk on dark beer and dance among the beer barrels. The most fascinating piece of equipment aboard each raft, by the way, is the toilet, a ramshackle enclosure held together by four planks.

One way Bavarians make it through the winter is by visiting one of the many saunas in Munich on a regular basis. Try the **Olympiabad** at the Olympic site in the north of town or the **Cosimabad**, where you can swim in artificial waves as well as sweat off a few pounds. The saunas are open to both sexes most of the time, and prices range from 13 to 20 marks per person. If the cashier asks for considerably more, chances are you're in a private "sex club" disguised as a sauna.

If you use the public transportation system, you will sooner or later emerge at **Marienplatz** in front of City Hall. At 11:00 a.m. sharp, every morning, the barrel makers and the knights of the famous **Glockenspiel** in the tower do their age-old stint, and 500 tourists watch, fascinated by the ancient mechanical device. The crowd of tourists, of course, provides the best show, and the Glockenspiel is one of the few places in the world where you can hear the phrase "Isn't that the cutest thing!" in a dozen languages.

While at Marienplatz, stroll down the pedestrian mall, considered one of the best in Europe. If you feel like a bit of exercise, climb up the 277 steps of the **Alte Peter Church** opposite City Hall for a superb view of the city. Another great view is from the **Olympic Tower** at the Olympic site. It has an elevator.

Finally, we know we promised not to discuss museums and such in this book, but there's an exception in Munich that we must include, the **Deutches Museum**. This place will be a blast for people who love to push buttons and crank handles at museum displays, because most everything in the Deutches Museum is "interactive." The exhibits trace the development of German technology, and they include the actual stuff—a turn-of-the-century transformer, classic cars, glass-blowing, etc. Many exhibits test your skill in some way, and there's a good planetarium and electricity demonstration. There are two drawbacks: the detailed information is all in German, and there's just too much stuff to see—you could spend a week in there. But if you like technology, or if you just like punching buttons, don't miss it.

LISTINGS

Nightspots

Ba-Ba-Lu, Ainmillerstrasse 1, phone 39-84-64.

Big Fifteen, Wittelsbacherplatz 1.

Blauer Engel, Wolfgangstrasse 11, phone 48-44-63.

Boccaccio, Briennerstrasse 10, phone 28-49-90.

Cabaret Eve, Maximiliansplatz 5, phone 55-40-70.

California, Feilitschstrasse, phone 34-85-58.

Capt'n Cook, Occamstrasse 8, phone 34-49-74.

Chez Otto II-Spinne, Ringseisstrasse 1, phone 53-51-94.

Domicile, Leopoldstrasse 19, phone 39-94-51.

Fred's Pub, Reisingerstrasse 15, phone 26-61-38.

Galerie Tangente, Kaulbachstrasse 75, phone 34-98-87.

Gaslight Club, Ainmillerstrasse 10, phone 39-16-40.

Haimhauser, Heidemannstrasse 26, phone 11-58-07.

Haus der 111 Biere, Franzstrasse 3.

J.A.M., Rosenheimerstrasse 4, phone 48-44-09.

Musicland, Siegestrasse 19.

Mylord, Ickstattstrasse 24, phone 2-60-44-98.

Nachteule, Occamstrasse 7.

Pom Pon Rouge, Hans-Sachs-Strasse 10, phone 26-34-69.

Puff, Occamstrasse 5, phone 34-99-01.

Beer Gardens

Aumeister, English Gardens, phone 32-52-24.

Chinesischer Turm, English Gardens 3, phone 39-50-28

Donisl, Weinstrasse 1, phone 22-01-84.

Hackerkeller, Theresienhohe 4, phone 50-70-04.

Hofbrauhaus, Platzl 9, phone 22-16-76 or 22-08-59.

Mathaser Bierstadt, Bayerstrasse 5, phone 59-28-96.

Osterwald Garden, Keferstrasse 12, phone 34-63-70.

Platzl, Munz 8, phone 29-31-01.

Pschorrkeller, Theresienhohe 7, phone 50-10-88.

About the Authors

Rollin Riggs and **Bruce Jacobsen** are the authors of two other popular travel guides, *The Rites of Winter: A Skier's Budget Guide to Making It on the Slopes* and *The Rites of Spring: A Student's Guide to Spring Break in Florida*. When they are not travelling or skiing, Riggs is a photojournalist in Connecticut, and Jacobsen is getting his MBA in California. They are both single. And available.

Our Research Team

Louise Burnham	London
Adrian Calisi	Cinque Terre
JoAnn Cavallo	Barcelona and Madrid
Harlan Coben	Costa del Sol
William Echikson	Pyla-sur-mer and Etretat
Lisa Gosselin	Paris and Canals
Steve Hughes	Lisbon and the Algarve
Ted Jefferson	Naples and Rome
Alex Myers	Greece
Amir Pasic	Yugoslavia
Karen Raber	Venice
George Semler	Costa Brava and San Sebastian
Judi Suben	Berlin and Vienna